QUEEN OF HEARTS

By the same author

Marcel Proust
The Galley Slaves of Love
Alfred
Mozart
Daughter of Paris
Tempest over Tahiti
The Last Great Empress of China

Marguerite of Valois in 1570 by François Clouet

QUEEN OF HEARTS

Marguerite of Valois ('La Reine Margot') 1553–1615

by CHARLOTTE HALDANE

THE BOBBS-MERRILL COMPANY, INC.
Indianapolis • New York

The Bobbs-Merrill Company, Inc.
A Subsidiary of Howard W. Sams & Co., Inc., Publishers
Indianapolis · Kansas City · New York

Contents

Illustrations

Part One

_1_ _Daughter of France_

Marguerite of Valois, Queen of Navarre, was born at St Germain-en-laye, near Paris, on 14 May 1553.

Her English contemporary, William Shakespeare, might have truly said of her also that at her birth a star danced.

She was born under the sign of Taurus, of which the ruling planet is Venus. And throughout her life she was ruled by love, passion, as well as taurine courage and tenacity.

She was the third daughter of the Valois King Henri II and his wife, the half-French, half-Italian Catherine de Medici.

As a child she was called Margot, and by this endearing diminutive she remained known ever afterwards—to her lovers, to the people of France, and to posterity.

In the maternal line Marguerite was descended from the famous Lorenzo de Medici; her French grandfather was the illustrious and enlightened Renaissance King François I. As a small child she was exceptionally pretty, but as her beauty blossomed into girlhood it appeared to all those at Court that she was almost as intelligent as she was lovely.

Catherine de Medici was orphaned in her cradle. Her French mother, Madeleine de la Tour d'Auvergne, lost her life in giving

3

birth to her; her father, Lorenzo, Duke of Urbino, died five days later. Catherine was brought up under the direction of her cousin, Pope Clement VII, who, because the little girl was young enough to have been his granddaughter, preferred to call her his niece.

According to the customs of the period, after a great deal of diplomatic and political haggling, on 28 October 1533 Catherine was married in Marseilles to Henri, Duke of Orleans, the second son of François I, who succeeded his father as Henri II. The Pope journeyed specially to France to perform the nuptial ceremony.

Husband and wife were both fourteen years old. Yet the marriage was immediately consummated, to the amusement and pleasure of François and His Holiness.

Catherine began her married life with two considerable handicaps.

She was far from beautiful, with slightly bulging eyes, a long foxy nose and a protruding lower lip. She was dumpy and inclined to become even more so owing to her chief vice, which was greed. Her appetite was enormous.

Far more serious, however, than Catherine's obvious lack of sex appeal was the fact that she was also, apparently, barren. For ten years the young Dauphine was tortured by the fact that she was unable to conceive. In her desperation and fear of being divorced on this ground she took the initiative by offering to her father-in-law to retire to a convent, or even, she humbly added, 'to serve whichever princess might be chosen to succeed her as the Dauphin's wife'. Fortunately for Catherine, however, François I was genuinely fond of her. Almost from their first meeting he had been struck by her modesty, charm of manner, and intelligence. She had used all the arts of her Italian femininity to win his affection and had succeeded so well that he assured her she had nothing to fear as the consequence of her unfortunate sterility.

As a close relative of two pontiffs Catherine was and always remained a good Catholic. Yet prayers and pilgrimages were ineffective in producing the miracle she longed for—a child.

In the sixteenth century, however, religious piety was not in the least incompatible with every superstitious and pagan belief, with magical rituals and the brewing of potions, with recourse to practices, some of which were merely silly and others sinister.

The Italians in particular were adepts at such arts. Catherine de Medici arrived in France with a train of her own countrymen and women, whom all her life she kept in her service. Whether it was due to her religious devotions or their magical prescriptions, in the end the miracle did at last occur. After nine years of sterility, in April 1543 Catherine conceived. Her first child, a son and heir to the Valois throne, was born at Fontainebleau.

This triumph after so many years of anguish patiently endured was, however, only the beginning of Catherine's late but astonishing fertility. In the next eleven years she bore nine more little princes and princesses. Her children were:

François (François II), b. 19 January 1544
Elisabeth of France (Queen of Spain), b. 2 April 1545
Claude of France (Duchess of Lorraine), b. 12 November 1547
Louis, Duke of Orleans, b. 3 February 1549; d. in infancy
Charles-Maximilien (Charles IX), b. 27 June 1550
Edouard-Alexandre (Henri III), b. 20 September 1551
MARGUERITE ('Margot', Queen of Navarre), b. 14 May 1553
Hercule (François, Duke of Alençon), b. 18 March 1555
Jeanne and Victoire, twins, b, 24 June 1556; d. in infancy

The baptismal names of two of Catherine's sons were changed at their confirmations to those under which they became known to history as the last Valois kings. Two of her daughters, Elisabeth and Margot, were to become queens.

Henri II was strikingly handsome; Catherine adored him. But almost exactly three years after their wedding, when they were both only seventeen still, the Dauphin fell madly and permanently in love, not with his plain little wife but with Diane de Poitiers. The fact that Diane was then thirty-eight, old enough to be his mother, made not the slightest difference to the prince's passion for her. And even in her forties this widow of Louis de Brézé, Grand Seneschal of Normandy, was still marvellously beautiful. Her flawless body inspired the painters and sculptors of the Valois Court to such masterpieces as Jean Goujon's statue of her goddess, Diana, with the crescent in her hair, the huntress with the traditional stag and greyhounds.

Diane was also a huntress. Inside that exquisite body, toughened by daily exercises and cold-water baths, was an equally tough and predacious mind. Diane was greedy for wealth and power and even her greed was satisfied by the immensely valuable gifts Henri made her. Without hesitation he gave her the Crown Jewels as well as the superlative castle of Anet. After his accession in 1547 he created Diane Duchess of Valentinois. On public occasions she took precedence after the Queen over all other women at Court, even the princesses of the Blood Royal.

Diane had no cause to be jealous of the plain little Medici, who showed none, either, of the royal favourite, so many years her senior. Diane treated the Dauphine with a kind of contemptuous affection, even nursed her—to Henri's delighted gratitude—when Catherine had scarlet fever. When the Dauphin became too pressing, his mistress would smilingly order him to his marriage bed to provide himself, she said, with an heir. The arrival of the royal brood after ten years made no difference to the relationship between the three of them. The King always showed affection towards his wife and children, but for twenty-two years Diane de Poitiers remained the queen of his heart.

And although Catherine accepted the situation with apparent equanimity at least two instances on record reveal her true feelings during those long years. In 1558, when Henri II abandoned the Italian conquests of his predecessors, she dared to quarrel violently with the King and his mistress in defence of the country of her birth.

'I have read the histories of this kingdom,' Catherine disdainfully informed the favourite, 'and I have found in them that from time to time at all periods whores have managed the business of kings.'

At a later stage, after Henri's death, when giving directions to Bellièvre, her superintendent of finances, with regard to Margot's conduct, Catherine wrote: 'I was hospitable to Mme de Valentinois; he was the King, yet even so I always let him know that it was to my great regret; for never has a woman who loves her husband liked his whore; for even though this is an ugly word for us to use, one cannot call her anything else.'

Catherine, alone in a strange country, despised at first for her sterility and for much longer on account of her relatively lowly birth, had only her wits, her innate craftiness, to help her in her difficult situation. She also possessed unusual physical courage. Even as a child, during serious rioting in Florence when she was only eleven years old and her life at one moment was in great danger, she behaved with extraordinary self-control and presence of mind. She was a passionate lover of beauty and the arts, an intellectual, and a tremendous reader. Her library contained more than five thousand books. With her sister-in-law and close companion Henri's sister Marguerite—who became Margot's godmother—she read the classics as well as the great contemporary French poets, of whom Ronsard was appointed poet-laureate.

But Catherine de Medici's favourite book, which as she rose to the position of autocratic power she held during the reigns of three of her sons, became her political Bible, was *Il Principe* (*The Prince*), a manual of statecraft written by her compatriot Machiavelli, and dedicated to her father, the Duke of Urbino.

Henri II was no intellectual. He was mentally lazy and, apart from his interest in his Navy, affairs of State bored him, so that he left enormous power to his Lord High Constable, Anne de Montmorency. The King's passion was for hunting and the open-air sports of his time, even those of an earlier date. He loved nothing more than dressing up in armour, and with his courtiers similarly and magnificently accoutred and mounted, to stage joustings and tournaments lasting for several days on end.

Marguerite began her famous Memoirs with a description of an occasion when she was still a little girl. She was sitting on her father's lap, watching a mock bout between two young lordlings, only a few years older than herself. They were the little princes Henri of Joinville, who later became the powerful second Duke of Guise, and Henri of Bourbon, Marquess of Beaupréau, who when he was fifteen was killed by falling from his horse, which trampled him to death.

Smilingly, the King asked his little daughter which of these two young princes she would choose as her cavalier?

'I told him I preferred the Marquess.'

' "Why?" he said. "He's not so handsome as the other one." (For the Prince of Joinville was blond and fair, whilst the Marquess of Beaupréau was dark, with brown hair.)

' "Because," I said, "he is good, and the other one has no patience and always wants to hurt someone and be the master." '

Whether or not Margot reported this anecdote truly, ten years afterwards she was to change her mind very definitely about that young nobleman.

Only a few days later, at this same tournament, the scene was one of major tragedy. In a bout with Montgomery, a captain in his Royal Scots Guard, the King was accidentally pierced through the eye by his adversary's spear.

Catherine claimed to have foreseen this horrible calamity in a dream. It certainly confirmed her faith, already strong, in astrology. The most famous astrologer of her day was her fellow-countryman, Lucca Gaurico, a bishop whose prophecies were even taken seriously by no fewer than four popes. It was he who warned Henri II 'to avoid all single combat, especially in his forties, as at that period of his life he would be in danger of a head wound which might lead to blindness or death.'

In March 1555, when Margot was only two, another astrologer, a Frenchman destined to become even more famous, published his book of *Centuries* under the pen-name of Nostradamus. In one of its quatrains this extraordinary work contained an almost exact description of the death of Henri II:

> Le lion jeune le vieux surmontera
> En champ bellique, par singulier duelle,
> Dans cage d'or les yeux lui crèvera,
> Deux classes une, puis mourir, mort cruelle.

Yet in spite of Catherine's impassioned pleas the King had insisted on going ahead with his jousting. He died ten days after this tragic mishap, in great pain, on 10 July 1559.

Diane de Poitier's reign was also over.

Henri II left his realm desperately weakened, damaged in military, financial and political power. On the mistaken advice of Montmorency, he had allowed himself to become involved in war with the two greatest Powers of his day, Spain and Austria. In 1557, two years before the King's fatal accident, Montmorency was utterly defeated at the Battle of St Quentin by Emmanuel-Philibert of Savoy, the brilliant commander of the Spanish forces.

This disaster was only partly retrieved by the reconquest of Calais from the English by François, Duke of Guise, head of the great House of Lorraine.

The subsequent Treaty of Cateau-Cambrésis, concluded in 1559 with Elizabeth I of England, Philip II of Spain and Emmanuel-Philibert, was deeply humiliating to the French.

This gloomy aspect of France's European situation was, however, only one of the strands of the threefold problem confronting Catherine on the accession of François II, the boy King. The other two were the acute menace to Valois power of the great feudal families, and the growing tempo and violence of the religious conflicts between Roman Catholics and Reformationists —the Huguenots.

Among the feudalists who then only reluctantly supported the Valois dynasty, the Guises were the most powerful and potentially threatening. They were six brothers, descended from the semi-royal House of Lorraine. Their chief was the warrior Duke François, known as the result of a great scar on his head received in battle as Scarface (*Le Balafré*). The Guises considered themselves fully equal in descent to the princes of the Blood. Their most astute member was a great prince of the Church, Charles, Cardinal of Lorraine, who was richer than the King and, in addition to his ecclesiastical eminence, wielded enormous power in the State. Another brother, Louis, was also a Cardinal of France.

Unlike the Guises, their chief rivals during the reign of Henri II, owing to the King's personal affection and reliance on the Lord High Constable, the Montmorencys could claim no semi-royal ancestry. Yet the Constable's nephew, Châtillon, was also a cardinal, and Coligny, Admiral of France, was to become the most famous of them all, the pivotal figure of the Wars of Religion.

The closest relatives of the Valois, however, and their acknow-ledged successors in the event of the dynasty coming to an end in default of a direct male heir, were the Bourbons. They were princes of the Blood. Yet the head of their House at that time, Antoine, King of Navarre (a small kingdom sandwiched between France and Spain in the extreme south-western corner of the realm), was no match either for the cunning of the Medici Queen Mother or the military and political brilliance of the Guises. Antoine's younger brother, the Prince of Condé, was both brave and cunning; he was also wildly ambitious. But he was a cripple, hunchbacked, with a large family to support on rela-tively very small means.

With the accession of François II, the Guises immediately moved into power. For the boy King, aged fifteen, was married to their niece, the lovely, high-spirited, spoilt and quick-tempered Mary Stuart, who openly sneered at her mother-in-law, the 'Florentine shopkeeper'. Catherine kept silence and her temper. She punctiliously saw that the Crown Jewels, so wantonly given by Henri II to Diane de Poitiers, were returned by that fallen favourite to their rightful owner—not to herself, but to the proud young Queen, Mary, to whom she also gave some of her own most precious pearls in celebration of the accession.

François II adored his beautiful young wife. But his endocrine glands were still so undeveloped that he was unable to consum-mate their marriage, which remained infertile. Aware of his youth, inexperience and need of guidance, on ascending the throne he had conferred the title of Governor of France on his mother. But, being wholly under the influence of Mary and her powerful uncles, the King informed his late father's intimate friend and counsellor, the Lord High Constable, Montmorency, that he might now retire. In his place the Duke of Guise took over the supreme military command, whilst the Cardinal of Lorraine controlled the realm's finances and internal policies.

In spite of her prerogative, at that moment Catherine carefully refrained from any direct interference in affairs of State. She knew, as did all at Court, that the young King's reign would be a brief one. And with Machiavellian guile she allowed the Guises their short term of authority. For she was holding the ace of trumps and needed to play no other card meanwhile.

Only four years after coming to the throne François II died at the age of nineteen of acute mastoiditis. Mary, his beautiful and tragic young widow, left on her sad path to the dour cities and bleak moors of Scotland and in due course to the block provided by Elizabeth I of England.

The successor to the crown was François's next brother, Charles IX. But this new king was still a small boy, a minor. And at that point there was no longer any question as to who was to be the real ruler of France during his minority. Catherine de Medici at last came to full and undisputed power.

This did not mean that the Guises and their rivals abandoned their plotting and intrigues. The Queen Mother's problems, both internal and external, might have intimidated the most courageous male ruler.

Nothing would be more erroneous than to imagine that the Wars of Religion that reached their horrible climax during the reign of Charles IX were a series of straightforward, although appallingly violent, conflicts between Roman Catholics and Protestants. They were also civil wars, in which the Valois dynasty and the great feudal families were locked in constant life-and-death wrestling for political power, with the ever-present menace of Spanish intervention. Both sides—Catholics led by the Guises, Huguenots by Montmorencys and Bourbons, especially Condé and Coligny—unhesitatingly called in or hired foreign aid. Time and again the country was devastated by foreign mercenaries, and very nearly bled to death as the battlegrounds shifted to and from blood-soaked, pillaged, burning towns, villages, and lands. On at least one occasion the Queen Mother and the King, with the younger princes and princesses, were compelled to fly from the Louvre to the safety of a Royal castle and back again, owing their lives to the protection of the foreign troops in their service.

According to Catherine's champions, she hated violence and bloodshed. Although this claim need not be taken too literally, it was largely borne out by her diplomatic and political manœuvring, her dealings with both Catholics and Huguenots, right up to her one fateful and ghastly lapse immediately after Marguerite's wedding, on the Eve of St Bartholomew, 24 August 1572, when she was overwhelmed by panic.

The persecution of the Reformationists had been steadily growing under François I and Henri II. Like all fanatical minorities, the Huguenots throve and increased on it. Whilst the Guises headed the Catholic movement for their utter extermination, the Montmorencys, led by the Admiral, Coligny, and the Bourbons, particularly Condé and Jeanne of Albret, the remarkable wife of Antoine of Navarre, became ever more fervent supporters of the French refugee, Calvin, who was directing their aggressions from his hive of asceticism in Geneva.

Catherine was too much a Medici, a daughter of the Renaissance, and a convinced follower of Machiavelli's precepts to be fanatical. The irreconcilable antagonisms between the powerful feudalists could be exploited advantageously to weaken them and increase the strength of the Valois. Above all, her innate realism, her acute awareness of the opportunities civil war would offer Catholic Spain and Austria on the one side, and Protestant England and the minor German States on the other, to intervene in the French internal conflict, made her search ever more desperately for a reasonable, a civilized solution to this fearful problem. Time was her greatest need—time for talking, debate, persuasion, the passing of pacifying laws and measures. In order to gain it, her first objective was to come to terms with the other great European Powers.

Her proposed solution for containing the designs of Spain, Austria, and England was an essentially feminine one. The instruments she proposed to use for her purpose were her children. Through their marriages she would convert her potential external enemies into allies. And having done so, she would then be able to concentrate on solving France's internal politico-religious dilemma.

2 *Princess in Pawn*

Under Catherine de Medici the Court of the Valois became the most brilliant in Europe.

When François I built Fontainebleau he employed the finest French architects, landscape gardeners, sculptors, and painters to create and embellish it. He sent to Italy for the most renowned artists of the period, headed by the immortal Leonardo da Vinci, a Florentine like Catherine. And when she became Queen Regent the Italian influence was firmly established.

Fontainebleau, Amboise, and later Chenonceaux—Catherine's favourite residence—provided the fairy-tale settings for the ceaseless rounds of magnificent entertainments she organized at fantastic cost to the royal and national treasuries.

Catherine, granddaughter of Lorenzo the Magnificent, undoubtedly did love beauty for its own sake. Yet as Machiavelli's disciple her motives were not purely aesthetic ones. Her superlative balls, banquets, and masques were carefully planned to dazzle and charm the turbulent leaders of the powerful feudal factions as a lure and means of distracting them from their incessant bitter rivalries and murderous hatreds.

'I used to hear the King, your grandfather, say,' the Queen

13

Mother wrote to one of her sons, 'that two things were necessary to live in peace with the French—that they should love their King and be kept happy and entertained.'

To this end Catherine perfected another, more subtle instrument. Although she was so plain, she never showed the least jealousy or envy of beautiful women. She appeared in fact to delight in surrounding herself with them.

Brantôme, the fond chronicler of the charmers of the Valois Court, described with sincere flattery 'this lovely troop of girls and ladies, more divine than human'.

First and foremost amongst them were the princesses of the Blood Royal, Henri II's sister, Marguerite, and his two elder daughters, Elisabeth and Claude of France. When Mary Queen of Scots married François II she was sixteen, and to see her, said her mother-in-law, was to fall in love with her. This bevy of beauties also included Anne of Este, Duchess of Guise, celebrated by the Court poet Ronsard as a saintly Venus, in whose eyes shone all the lights of love.

Catherine chose as her maids-in-attendance and ladies-in-waiting eighty girls and women of the highest nobility, whom she 'dressed in silks and gold like goddesses', but who were trained to be 'friendly and welcoming as simple mortals'. These 'Dames galantes' as Brantôme called them, 'very beautiful and honest maids', were scathingly referred to by the Queen Mother's Huguenot enemies as her Flying Squadron, whose mission it was to ensnare those noblemen and princes—including even her own sons—whose weaknesses she ruthlessly exploited to increase her own authority. In spite of the public glamour these beauties enjoyed, Catherine subjected them to rigid discipline, not hesitating at physical punishment, such as a good whipping, if one of them displeased her.

As time went on the Valois Court became increasingly a centre of sexual intrigues and vices and the mutual hatred and jealousies they aroused, to all of which the Queen Mother turned a blind eye when it suited her and which she severely curtailed when it did not. And it finally degenerated into seething and orgiastic corruption.

After the signing of the Peace Treaty of Cateau-Cambrésis, the Royal match-maker's policy of creating alliances with those powerful and dangerous neighbours who had routed the Lord High Constable at St Quentin had its first successes. The marriages of Elisabeth of France to Philip II of Spain and Margot's aunt and godmother, Marguerite of Valois, to the heroic Emmanuel-Philibert of Savoy were the occasion for the festivities during which Henri II lost his life. Soon afterwards Catherine began to lay her plans for the disposal of her youngest daughter, Marguerite, in the interests of French statecraft.

The little princess spent her infancy and early childhood away from Court, at St Germain and Amboise, with her small brother, the Duke of Alençon. Her governess was a remarkable woman, Charlotte de Curton, of whom she was very fond, for she was an affectionate child who received very little love from her mother. Mme de Curton's training had a lasting effect on Margot's mind, which even then was unusually bright and eager.

Marguerite was barely twelve when her mother decided that she should join her in the protracted tour of France of 1564. During this leisurely voyage the whole magnificent Court swept through Champagne, the two Burgundies, Lyons, Provence, Languedoc, and Guyenne. The journey lasted from March of that year until May 1566.

The country had already been torn by civil and religious warfare. Catherine's plan was to attempt to come to terms with the rival factions by her own on-the-spot investigations into local conflicts. But as her personal interest always lay in the strengthening of the dynastic power, she took with her as the living symbol of Valois majesty the young King, Charles IX, whom she thus would show to those of his people who otherwise would never have had a glimpse of him.

The reason for Marguerite's inclusion, however, was not the least important of Catherine's motives. For at Bayonne there was to be an historic meeting on French soil with Philip II of Spain and his Queen, at which Catherine was hoping to arrange the marriage of Margot to the Spanish Infante, Don Carlos. For some time previously she had been corresponding on this project with her daughter Elisabeth, to whom she had sent portraits of the Royal Family to show to her Spanish relatives. When the Infante had seen Margot's, so the Queen of Spain wrote to her mother, he had laughingly told her three or four times that the youngest princess was the prettiest—'*Mas hermosa es la pequeña*'. 'The King also thought she was very lovely and asked me if she was tall.'

Catherine's hopes of this match were not to be realized. Philip II was no less cunning than the Queen Mother. As a fanatical Catholic, he viewed with constant and deep suspicion her apparent efforts to pacify her heretical subjects by granting certain rights and concessions to the Huguenots. At the last moment Philip withdrew from the Bayonne meeting, sending instead the notoriously intransigent Duke of Alba as his representative.

But, artfully saving face, Catherine did not allow this setback to mar the regal splendour of the entertainments she had planned for the occasion.

It is scarcely surprising that when writing her Memoirs nearly thirty years later Marguerite remembered relatively little of that grand tour of France and left it to others, she wrote, 'to recall the magnificence everywhere'—at Bar-le-Duc, on the occasion of the christening of her little nephew, her sister Claude's son; at Lyons, where they were met by her godmother, Marguerite of Savoy and her husband.

She did, however, remember, and described in detail, the banquet given for the French and Spanish Courts at Bayonne by Catherine on 25 June 1565 and the marvellous water-party on the River Adour. This took place on an island in the river, where in an open meadow 'the Queen my mother had alcoves built, each one containing a round table to seat twelve persons, with the royal daïs at one end raised on four banks of grass'. The royal barge was accompanied by 'river gods, singing and reciting verses of welcome'. As Their Majesties and suite disembarked, 'shepherdesses' lined the long avenue leading to this open-air banqueting-hall, 'in picturesque groups, each one of which was dressed in the regional costume of every province of France, but in cloth of gold and satin, dancing and singing to the traditional instruments of their provinces'. During the banquet there was an elaborate transformation scene, when, escorted by 'satyrs' playing musical instruments, there appeared 'a great luminous rock, but still less dazzling than the beauty and the jewels of the "nymphs" who made their appearance under it'. There then followed a ballet.

The festivities were unfortunately brought to a sudden end by a violent thunderstorm that burst upon them. The whole gorgeous company, the Royal Family, ladies, courtiers, 'nymphs', and 'satyrs', rushed helter-skelter to the boats to carry them out of the downpour which had overtaken them 'as if the heavens were jealous of such glorious beauty'.

Marguerite's description of this unplanned fiasco reveals one of her most endearing qualities: the sense of humour which so often came to her help in far worse predicaments than a drenching. For she wrote that this anticlimax provided all the Court with a good laugh on the following day.

With such a youthful background, it is not surprising that, like her mother, Marguerite all her life adored beauty and the arts, festivities and luxury often far beyond her means. When many years later she was rightfully accused of the most wanton extravagance, she replied simply and truthfully, 'I was brought up to it,' and it never occurred to her that a Daughter of France should live in any other fashion.

To Catherine the failure of her negotiations with the Duke of Alba at Bayonne was a serious disappointment. They could not come to satisfactory terms politically, and Philip II withheld his consent to the match between Marguerite and Don Carlos, whom he was even considering marrying to the Protestant Queen of England.

Two other possible foreign matches for Marguerite remained. Philip II's nephew was the young King of Portugal, and there were prolonged negotiations through the French Ambassador at Madrid to bring about this marriage. These dragged on until Charles IX, by then having reached his majority, irritated and insulted beyond endurance by Philip's machinations, abruptly broke them off. Philip also foiled Catherine's plan to marry the King of France to the elder daughter of the Emperor Maximilian of Austria; Charles IX had to content himself with her younger sister. And the Emperor showed no more enthusiasm than Philip to receive Marguerite as his daughter-in-law, wife to his son Rudolph, King of Hungary.

Margot was growing prettier every day, yet these successive failures of her mother's plans to find her a throne, in which she knew herself to be no more than a political pawn, were unlikely to add to her happiness or increase her self-confidence.

In a rare moment of intimacy, Catherine once remarked to her daughter, 'My child, you were born in an unhappy age,' and in early childhood Margot was to experience the fact. Her entire life was passed during the bloody Wars of Religion, the first of them in 1562, when she was only nine. With only brief intervals of peace, they lasted throughout her girlhood and early womanhood, involving the Royal House, the nobility, and the common people.

Catherine appeared to have settled the country after the first war by the Peace of Amboise in 1563. But the Catholic leaders were far from appeased by the growing influence at Court, as they saw it, of their Huguenot enemies. The old Constable, Montmorency, still influential even after St Quentin, formed an alliance with his former rivals for power, Guise and St André, which was known as the Triumvirate. The Duke of Nemours, in love with Guise's ravishing wife, Anne of Este, was said to be plotting to kidnap the heir-presumptive, the Duke of Anjou, and to set him up against the Queen Mother and Charles IX, whom they claimed to be already tainted by heresy. Nor, at that early stage in his life, was Henri of Anjou immune from the Protestant influence that had infiltrated the Court.

In her Memoirs Marguerite told how Henri ceaselessly tormented her on account of her childish piety: he threw her Book of Hours in the fire, trying to replace it by Huguenot prayerbooks, which the little girl promptly passed on to her governess, Mme de Curton, with whom she visited the old Cardinal of

Tournon, 'that good old man, who encouraged me to remain true to my religion and gave me new Books of Hours and rosaries to replace those that had been burnt. My brother Anjou and other souls who had determined that I should lose mine were furious when they found them and taunted me with my childishness and stupidity, saying it was clear that I had no sense and that everyone who did have any, whatever their age or sex, having heard the true preaching, gave up such bigotry, but that I was as stupid as my governess. And my brother Anjou threatened me that my mother would have me soundly whipped for it. But he was only speaking for himself, for the Queen, my mother, did not know that he had fallen into error', and as soon as she did find out, Marguerite asserted, Anjou was sternly brought back to the true faith of his forefathers.

She was only seven or eight at the time and, 'bursting into tears, I told him that he might have me whipped or killed if he liked, for I would rather suffer anything than be damned'. Henri might merely have been teasing his pretty but precocious little sister; yet the fact that such brotherly teasing could be based on so serious a matter as their religion and the salvation of their souls was a reflection in miniature of the tremendous drama that dominated their lives even in childhood.

In August 1566 Philip II sent an expedition under the cruel Duke of Alba to the Low Countries, to exterminate his dissenting subjects there. The close proximity of these Spanish troops led Catherine to raise an army of French and Swiss mercenaries to protect France's frontier. In September a year later the Huguenots, led by the Bourbon Prince, Condé, and Coligny, suspecting the Queen Mother of being in league with Philip and planning their destruction similarly, decided to take the initiative. They plotted to kidnap the Royal Family from Montceaux-en-Brie, where the Court was then in residence. They were foiled only in the nick of time by the Swiss Guards, who arrived at midnight at Meaux. At three in the morning these dependable infantrymen formed a square, in the midst of which were placed the King, the Queen Mother, and her ladies, whilst 300 mounted cavaliers escorted it in safety to Paris and the Louvre. Condé and a small column of his men, however, pursued them there.

Throughout these wars the Parisians remained stolidly on the Catholic side—on the side of the country's traditional religion, which they equated with the monarchy. The populace rose to repel the Huguenots, whilst the Royal defenders were commanded by the Lord High Constable. At the Battle of St Denis the old warrior, aged seventy-four, was mortally wounded.

Catherine had always resented and feared Montmorency's influence over her husband. After his death she had little difficulty in persuading Charles IX to abolish the post of Lord High Constable. But against all his inclinations she cunningly induced him to appoint his younger brother, Anjou, Lieutenant-General and head of the Catholic army which was being prepared to annihilate the Huguenots.

As her sons grew up Catherine's difficulties in managing them grew greater. Charles had been a fine and apparently healthy baby. And although later he was tall and physically unusually strong, he became tuberculous, like his brother François. Charles was also mentally unbalanced to the point of insanity. Mere hunting and field-sports did not satisfy his blood-lust. He had murderous bouts in which he amused himself by torturing and dismembering even domestic animals. And at any moment he might burst into fits of such maniacal rage that even the Queen Mother feared him. His narrow escape at Meaux brought on one of these furies, for he was no physical coward and wanted to do battle against the Huguenots. Only by constantly playing on his jealousy and fear of his brother Anjou, whom he knew to be waiting impatiently to succeed him, did Catherine bring him to reason.

The Queen Mother's own compensation for her sexual frustration was her passionate, obsessive love for this son, Henri, 'the apple of her eyes' as she called him. Whilst in every other respect her coolly calculating mind successfully controlled her feelings, Catherine was secretly dominated by this morbid passion.

In the Battle of Jarnac on 13 March 1569 Anjou was victorious. He killed Condé, the rebellious Bourbon cousin, and had his corpse brutally dragged around the Catholic camp, to the delight of his soldiery. After this victory he was confident that he would also defeat Coligny. But before taking on this second venture, which might bring him death as well as triumph, he said, he wished 'to render an account to the King, his brother, and to his mother', of the battle he had won. The reporter of the meeting at which he did this was his young sister, Marguerite.

As any other sixteen-year-old girl might have done, the Princess had long ago forgotten their childish religious squabbles, and forgiven Henri for them. Instead, she had formed a gushing adoration for this romantic elder brother, whom his doting mother was only too eager to rejoin.

'So she suddenly decided to leave with the King, taking with her as well the little troop of her women . . . and myself. Flying on wings of maternal devotion, she made the journey from Paris to Tours in three and a half days, which were not without considerable inconvenience and many comical incidents. . . .

'At Plessis-les-Tours we met my brother Anjou with his Army chiefs, the flower of the princes and nobility of France, in whose presence he gave an account to the King . . . with so much art, eloquence, and grace that it won general admiration, all the more so as his extreme youthfulness emphasized the wisdom of his speech, more appropriate to a greybeard than an adolescent . . . and whose beauty was so striking that it rivalled his good fortune and glory.'

Marguerite may even then have been exceptionally observant, or her next paragraph could have been an afterthought when she recalled this illustrious occasion. In any case, it throws a sharp flash of light on Catherine's handling of the dangerous rivalry between her sons:

'What my mother felt, who loved him alone, cannot be put into words. . . . In anyone else one would easily have observed the transports of joy she was feeling; but she never failed in caution and with perfect self-control, making it quite clear that a person of discretion never does anything involuntarily, she refrained from showing her joy and praising the behaviour of so perfect and beloved a son as it deserved, but only took up the points in his speech relevant to the war situation, for discussion by the princes and noblemen present.'

Yet in spite of Catherine's carefulness it was inevitable that the King should be far less enthusiastic than their mother and sister about Anjou's brilliant success, both on the battlefield and in council. It only hardened his jealousy and bitter hatred.

Anjou was no fool. Machiavelli advised *The Prince* to be half lion and half fox; Henri half a Medici, certainly had his share of foxiness as well as courage. Clearly aware of Charles's enmity, he exploited their mother's adoration to the utmost limit. Yet at that moment he was still uneasy. When, as he was shortly to do, he returned to the battlefield, there had to be someone with the adoring Queen who would keep her idol in her thoughts night and day. And fortunately for him the right person was available.

'One day', Marguerite continued her narrative, 'when the Queen, my mother, was walking in the park with some of the princes, my brother Anjou asked me to walk down another avenue with him.' There he first of all reminded her of how much they loved one another; but until then there had been no utilitarian afterthoughts in their mutual devotion.

'That', Henri continued, 'was all very well in our childhood, but we are no longer children. You see the great destiny to which God has called me, and to which the Queen, our good mother, brought me up. You know that I love you more than anyone in this world and that I will never have any fame or possessions in which you will not share. I know that you have enough intelligence and good sense to be of great use to me with the Queen, and to help me to preserve my present good fortune. But I fear that my absence may do me harm whilst my brother is always with her, flattering her and doing everything to please her.'

He was afraid, he went on to tell Marguerite, that the King might not always be satisfied with hunting animals, but might be inclined to hunt men also, depriving Henri of his post as Lieutenant-General and personally taking over command of his army, which he, Anjou, would find so unbearable that he would prefer a cruel death. For that reason he considered it necessary to have a very faithful friend to keep him constantly in his mother's mind. He knew of no one more suitable for this task than Marguerite, his 'second self'. She had all the necessary qualities—he repeated this again—intelligence, good judgment, and loyalty. And he requested his sister to be continually at their mother's side, morning, noon, and night. He, in return, would persuade the Queen no longer to consider her youngest daughter a mere child, but to treat her in his absence as she would himself, 'which', he added, 'I'm sure she will do. Forget your timidity with her, speak to her confidently, as you do to me, and be sure she will like it; it will do you great honour, too, to be loved by her. And after God, I shall owe my good fortune to you.'

This was the first great turning-point in Marguerite's life. Until then, she said, all she had thought about was hunting and dancing. Although she was sixteen, she had not yet begun to take an interest in wearing lovely clothes or looking pretty. 'And I had been brought up in such awe of the Queen, my mother, that not only did I not dare to speak to her, but if she merely looked at me I trembled with fear of having done something to displease her.'

This awe in which Catherine held her children, her Court and her Ministers was one of her most powerful psychological weapons. She had acquired her supreme authority in a hard school, after many years of patient humility, and having at last done so was determined to retain it to the end.

At first Marguerite was so joyfully overwhelmed by her brother Anjou's flattering trust in her that she wanted to answer him, she wrote, in the words of Moses during his vision of God in the burning bush: 'Who am I that I should go unto Pharaoh?' But she quickly recovered from this delightful shock, which opened up an entirely new prospect for her. 'His words pleased me; it seemed to me that I had suddenly become something more than I was until then.' They had aroused in her a latent ambition, a sense of her own possible importance as an individual, which never afterwards left her, even at times of greatest depression. She answered Henri that she would be only too happy to do what he asked of her.

Anjou kept his promise and spoke to the Queen Mother about

Marguerite. Catherine then sent for her and for the first time in the young Princess's life put her at ease in her presence.

'Your brother,' the Queen Mother benevolently said to her, 'told me of your conversation with him; he no longer regards you as a child, nor will I, and it will give me great pleasure to talk to you as I would with him. . . . So do not be afraid to speak to me quite frankly, for that is what I wish.'

'I obeyed her only too happily and never failed to be the first person present at her rising and amongst the last at her retirement. She did me the honour of sometimes talking to me for two or three hours and by the grace of God was so satisfied with me that she could not praise me enough to her women. I always talked to her about my brother and kept her informed of all he was doing with such loyalty that I was nothing but his shadow.

'I remained in this happy relationship with the Queen my mother for some time'—a couple of months—'during which the Battle of Montcontour took place, when the news came from my brother Anjou (who always wanted to be close to the Queen my mother) that he was about to besiege Saint-Jean-d'Angely and that it was necessary for the King and herself to be present there. She, wanting to meet him again even more, suddenly decided to leave, taking me with her . . . and I went very joyfully indeed, never dreaming of the misfortune that Fate had in store for me.'

What suddenly happened to throw Marguerite into such despair from the height of her happy pride during those two months?

'Since he left'—she explained it—'his closest companion was de Guast, by whom he was so completely dominated that he could only see through his eyes and speak through his mouth. This wicked man, born to do evil, but by whom he was utterly fascinated, filled his mind with a thousand obsessive maxims, such as that "one should never love nor trust anyone saving oneself, nor rely on them, neither sister nor brother" and other fine Machiavellian principles, which he seriously took to heart and determined to carry out.

'As soon as we were alone, after the first greetings were over, my mother praised me to him and told him how faithfully I had served him at her side. He answered her very coolly that that was

Catherine de Medici

Henri II of France by François Clouet

a good thing, as he had asked me to do so, but that "prudence forbade one to use the same expedients all the time and that what was useful at one point might be harmful at another".

'She asked him why he said this and he, finding the moment propitious to bring out the fabrication with which he was determined to ruin me, told her that I "was growing beautiful and that M. de Guise was courting me and that his uncles were hoping that I would marry him; that if I were to feel any affection for him there would be a danger that I might reveal to him everything she told me; that she well knew the ambitions of that House, and how they had always set themselves up against ours. For that reason it would be a good thing if she ceased to talk to me about our affairs and gradually withdrew her intimacy from me."

'That very same evening I noticed the change in her manner as the result of this pernicious advice, and, seeing that she was afraid of speaking to me in front of my brother, and told me three or four times to go to bed, I waited until he left her room and then drew near to her and begged her to tell me if I had been unlucky enough to do anything to displease her? At first she tried to evade answering me, but then she said:

'"My girl, your brother is wise and you should bear him no ill-will for what I am going to tell you, which is all to the good." And then she ordered me not to talk to her about my brother any more.

'These words hurt me as deeply as her first ones, when she had taken me into her favour, had made me happy. I did everything to convince her of my innocence, and that I had never heard anyone mention it'—the suggestion that she should marry Guise—'and that if he ever did as much as mention it I would immediately tell her of it. But it was useless; my brother's words had made such an impression on her mind that they left no room in it either for reason or truth. Seeing that this was the case, I told her that I felt the loss of my happiness no less deeply than my previous joy in it; that my brother had taken it from me as he had bestowed it on me, without my deserving it, on purely imaginary grounds that were mere fantasies; and I assured her that I would remember for the rest of my life the injury my brother had done me.'

And indeed Marguerite did so. For this was the beginning of the enmity between herself and Anjou that was to become steadily deeper and more embittered with the years.

When Marguerite dared to tell her mother so, Catherine not surprisingly 'became angry and forbade me to show it to him in any way'. It was her last chance of speaking so frankly and intimately with the Queen, for 'from that day forward she gradually withdrew her favour from me, making an idol of her son, satisfying him in this matter and in everything else he desired of her'.

As the result of this emotional shock and 'of the bad air which was then in the Army', Margot became desperately ill. Probably she caught scarlet fever. Her mother—perhaps secretly regretting the necessity of withdrawing her intimacy from her, of which she had nevertheless been thoroughly convinced by Henri —unbent sufficiently to visit her sickbed frequently in spite of the risk of infection.

Anjou, having achieved his objective and possibly also secretly sorry for his abrupt unkindness to his young sister, did the same, 'not leaving my bedside day or night and caring for me as kindly as if we were still at the time of our greatest intimacy'. He went even further, for when Marguerite was convalescing at Angers, 'sick in body but with my soul even more sickened, I found to my dismay that M. de Guise and his uncles had arrived there, which pleased my brother, since it lent colour to his story and increased my apprehension and suffering'. Anjou went as far as bringing Guise to see her, pretending 'that he was very fond of him, and in order to convince him of it 'he often embraced him and said to him, "Would to God you were my brother!" which M. de Guise pretended not to hear, whilst I, knowing his malice fretted at not being able to tax him with it.' All she could do was to 'reply to his hypocrisy with sighs'.

Did Marguerite protest too much when writing these recollections? Was there any substance in Anjou's contentions based on de Guast's advice? Other historical evidence indicates that this was so.

The clue to Anjou's erratic behaviour was his homosexuality. He never hesitated to exploit the devotion he knew how to arouse in women by flattery and charm; he exploited to the utmost his mother's incestuous passion for him and his sister's loyalty, taking from them all the advantages these gave him, but giving them next to nothing in return. He was certainly wildly jealous of his brother the King and in Marguerite's case to a lesser degree of Guise, for whom he may also have had more than brotherly affection. He was to continue for many years playing his cat-and-mouse game with poor Marguerite, making her increasingly angry and unhappy. Although he had distinguished himself in battle with the help of his military staff, Henri of Anjou was temperamentally more of a fox than a lion, yet, like his father, he became the tool of his favourites, who unabashedly exploited his homosexuality and depravity as de Guast did.

The young Duke of Guise, who at that time was twenty, was the boy whom little Margot had told her father she would not choose as her cavalier because he was 'impatient, always wanting to hurt someone and be the master'. But Marguerite's feelings towards him also changed as she grew into girlhood. Ten years later than that early episode he was even more handsome, fair, tall, and brave. He had not much love for Anjou, who was given the military leadership of the Catholic army to which he himself aspired. But he fought well in those battles and was wounded in the foot. He was the son of Duke François I, Scarface, and after he was similarly scarred in battle inherited this nickname. His uncle was the immensely rich and powerful Cardinal. Princess Claude of France had married the head of their House; and in order to strengthen their ties with the throne still further, the Cardinal was planning the marriage of this nephew with her younger sister, letting it be known that in that event he would give him a vast fortune.

Catherine de Medici always deeply distrusted the Cardinal and particularly feared his treasonous intrigues with Philip of Spain. When news of his aspirations for his nephew reached her, the Queen went to visit him, as the Cardinal was at that time ailing. Catherine always believed in taking the initiative in every possible case, and this was one of the mainsprings of her astute statecraft. She reproached the Cardinal for the rumours of such an impending match that had reached the Spanish Court and made it clear to him that it would not be to her liking, since she was still hoping for the Portuguese alliance for Marguerite.

More than probably, Margot was at that time in love with Guise and would gladly have married him. It was said that their relationship had reached the flirtatious stage and even gone a great deal further. Malicious gossips reported that Guise had access to the Princess's private apartments in the Louvre and had brought a friend there on one occasion, when he paraded his intimacy with her. In all the freshness of her eighteen years, Marguerite had become extremely pretty, with the sparkling eyes of the Valois, a flawless skin, and a delightful little bosom, which the costumes of her period by no means concealed.

They exchanged notes and letters through a lady-in-waiting and one version of this episode stated that it was Marguerite's enemy, de Guast, who managed to steal one of these notes—certainly nothing would have given him greater pleasure. He arranged to have it seen by the King, whereupon Charles flew into one of his rages and ordered his bastard brother, Angoulême, to arrange to kill the presumptuous young Guise during the next day's hunt. Marguerite, however, was able to warn him in time, so that for some days he did not appear at Court. When he did so, Charles IX furiously ordered him out of his sight.

According to the version sent to Madrid by the Spanish Ambassador, it was Catherine who discovered this secret correspondence. Hearing of it, Charles, wearing only his nightgown, burst into the Queen Mother's room at five o'clock in the morning, demanding that his sister be sent for immediately and severely punished for disgracing a Daughter of France.

Terrified by this sudden summons, Margot hurriedly dressed and rouged her face to hide her pallor. When she entered her mother's room, the King placed a guard at the door and then himself savagely attacked her with his fists. The poor girl fell to the floor, fainting, and it took the Queen Mother more than an hour to revive her.

Whether the situation did take so melodramatic a turn or not, Marguerite herself described in her Memoirs how wretchedly she was tormented by it. She knew that without Royal consent the marriage to Guise could not take place; it was clear enough that such consent would be withheld. In desperation she wrote to her sister Claude, Duchess of Lorraine, 'asking her to arrange for M. de Guise to leave the Court, and begging her to see that he was married as soon as possible to his mistress, the Princess of Porcian . . .'.

The Duchess immediately took the necessary steps; Guise was very soon afterwards married to the Princess—a rich widow—'thus', Marguerite wrote half sorrowfully and half relieved, 'delivering me from that calumny and proving to the Queen my mother the truth of what I had always told her . . . and giving me peace'.

Such as it was, this peace of mind was only temporary, and a poor substitute for the hopes she might have had of marrying her handsome young Duke. The Lorraines having thus been put in their place by the House of Valois, Catherine once again turned her mind to her more ambitious marriage projects for her unhappy little daughter.

3   Ill-omened Wedding

Never was there less of a love-match than the marriage of Marguerite of Valois and Henry of Navarre. It was a union based solely on external and internal State policy by the bride's mother and brother in collaboration with the Huguenot leaders, Coligny and Jeanne of Albret.

Catherine and Charles IX had been deeply offended by the refusal of Philip of Spain and his nephew, the young King of Portugal, to accept the Valois Princess into their House. France was becoming more and more alarmed by Spanish activities in the Netherlands; Coligny was ceaselessly urging an expedition to rescue his co-religionists there from Spanish atrocities.

Catherine had been so deeply impressed by Nostradamus's prophecy of the death of her husband that she had appointed him Court astrologer. When he also predicted that all her children would become kings and queens she never ceased to endeavour to prove him right. Her chief preoccupation was to find a kingdom for her beloved Anjou, and the crown she was then attempting to secure for him was that of England.

Two of the Huguenot leaders, the Cardinal of Châtillon and the Vidamus of Chartres, had crossed to England during the previous War of Religion and were well received at Court. Catherine was using them as intermediaries in approaching Elizabeth I regarding this marriage she so ardently desired. The Virgin Queen, who was Henri's senior by eighteen years, and Henri himself, dashed the Queen Mother's hopes, however, since neither of them was willing to form so ludicrous an alliance. Undaunted, Catherine then quite seriously proposed to Elizabeth her youngest son, the Duke of Alençon, with equally negative results and to the Virgin Queen's sardonic amusement.

France was successful in 1570 in bringing about a treaty with England and the German Protestant princes against Spain and the Holy Roman Emperor. These alliances and manœuvres revealed how far the House of Valois had gone and was going in the Protestant direction.

By giving Marguerite to Henry of Navarre a crown would be obtained for her also, even although only of a small kingdom lying on the slopes of the Pyrenees in the extreme south-west corner of France, adjacent to the Spanish frontier. Until 1234 the whole of Navarre had belonged to Spain, but then passed to the Albret line. In 1511 Ferdinand of Spain took back High Navarre, south of the Pyrenees, from Jean III of Albret, leaving him only a restricted territory in the lowlands and the province of Béarn. In spite of the small area it then occupied the strategic importance of Navarre was considerable, since it was a wedge between its two powerful and antagonistic neighbours. If the King of Navarre were to repudiate his loyalty to the King of France his kingdom would offer the Spaniards a foothold for invasion; so long as he did remain loyal it provided a bastion between the rival Powers.

Marguerite, Duchess of Angoulême, was the only and dearly loved sister of François I, Margot's great-aunt. She was plain but unusually intelligent, a poetess and author of eight romantic autobiographical tales in the Italian fashion, the *Heptameron*. She was a widow aged thirty-three when she fell in love with young Henri of Albret, who was only twenty-two. But the Albrets had a flair for making advantageous alliances and to marry the King of France's sister was clearly the best match Henri could make. They had a daughter and a son; the boy died in childhood but the girl, Jeanne, became a formidable figure as Queen of Navarre.

Henri shared the Duchess of Angoulême's enlightened views on the Reformation and under their rule Navarre became a refuge for many persecuted Calvinists. But much as King François loved his sister, he thought it wiser to retain their little daughter in France, in case her parents might in self-protection be tempted to marry her to a Spaniard. Jeanne, however, was a natural rebel, astonishingly strongminded even as a child. When she was only twelve she defied her royal uncle's plan to marry her to the German Duke of Cleves and had to be carried to the altar by the Lord High Constable in person, at the King's command. The marriage was never consummated and was in due course annulled by papal authority. Jeanne of Albret virtually had a Court of her own in Paris and her mother complained bitterly of her extravagance, but to no effect.

After the death of François Henri II, Margot's father, fearing that his temperamental female cousin might still marry a Spaniard, suggested as her second husband Antoine of Bourbon, the handsome, dashing young First Prince of the Blood, who, in the event of the Valois dynasty dying out—at that time a highly unlikely prospect—was next in line to the throne of the Lilies. Jeanne, as ambitious as she was strong-willed, fell madly in love with Antoine.

Antoine was Lieutenant-General of the realm and was killed in a very peculiar and almost hilarious incident at the siege of Rouen in 1562. As a gesture of contempt towards the defenders of that city he had taken down his trousers and was publicly relieving himself against the ramparts when he was hit by a musket shot. Antoine had certain excellent qualities; he was brave and broadminded, and it might be said that he had forfeited his life to his sense of humour. These qualities were inherited by his and Jeanne's only son, Henry of Navarre, who with his younger sister Catherine was still a child when his father was killed.

But Jeanne, the Queen Mother, after her return to Navarre became converted to Calvinism, and as she never did anything by halves she became one of the Geneva Master's most ardent disciples, a fanatical Puritan and leader, with the Prince of Condé, her brother-in-law, of the French Huguenots. Her obstinacy deepened into fanaticism, her love of luxury was transformed into the extremes of austerity and meanness. Her small kingdom became a stronghold of The Religion, where the pastors, their endless prayer-meetings and austerely controlled flocks were encouraged and protected, whilst Jeanne vindictively pursued priests and nuns, forbade all Catholic ritual, burned down churches and pillaged those of her subjects who remained loyal to France's traditional religion.

This ruthless, despotic and selfish woman was to become poor Margot's mother-in-law, hardly the one a spoilt, gay, rather naughty and beautiful young princess loving luxurious clothes, festivities and the arts would have wished for.

Yet Jeanne was punctilious in observing her fealty to the Valois ruler and invariably addressed the Queen Mother and the King with the respect due from a vassal.

During his mother's lifetime Henry of Navarre took little part in the government of his small realm. He was born at Pau on 14 December 1553, seven months later than his future bride. He had a healthy, tough childhood; as a boy he went about barefoot, like any of his peasants, and took no interest in the lessons of his tutors. But he was brave and a good soldier. After Condé's death at Jarnac his mother and Coligny appointed the young Prince head of the Huguenot forces; his second-in-command was his cousin, Condé's heir and successor, who was a year older.

Navarre was far fonder of girls than his severe mother might have wished, but his love affairs were brief and bucolic, with whatever rustic beauties happened to attract him; he knew nothing of the arts and intrigues of erotic intercourse as they were so subtly practised at Court, where Marguerite had grown up. Henry was more than casual regarding his dress and appearance; it was said that he was averse to water, hardly ever washed and, frankly, stank. Before his marriage Navarre undoubtedly appeared to be little better than a provincial oaf.

This was however, no deterrent to the Queen Mother in deciding that he was a fit young man to become her son-in-law. She had little doubt that when he did arrive at Court and saw his beautiful young bride Henry would be cleansed, groomed, civilized, and above all converted. For there were two serious obstacles to the marriage which would have to be overcome before it might take place. The prospective bride and bridegroom were third cousins and would need a Papal dispensation owing to their consanguinity; much more important to Rome, Navarre was a heretic.

According to Marguerite's own account, the match was first suggested to the Queen Mother at dinner by a son of the late Constable, Montmorency.

'When we rose from table he told me that she had asked him to speak to me about it. I said to him that it was superfluous to do so, since I had no will in the matter but my mother's.' And Marguerite was obliquely addressing Catherine's implacable will when she added that 'I begged him to remind her how deeply Catholic I was and that it would distress me to marry someone who was not of my own religion. After this the Queen my mother called me into her cabinet and told me that the Montmorencys had suggested this marriage to her and that she would like to know my will about it, to which I answered that I had no will nor feelings except her own'—and again Marguerite begged her mother to remember that she was deeply Catholic. Whereupon, according to another account, Catherine reassured her daughter, saying that 'that might easily be remedied, as they were hoping that he would become a Catholic'. And without doubt that was Catherine's hope and intention; if Navarre did so she felt sure of obtaining the Papal dispensation regarding their distant relationship.

Jeanne of Albret, however, by no means jumped at the proposed alliance, which, apparently, had already been mooted many years previously, in Henri II's time, when Marguerite and Navarre were still children, and before the religious conflict between their parents had become so acute. In spite of the advantages to be gained from it at this later date, an easy acceptance would not have been in Jeanne's fanatical and grasping character. There ensued a long correspondence between the two Queen Mothers: Catherine playing her hand with all her Italian guile and synthetic charm; Jeanne, deeply suspicious of her Papist tricks, reluctant to accept her cordial, even pressing invitations to visit her to draw up the marriage contract. In spite of her moral rigidity, Jeanne of Albret had a grim sense of humour.

'I do not know, Madame', she wrote, 'why you tell me that you wish to meet me and my children and that it is not that you want to do us any harm. Forgive me if, when reading your letters, I felt like laughing, for you were trying to reassure me about something I never feared, for I never thought that, as the saying goes, you ate little children.'

But on 15 February Jeanne did meet Catherine at Chenonceaux for the relevant discussions. She took her young daughter with her, but ordered her son to remain in Béarn until she had settled matters to her satisfaction. Apart from the haggling that took place with regard to the future bride's dowry and landed property, Jeanne may have been afraid, as her letters to him indicated, that Henry would be so impressed by Marguerite's beauty that he would agree to the Valois terms unconditionally, but especially that he might allow himself to be converted to her religion. She also realized quite clearsightedly that in the eyes of the Valois Court, the most brilliant in Europe, Henry, unless he was first properly groomed and fitted out, might cut a poor and ridiculous figure.

Even Jeanne of Albret was impressed by Marguerite's beauty and charm. On 21 February she wrote to her son that Madame —this was the courtesy title of the unmarried Princesses of the Blood Royal—had received her very kindly. His fourteen-year-old sister Catherine added a postscript to her mother's letter, saying that Marguerite was very beautiful and had given her a sweet little dog as a present. But when Jeanne tried to sound out her future daughter-in-law in the hope of converting her to The Religion, she was greatly disappointed by her firm resistance.

'I find', she wrote on 11 March, 'that Madame has become very cool towards me', and when she asked Marguerite outright whether she would agree to follow her husband's religion, the reply, polite yet definite, was that 'If it pleased God that their marriage should take place she would not fail to obey him and her mother-in-law in all reason, but even if he were king of all the world she would not change her religion, in which she had been brought up'. Then Jeanne, losing patience, declared that the marriage was off and they parted very coldly.

At Chenonceaux, Blois, and, later, Paris, the Queen of Navarre found everything increasingly annoying and irritating. Catherine was no longer wooing her and occasionally even made fun of her provincialism with malicious amusement.

'As for Madame', Jeanne complained, 'I only see her at the Queen's, where she stays all day, going to her own apartment at times when it is inconvenient for me to talk to her and even there Madame de Curton'—Marguerite's governess, who was still with her and was no doubt supporting her Catholic resolution—'never budges from her side, listening to everything I say.'

Jeanne reluctantly admitted that Marguerite was 'beautiful, polite, and gracious, but brought up in the most damned and corrupt company there has ever been . . . here it is not the men who court the women, but the women who make advances to the men', and with increasing maternal anxiety she wrote to her son that not for the world would she wish him to live there: 'that is why I want you to marry, so that you and your wife may withdraw from this corrupt environment; if you remained, you would never escape from it', and she ended her letter by admonishing Henry to pray with all his might for God's help, which he would badly need.

In another letter Jeanne wrote that 'as regards Madame's beauty, I admit that she has a good figure, although she laces herself very tightly. As for her face, she uses so much make-up that it disgusts me, for she will spoil it, but in this Court they all use almost as much make-up as in Spain.'

The marriage contract was at last signed on 14 April. The King, the Queen Mother, her brothers, Anjou and Alençon, together endowed Marguerite with a fortune amounting to more than a million and a half *écus* in gold—which, however, was never subsequently paid—as well as a casket of immensely valuable jewels, to which Navarre later added another collection worth 30,000 écus, in addition to the wedding ring, in which was mounted a diamond which alone was worth 10,000 écus. Jeanne of Albret was unable to obtain the settlement on Marguerite of certain lands and properties for which she had been haggling, but when the engagement was celebrated her fiancé assigned to his bride the rights and revenues of other lands and domains he owned in France.

Jeanne of Albret's health had been failing even before she left her kingdom to meet the Queen Mother. In spite of a cure she took during the negotiations, it did not improve. On 14 May she arrived in Paris, where she was expecting her son to join her for his wedding. But the strain of the past months was too much for her. She fell ill of a fever and died five days later, on 9 June. She was only forty-four.

Jeanne's sudden and dramatic end threw her Huguenot colleagues and followers into furious consternation. They immediately spread the rumour that she had been poisoned by the detested Florentine, Catherine de Medici, whose countrymen in her employment were famous for concocting lethal potions. An autopsy appeared to prove that Jeanne had died a natural death; nevertheless, the rumours persisted.

In view of the fact that the contract was by then signed and therefore Jeanne of Albret, had she lived, could no longer be as tiresome to Catherine and Charles IX as she had been during the preceding months, there would seem at that point to have been no urgency for them to rid themselves of Marguerite's future mother-in-law. But to the bride her death certainly was a relief. Margot was well aware of the fact that as soon as she was married to Navarre, Jeanne would have left her no peace and would have nagged her and her husband unmercifully until she changed her religion and her whole way of life. It was bad enough to have to marry a man not of her own choice, but one forced on her by maternal and brotherly authority as a political manœuvre; to be saddled with such a mother-in-law as well would have been a burden from which she was undoubtedly glad to be freed. And how Margurite did feel about Jeanne she made clear in a cynical little story she told in her Memoirs. This was addressed personally to her devoted admirer, Brantôme.

'The incident', she wrote to him 'was so amusing that although it is not worthy of passing into history, it should still not be passed over in silence between ourselves.'

The occasion was the official visit of mourning Madame paid to the deathbed of Jeanne of Albret. She was accompanied there by the Cardinal of Bourbon and several great ladies of the Court who were related to the late Queen of Navarre, 'to pay her the last respects due to her rank and our connections with her, not with the pomp and ceremony of our religion, but merely with the minor ceremonial allowed by Huguenoterie', she explained disdainfully, 'namely, she being in her usual bed, with the curtains undrawn and no candles, no priests, no cross and no holy water; we, standing five or six paces away from her bed with the rest of the company, merely gazing at her. Madame de Nevers, whom, as you know, during her lifetime she had hated more than anyone else on earth and with whom she had frequently had high words (and, as you also know, she knew very well how to use them towards those whom she hated), left our group and with several splendid humble and profound curtsies approached her bed and, taking her hand, kissed it, then with another deeply reverential curtsy rejoined us. We who knew how they had hated one another appreciated it. . . .'

In other words, at Jeanne of Albret's deathbed Marguerite and her friends could hardly restrain their smiles at the Duchess of Nevers' impudent gesture. Her account of this incident reveals Marguerite's naughty sense of humour, and how superbly she was able to observe, remember, and report a scene many years later; it also makes quite clear where her sympathies lay. Possibly it was some little consolation for her private misery at that time, when, it was said, she wept a great deal. After telling this anecdote, Marguerite proceeded:

'Some months later the King of Navarre, wearing mourning for the Queen his mother, arrived, accompanied by 800 gentlemen, also all in black, and was received with great honours by the King and the whole Court; and our wedding took place a few days later, in such triumph and magnificence as no other person of my rank had known until then; the King of Navarre and his troop having changed from mourning into very rich and handsome costumes and all the Court arrayed as you know and would be able to describe far better; I, in royal garb, with crown and ermine stole, leading the procession, the precious stones in my crown flashing, and my great blue cloak with four trains carried by three princesses; the stands which had been put up as usual for the weddings of Daughters of France, from the Bishop's residence to Notre Dame, covered and draped in cloth of gold; the people packed together down below to watch the wedding procession and all the Court passing along above them. So we arrived at the Cathedral porch, where the Cardinal of Bourbon was officiating, and when he had received us and we had said the usual words, customary in such cases we passed along the stands to the platform separating the nave from the choir, where there are two flights of stairs, one to go down into the choir, the other leading out of the church through the nave. The King of Navarre went out by those of the nave, we . . .'

At that point there is a dramatic gap in Marguerite's narrative. When she wrote it she had her reasons for breaking off so abruptly what until then was an account of her personal triumph, of her superb and glamorous appearance and procession, to the delight of the populace below. One clue lies in a sentence written long afterwards: 'All the harm that ever came to me in life came through marriage, the greatest calamity that ever befell me. . . . Ah! do not let anyone say that marriages are made in heaven; the gods would not commit so great an injustice!'

The wedding did not in fact go off as smoothly as the reluctant bride reported.

When it was learned in Rome that Catherine de Medici was intending to marry off her daughter to the heretic Navarre, Pope Pius V made a strenuous last-minute effort through his legate to bring about the Portuguese alliance, but too late. By then the King of France was implacably opposed to Spain.

The Huguenots saw in the marriage between their King and leader and the King of France's sister an opportunity to strengthen their ties with the Crown and to oust from favour the hated Guises, who fully returned their enmity and were at the head of the Papist faction. At the time when Jeanne of Albret was bitterly complaining of the Queen Mother's levity and mockery, Charles IX apparently on at least one occasion went out of his way to soothe and reassure her. When Jeanne had expressed her doubts to him regarding the arrival of the Papal dispensation authorizing the marriage, he replied to her, 'No, my aunt. I honour you more than the Pope, and love my sister more than I fear him. I am not a Huguenot, but nor am I a fool. If the Pope becomes too tiresome, I myself will take my sister's hand and lead her to her wedding in chapel.'

As far as his irritation with the Pope went, Charles was certainly sincere in making this remarkable declaration. His love for his sister was, however, as she very well knew, conditional on her total obedience to his royal command.

Whether or not Marguerite's girlish passion for the Duke of Guise had gone beyond conventional limits, whether or not her eldest brother had beaten her in a fit of fury when their correspondence was brought to his notice, he knew perfectly well that had she been allowed to make her own choice the last husband she would have wished for was Henry of Navarre. Marguerite really was a sincere Catholic, but by then she was also aware that she had become a beauty admired by the entire Court; she was nearly nineteen and was thoroughly enjoying the life of luxury to which she was accustomed. She also had her full share of the Valois temperament. In marrying that malodorous provincial young King she would at least become a Queen of a small kingdom, but was that sufficient consolation for losing her lover and having been publicly repudiated by the greatest Catholic monarchy in Europe? The prospect of having to spend the remainder of her life in Béarn, that remote little corner of French soil over which Henry ruled, was a profoundly depressing one, especially in that stiff-backed and sombre Huguenot atmosphere that was so repugnant to her. She might well have hoped against hope that the Papal dispensation would be withheld and even until the last moment that the marriage would not take place. But Marguerite was no more than a pawn in her brother's and mother's policies.

The old Pope, Pius V, did in fact withhold his consent. When he died on 1 May Catherine and Charles thought that they might expect his successor, Gregory XIII, to be more amenable. They used every wile to persuade His Holiness that Henry of Navarre's conversion was imminent and that the dispensation, on the grounds of blood relationship alone, might safely be granted. But Gregory, like his predecessor, refused to be foxed by Medici or Valois guile. When the wedding was about to be celebrated the Papal dispensation had still not been received.

Catherine's audacity when faced with this crisis was as indomitable as usual.

The Cardinal of Bourbon, who was to perform the ceremony, was an uncle of the bridegroom and exceedingly pleased at the prospect of this royal alliance. He pointed out to the Papal legate in Paris that according to the marriage contract Navarre's children would be brought up in the Catholic faith even if their prospective father did not yet belong to it. Still the Holy Father remained obstinately unco-operative. Thereupon there ensued one of those conveniently ambiguous incidents which gave a touch of comedy to the solution of this grave religious and dynastic problem. The Cardinal allegedly received from his colleague in Rome, the Cardinal of Lorraine, a letter purporting to inform him that the Papal dispensation was imminent. According to one account, this was in the form of a sealed packet which the nuncio Salviati presented to the Queen Mother and which she did not even have the curiosity to open, knowing perfectly well that the contents were not as assumed, but passed straight on to the Cardinal of Bourbon, who likewise refrained from burning his fingers by doing so. It was simply taken for granted that the dispensation had been given. But to make doubly sure, all the same —and this was not rumour, but fact—Catherine gave strict orders that there was to be no further communication with Rome until after the wedding.

The ceremony was fixed for Monday, 18 August 1572. On the previous Thursday Catherine herself wrote to Mandelot, the Governor of Lyons, ordering him for love of his King and in his official capacity 'not to allow to pass through any courier from Rome, whether he was or was not bringing any despatches to his said Lord'—the King—'or anything else, until after Monday'. As the journey from Rome to Lyons took at the minimum four days, there was thus no danger that the Pope's refusal to sanction the marriage would arrive in Paris until after it was over. Charles IX personally confirmed this order. And to safeguard herself Catherine also wrote to the Holy Father explaining that it would have been impossible for various reasons to postpone the wedding any longer and hoping that he would take it in good part.

Valois impudence went even further. It was usual on such festive occasions for a medal to be struck, commemorating them. This was also done. On one side were the interlaced monograms of bride and groom surrounded by the Latin phrase, *Constricta hoc vinclo Discordia*; on the reverse was the Pascal Lamb with the quotation from the Gospels, *Vobis annuntio pacem*.

On the evening before her wedding the bride was escorted in great splendour from the Louvre to the Bishop's residence adjacent to Notre Dame Cathedral, and next morning the whole Court arrived there to conduct her to the ceremony. The procession was headed by the King and the bride's two other brothers, the Dukes of Anjou and Alençon, with the Queen Mother, her ladies, Ministers, and officials.

In the forefront of the Catholic courtiers were the still immensely powerful Guises, Aumale and Nevers; the Huguenots were led by Navarre's cousin, the Prince of Condé and the Admiral, the irreconcilable opponents in the Wars of Religion which were to reach their furious climax only six days later. The King, his brothers and Condé, who was also of the Blood Royal, wore similar costumes of heavily embroidered pale yellow satin flashing with gold and jewels. The Catholic noblemen were dressed with equal magnificence, but in marked and deliberate contrast the Huguenots appeared in the simplest and plainest clothes such a State occasion allowed.

In view of the bridegroom's religion, it had been arranged beforehand that the wedding should not be solemnized in front of the High Altar, but should take place on the Cathedral porch in full sight of the populace. Marguerite's statement that the onlookers below were tightly and enthusiastically packed together was not corroborated by other accounts, for the stolidly Catholic Parisians only coolly supported this mixed marriage. And when it had taken place they beheld an unedifying sight which was unlikely to increase their warmth for it.

As Henry of Navarre was unable to hear his nuptial Mass, it had been agreed that at the relevant moment he should turn to one of the royal Dukes, praying him to do so on his behalf. But whether he was drunk or sober, whether his indifference was due to his marked lack of devotion to his beautiful bride as well as to her religion, Henry, with a misplaced levity on so solemn an occasion, after the Catholics had entered the Cathedral brashly walked about on the porch, talking loudly to his supporters and co-religionists, who had joined him there as soon as the liturgy began.

Marguerite's glamorous but brief account of her wedding understandably enough made no mention of the fact that amongst those splendidly arrayed noblemen attending it was her former love and suitor, the Duke of Guise. And when the bride was asked by the Cardinal for the usual assent Guise unabashedly 'rose and stood up in front of the other noblemen to take a closer look at Marguerite's face and eyes', a cruel gesture which did not pass unobserved by the bride's brother, the King, 'who gave Guise a look which expressed his feelings more loudly than words'.

For a crucial instant Marguerite was speechless, motionless. Charles, irritated by Guise's behaviour and his sister's reluctance even at that last second, gave her a smart tap on the neck which compelled her to bow her head in assent. Whether the account of this brutal incident was fact or legend, such marriages, as Marguerite wrote, are not made in heaven.

After the bride had entered the Cathedral and heard her nuptial Mass, with no groom at her side, the procession re-formed and returned to the episcopal residence, where at the wedding banquet the King of Navarre did publicly embrace his new Queen. But from that day to the end of their marriage they never loved one another. In spite of her beauty, charm, and intelligence, which in due course won her more lovers and admirers than any Queen of France ever attracted, Marguerite had no sex appeal for her husband, who from the outset felt himself her inferior in cultural accomplishments and refinements of outlook and taste, to which he attached little importance.

When the banquet was over the bridal procession returned to the Louvre. Observers noted that the watching Parisians then expressed their true feelings regarding this triumph of Huguenoterie, for the warmest cheers were not given to the Royal Family; they were given to the Duke of Guise, leader of the Catholic party.

There followed three days of elaborate festivities so enjoyed in happier times by Marguerite of Valois. She did not refer to them, either, in her story. For 24 August 1572 was St Bartholomew's Day, the day that caused her marriage to Navarre to be remembered ever afterwards as the Blood-stained Wedding.

4 *Massacre*

Of all the masterpieces of François Clouet and his school, Court painters to the Valois, none is greater than the portrait of Gaspard de Coligny, sacred martyr of the Huguenots, traitor and arch-villain to the Catholics. It reveals a man at the height of his powers. Under a high, intellectual forehead, the clear eyes look out on a rather distasteful world, coolly, reflectively, slightly smiling. The lips have a sensuous curve, yet the set of the mouth is firm and determined, and under the short beard the jaw-line seems to emphasize this moral courage and relentless obstinacy.

Coligny was one of the three Châtillon brothers who were nephews of Montmorency, to whose protection they owed their advancement. All three were converted to The Religion in 1556. They nevertheless claimed to remain completely loyal to the Throne, their special mission, as they saw it, being to free the King from the sinister influence of the Catholics, especially of their arch-enemies, the Guises.

Elizabeth I was still hoping to regain Calais from France. The Huguenots were asking the price of 300,000 crowns and 10,000 men for this port, and pending its return Coligny offered England Le Havre, of which the Lord High Admiral was Governor. A treaty between them to this effect was signed at Hampton Court on 20 September 1562.

On 27 September English troops invaded Normandy, although France and England were not at war, 'with good and sincere intentions'—so Elizabeth's proclamation ran—'towards the King, our good brother', to save his Protestant subjects from annihilation and 'to procure for them by all good means repose, peace, freedom, and deliverance from the violence of the said House of Guise or any adherents of the same'.

Coligny was unable to fulfil the terms of the Treaty. France defended herself. The Queen Mother personally supervised the Siege of Rouen, held by the Huguenots, but in danger of capture by the English. Catherine managed to win over the Prince of Condé, who was in charge of the defence.

The Triumvirs, the Catholic leaders, had no compunction either in calling upon their own allies; the defeat at Dreux of the Protestants was largely due to Spanish aid. Elizabeth I cooled off, and Coligny was obliged to retreat to Orleans.

It was during the siege of that city, led by François, Duke of Guise, whom his followers called Guise the Great, that he was murdered on 18 February 1563 by Poltrot de Méré. The Catholics were convinced that his assassination was plotted by Coligny, and from that day onwards they swore to annihilate him in revenge. The Admiral admitted that he had not 'dissuaded' Poltrot from it; he even declared that Guise's death was 'the greatest good that could have happened to this kingdom', to himself and his House.

The Guises never ceased to demand that Coligny be brought to justice for this crime. But Catherine refused to sanction his prosecution. Her paramount anxiety was to avoid another civil war. She also needed him to negotiate on behalf of the French monarchy with Elizabeth I, as well as to rebuild the royal navy. In the following February, 1564, the Admiral was declared 'purged, discharged, and innocent' of the assassination of Duke François.

The Second War of Religion ended with the Peace of Longjumeau, signed for the Protestants by Cardinal Odet of Châtillon.

But in 1569 the Huguenots, forestalling, as they thought, a new attack on themselves, made their abortive attempt to kidnap the King from Montceaux-en-Brie. The Queen Mother indignantly regarded this plot as open treachery, a flagrant breach of the Peace Treaty, and held Coligny directly responsible for it. She had protected him against his mortal enemies, the Guises, and this was his gratitude. Catherine convinced herself that Coligny was her personal antagonist. The duel between them now entered its last and bitterest phase.

Coligny had not accompanied Condé and his small troop from Meaux to Paris, from which the Huguenots were obliged to retreat after the Battle of St Denis. On the grounds of the Admiral's former plotting with Elizabeth I and his responsibility with his brothers (who would also be punished) for the Treaty of Hampton Court, Catherine arranged that in his absence he should be tried and condemned for high treason by the Parliament of Paris. Cardinal Odet and Andelot were stripped of their property and dignities. Coligny was condemned to death and, to the huge delight of the Catholic Parisians, he was publicly executed in effigy on 13 September 1569.

'In order to stress the infamy of his crime, he was ordered to be hanged, not beheaded, his coat-of-arms was broken and dragged in the gutter and his possessions confiscated.' But this symbolical execution did not satisfy the Queen Mother.

When the death sentence had been passed by the relevant tribunal, it was as a rule publicly carried out by the royal executioner, who, before setting about his gruesome task, always first asked his victim's pardon, to save his own soul from damnation for taking a human life. Executions of exceptionally infamous or distinguished persons were normally attended by the King, the Queen Mother, the Court, and many fair ladies. Poltrot de Méré, killer of the Duke of Guise, was sentenced to quartering. He was torn in four by the attaching of his limbs to four strong horses, whipped north, south, east and west. His end was so horrible that one young lady witnessing it died of heart failure— but only one.

There were occasions, however, when the Throne's enemies were not despatched so publicly, although still officially. The man who volunteered for the deed, after an edict condemning the intended victim, was known as 'the King's Killer'. A price of 50,000 *écus* was placed on Coligny's head.

'To all persons', the edict in his case ran, 'of whatever quality they may be, who may take and apprehend the body of the said Admiral alive, His Majesty will give 10,000 gold *écus au soleil* . . . and to whom will not take him alive, but will put him to death, His said Majesty will promise 2,000 *écus au soleil*.'

The volunteer for Coligny's murder—perfectly legal, since it was the King's will—was a Sieur de Maurevert, a renegade Huguenot 'who was at the camp and in the suite of the said Admiral'. Maurevert, however, was a very bad shot. His attempt misfired completely; the Admiral was unscathed, but the bullet meant for him killed M. de Mouy, who was with him at the time. Maurevert escaped and humbly apologized for his clumsiness to the Duke of Anjou, who thereupon 'sent him to the King, his brother, to confirm his grace and give him the 2,000 *écus* as promised. . . . The said Maurevert was kindly received and paid the said sum by the King. He made his oath at the King's hands to serve him faithfully in all matters. . . .'

The Queen Mother had once contemptuously referred to Coligny as 'more cowardly than a woman'. But Catherine's verdict was inspired by hatred, and incorrect. The Admiral was in fact a master of retreat, and when he retired from a battlefield it was with the firm intention to live to fight another day. Montcontour, at which he lost nearly his whole force, turned out a hollow victory for the Crown and the Catholics. Once again Catherine was compelled to make peace with the detested Huguenot leader. Her motives this time were her constant fear of the Guises and their ally, Spain, and her recent decision to arrange a marriage between Marguerite and Henry of Navarre, whose mother, Jeanne of Albret, was Coligny's most fervent supporter. Finally, she was forced to come to terms with him by the bitter enmity between her sons, which was growing like a cancer on the Valois body.

So Catherine invited Coligny back to Court at a price which she must have found heavy. He was offered sumptuous inducements to return to Paris, presented with 150,000 *livres* and— ironical touch which this fervent but clear-sighted Calvinist no doubt appreciated—the revenues of an abbey amounting to another 20,000.

Charles IX was then twenty-two. He was married to Elisabeth of Austria on 26 November 1570. His mistress, however, the lovely Marie Touchet, was a Huguenot. During his boyhood and adolescence Charles had been Catherine's pliant tool. But as he grew to manhood and saw that his brother Anjou was only too obviously envying him his throne, plotting against him, and supplanting him in their mother's affection, Charles became more and more restive. Whether or not he knew it and exploited it, he had one effective instrument with which to fight the Queen Mother: his sudden maniacal rages which Catherine, a brave enough woman otherwise, really dreaded. Since he was far more emotional than reasonable, Charles probably did not fake these furies, and when they seized him they were perfectly spontaneous.

His father had been accidentally killed when he was a child. It was not in the least surprising therefore that he should have been seeking some father-surrogate to counter the maternal dominance. In spite of his anger with the Huguenots at Montceaux, Charles now turned more and more to Coligny as his guide, philosopher and friend in all but religion, and the Admiral even had high hopes of his ultimate conversion as well. Coligny clearly realized the enormous advantages his party might gain from the mutual hatred of the royal brothers and their mother's part in it. Catherine and Anjou were ineluctably in the hands of the Catholics and the Guises. But the King's affection for him gave Coligny a trump card with which to counter their intrigues. He knew the danger in which he stood from them, but this did not deter him from taking advantage of his strong position. Very soon the Admiral was dominating the Royal Council, never ceasing to urge war on Spain, knowing that the King was longing for such an opportunity to outshine his brother's military glamour after Jarnac and Montcontour.

Catherine was keenly aware that she could no longer control Charles as easily as in the past. Yet she still had one considerable card to play. France was too impoverished in men and money to go to war with Spain without aid from Elizabeth of England, who at that point was not willing to fight the Catholic King. In consequence, at the Royal Council attended by the King, the Queen Mother, their Ministers and the Admiral in 1572, Coligny's proposal for such a war was unanimously defeated. Then, turning to the woman whom he knew to be his most implacable enemy, 'Madam,' the Admiral declared, 'the King renounces going to war. God grant that he may not find himself confronted by another one which he will no doubt not be able to renounce so easily.'

Catherine put only one interpretation on those words, the threat of yet another Huguenot rising that would inflame the kingdom. It was then that she chose the desperate weapon she would employ to avert it—Coligny's murder. Having reached this implacable decision, the Queen Mother in her turn then made a strategic retreat to Montceaux, leaving Coligny temporarily in undisputed possession of the King's favour, which he took immediate steps to exploit. By 13 August, 3,000 Huguenots were assembled at the French frontier to relieve the Siege of Mons by the Spaniards; in Paris Coligny had interviews with the English Ambassador in order to influence Elizabeth's policy more favourably, and he informed the Prince of Orange that he would shortly arrive at the head of 12,000 musketeers and 2,000 horsemen.

It was essential to Catherine's scheme that the Admiral's death should not be regarded as an illegitimate execution, which would raise the Huguenots against the Crown and threaten the impending marriage between Marguerite and Navarre. As the Guises and Châtillons were known by the whole world to be mortal enemies, what would be more natural than the murder of Coligny by a hireling of the Lorraines in revenge for the death of Guise the Great, for which they still thirsted? And so it was planned to appear.

Not surprisingly, Maurevert had gone into the service of the young Duke of Guise. For all the great feudalists, although with no royal prerogative, employed their own private bodyguards and assassins. After his first failure, however, it was slightly surprising that the Queen Mother should again revert to Maurevert as the Admiral's killer. Since Coligny was so firmly entrenched in Charles IX's favour, Henri of Anjou was only too pleased to make the necessary arrangements with the Guises. The Duke's former tutor owned a house in the Rue des Fossés—St Germain —which lay directly on the route the Admiral normally took from the Louvre to his own residence. This house had a ground-floor window from which Maurevert was to aim at his victim as he passed, and two exits for his escape immediately afterwards. The time and date were chosen with care. The attempt was not to be made until after Marguerite's wedding on 18 August and the festivities of the following three days: pageantry, banquets, and balls in which the leaders of both parties were to appear in Court dress and fancy costumes. But on the Saturday morning, 23 August, the King would be hearing Mass at the Hôtel de Bourbon; Anjou would preside in his place at the Royal Council to be attended by the Admiral and the attack was to be made on Coligny's returning home.

Everything proceeded perfectly according to plan, except that the incompetent killer missed for the second time. Maurevert did, however, succeed in escaping. The Admiral's right-hand little finger was shot off and he was also wounded in the left arm. Yet he made his way home to bed with complete calm and self-control.

When Charles IX heard of this wicked attempt on his friend and counsellor he insisted on immediately visiting Coligny to express his sympathy with him and his rage with the obvious instigator of the crime, as he thought, the Duke of Guise. The Queen Mother and Anjou also hastened to the victim's bedside to show their concern for him. Their real anxiety was to be masked by this hypocritical gesture, for Maurevert's failure had put them both in the greatest personal danger. Catherine was aware that Charles would very soon discover her own and his brother's complicity in the plot; whilst she herself might escape the vengeance of matricide by her infuriated elder son, she was terrified that Charles would kill Henri with his own hands for his treacherous alliance with Guise.

Marguerite, Queen of Navarre, bride of only five days, was in complete ignorance of the plot against Coligny and her mother's and brother's instigation of it.

When, after describing her wedding ceremony at Notre Dame in her Memoirs, Margot broke off her narrative so abruptly, the next paragraph continued:

'Fortune, which never allows human beings uninterrupted happiness, soon changed this blissful state of marriage and triumph into its absolute opposite, owing to this wounding of the Admiral, which so infuriated all those of The Religion that it threw them into utter despair. The elder Pardaillan and other Huguenot leaders spoke so strongly about it to the Queen my mother that they convinced her they were intending to avenge it. On the advice of M. de Guise and my brother [Henri] it was decided to forestall them—a decision of which King Charles knew nothing. For he was devoted to the Admiral, M. de la Rochefoucault, Teligny, La Noue, and some of the other leaders of The Religion, whom he was hoping to serve him in Flanders. And from what I later heard him say, it was very difficult to persuade him to agree to it, which he would never have done had he not been told that his life and throne were at stake ... and he was so furious with M. de Guise that he swore to bring him to justice. If M. de Guise had not hidden himself away on that day, the King would have had him arrested. ... So that although the Queen my mother pointed out to him that the death of the Duke of Guise, his father, brought about by the Admiral, exculpated his son, since, having been unable to bring him to justice, he had wanted to take his own revenge ...' the King 'would neither abate nor renounce his passionate desire ... and still ordered M. de Guise to be found and arrested, as he would not allow such a deed to remain unpunished.

'At last ... as the Queen realized that this accident had brought matters to the point when that very night, if their plot were not prevented, they [the Huguenots] would attempt an attack on the

King and herself, she resolved to have King Charles informed of the whole truth and of the danger in which he stood by the Marshal of Rais, from whom she knew he would take it better than from anyone else, being the one closest to him and highest in his favour.'

This Marshal was an Italian, Alberto Gondi, the son of a Florentine banker, who had accompanied Catherine de Medici to France and remained in her service ever since, raising money for her on the frequent occasions when the privy purse was nearly exhausted by her extravagance. In becoming thus indispensable to his Royal mistress, he also amassed an enormous personal fortune. He was given French nationality and ennobled under the title of Count of Rais, or, as it was later spelt, Retz. His wife, who was also Italian, had helped to bring up the Royal Family and remained a lifelong friend and confidant both of the Queen Mother and of Marguerite.

Gondi's task on that ominous evening, as Marguerite did not yet know, was a much more delicate one than merely to ask the King's forgiveness for Guise. Catherine and Anjou had reluctantly decided that he should break the fact of their own complicity in the attack on the Admiral to Charles, rather than that the King should learn of it in a matter of hours from one of his Huguenot protégés.

When doing so in tactful and courtierly terms, Gondi was to refer to a secondary reason for the Queen Mother's hatred of Coligny. Some time previously two of his henchmen had allegedly murdered the Admiral de Charry, one of her most devoted officers.

Towards nine or ten o'clock in the evening, Marguerite continued, Gondi visited the King in his study and told him that 'as his very faithful servant he could no longer hide from him the danger in which he stood if he carried out his threats against the Duke of Guise', and he then broke it to Charles that the Queen and Anjou had been involved. The Queen's reason for consenting to the attack on Coligny, said Gondi, 'was her extreme displeasure at Charry's murder', for she had had few such loyal servants during the King's minority, when all France was divided, 'the Catholics for M. de Guise, the Huguenots for the Prince of Condé, both wanting to deprive him of his Crown, which had only been preserved for him, under God, by the prudence and vigilance of the Queen his mother'.

And however much history was to blame Catherine for having given way to panic on the Eve of St Bartholomew—more for Anjou's sake than her own—that argument of Gondi's was no Italian sophistry, but stark truth.

'In that extremity,' Gondi continued according to Marguerite, 'she had no more faithful adherent than Charry, whose assassination the King knew she had vowed to avenge.'

Gondi then repeated Catherine's case against Coligny, with which Marguerite, a better Catholic than her mother, fully agreed. The Queen Mother's sole objective, according to her daughter, was 'to remove from the kingdom that pest, the Admiral, alone'; but, owing to bad luck, Maurevert's aim had been faulty. Now, in their desperation, the Huguenots were threatening to kill not only Guise, but the Queen and the Duke of Anjou, 'believing also that King Charles himself was on their side and that they would have recourse to arms that very night. So that he saw His Majesty in very great danger whether from the Catholics on account of M. de Guise, or the Huguenots, for the said reason.

'King Charles, who was very prudent and who had always been most obedient to the Queen my mother and a very Catholic prince, seeing how matters stood, suddenly decided to join the Queen his mother and to conform to her will, saving her from the Huguenots by using the Catholics for the purpose; but not without extreme regret, nevertheless, for being unable to save Teligny, La Noue, and M. de la Rochefoucault. And, having rejoined the Queen my mother he sent for M. de Guise and all the other Catholic princes and captains, when it was resolved to start the Massacre of St Bartholomew that very night. And immediately all the chains were fixed'—across the streets of Paris, to barricade their entrances and exits against all intended victims who might attempt to escape—'the tocsin rang and everyone rushed to his own post, according to the order that was given, in the Admiral's case just as much as of all the Huguenots. M. de Guise

went to the Admiral's lodging and M. Besme, a German gentleman, ran up to his room, stabbed him to death, and threw his
body out of the window to his master, M. de Guise.

'As for myself, I was told nothing whatever about all this. I
saw everyone in action'—in the heart of the Palace of the Louvre
itself—'the Huguenots in despair, fearing the Guises and whispering to one another. The Huguenots suspected me because I was a
Catholic, and the Catholics because I was married to the King of
Navarre, who was a Huguenot.

'So that nobody told me anything until the evening, when I
was at the Queen my mother's, seated on a coffer next to my
sister of Lorraine [the Princess Claude] who was looking terribly
sad. The Queen my mother, who was talking to some others, saw
me there, and told me to go to bed. As I was curtsying to her
first, my sister took my arm and stopped me, crying bitterly, and
said to me, "My God, sister, do not go there!" which frightened
me dreadfully. The Queen my mother, noticing this, called my
sister over and scolded her very angrily, forbidding her to tell me
anything. My sister answered her that there was no point in
sending me to be sacrificed like that, and no doubt that if they
discovered anything they would take their revenge on me. The
Queen my mother replied to her that by the grace of God I
would come to no harm, but that whatever happened I must go,
for fear that otherwise they might suspect something, which would
interfere with the plan.'

Catherine's passion for her son Henri allowed her no compassion for her unfortunate youngest daughter. In that moment,
when she was in such great danger, yet totally unaware of the
reason for it, Marguerite did not understand her mother's motive
for this hideously unmaternal and pitiless attitude towards her,
but in due course she understood it only too clearly:

'I could see that they were arguing, but I could not hear what
they were saying. Again she roughly ordered me to go to bed. My
sister, in tears, said good-night to me without daring to say anything else, and I went, trembling, completely at a loss, not knowing what it was that I had to fear.

'As soon as I was in my dressing-room I prayed to God that it might please Him to take me under His protection and that He would safeguard me, without knowing from what or from whom. Whereupon my husband, who had already gone to bed, told me to do so too, which I did. I found his bed surrounded by thirty or forty Huguenots whom I did not yet know, since I had only been married a very few days. All night they did nothing but talk of the accident that had befallen the Admiral, resolving that as soon as day broke they would demand justice from the King against M. de Guise, and that if he did not accord it they would take it upon themselves. My heart was still wrung by my sister's tears; I was unable to sleep owing to the fear she had aroused in me, without knowing the reason for it.

'So the night passed without my being able to close my eyes. At daybreak the King my husband said that he would go to play tennis whilst waiting for King Charles to awake, when he would, he suddenly said, demand justice of him. He left my room and all his gentlemen went with him. As I saw that day had broken, and assuming that the danger of which my sister had spoken was past, being dead tired, I asked my nurse to shut the door, so that I might go to sleep.'

'An hour later, when I was fast asleep, a man beat on the door with his feet and hands, crying, "Navarre! Navarre!" My nurse, thinking that it was the King my husband, ran to the door and opened it. A gentleman called M. de Léran rushed in, with a sword-wound in his elbow and a cut from a halbert in his arm, pursued by four archers, all of whom burst into my room after him. Seeking protection from them, he hurled himself on to my bed. Feeling this man holding me, I threw myself down by the bedside, but still he clung to me desperately, holding me over his body. I did not know the man, nor whether he was attempting to attack me or whether the archers were aiming at him or at me. Both of us were equally terrified and screaming with fright. At last by God's will M. de Nançay, Captain of the Guard, arrived, and seeing me in such a state, could not refrain from laughing, although he felt sorry for me. Sharply reproving the archers for their impertinence, he ordered them to leave my room instantly, and granted me the life of that poor man, whom I made lie

Marguerite of Valois in 1555 attributed to François Clouet

Charles IX of France by François Clouet

down in my dressing-room to have his wounds attended to. My nightgown was drenched in blood.'

Even in that terrifying moment when she rose from the floor in her blood-stained nightgown Marguerite could still note without resentment M. de Nançay's laughter at the beautiful young bride's plight. This was her *Noce vermeil*, her Blood-stained Wedding, as it was ever afterwards called.

'Whilst I was changing', she continued, 'M. de Nançay informed me of what was happening, but reassured me by telling me that the King my husband was in the King's chamber, and that no harm would come to him. He made me put on a dressing-gown and then took me to the room of my sister, Mme de Lorraine, where I arrived more dead than alive. As I came into the ante-room, of which all the doors were open, a gentleman named Bourse, fleeing from the archers pursuing him, was pierced by a halberd only three steps away from me. I almost fainted and fell to the other side, into the arms of M. de Nançay, thinking that we had both been wounded by that blow. When I had slightly recovered, I went into the little room where my sister slept. Whilst I was there M. de Miossans, first gentleman to the King my husband, and Armagnac, his first valet, came to find me and begged me to save their lives. I went and threw myself on my knees before the King and the Queen my mother, to ask them for this mercy, and at last they granted it to me.'

Whilst all this appalling bloodshed was taking place in the Louvre itself, even worse atrocities were being committed in the streets of Paris. As Marguerite stated with reticence amounting to indifference, Guise brutally avenged his father's murder by the assassination of the helplessly wounded Admiral, who faced his martyr's end with heroic fortitude.

The Queen of Navarre knew only from hearsay how King Charles had been persuaded to agree to the massacre. But according to a later personal account of this dramatic decision by Henri of Anjou—shortly afterwards to become King of Poland for a brief period—it was he and the Queen Mother who on that sinister Saturday evening finally convinced Charles IX of the inevitable necessity for commanding that it should take place. They spent two hours urging their case on him, and at last Catherine succeeded in averting what she had most dreaded— Charles's vengeance on herself and Henri for their instigation of the plot against Coligny, which they freely admitted. But she only succeeded in turning the King's wrath away from themselves.

Whether or not Charles was finally convinced by their argu- ments that his own life and throne were at stake, the sight of those two—his mother and brother, as usual in collusion, himself as usual unloved by that mother and merely her tool—brought on, as Catherine had feared it would, the fit of maniacal rage this emotional strain was bound to arouse. He was 'thrown into a state of murderous intoxication by his bitter jealousy; he had a definite attack of mania. He cursed and fled, and as he did so, like an exhausted boar, he shouted at his mother and brother, and the four men who had forced his hand'—the Councillors who had accompanied them to this dangerous interview—'the famous invective: "Kill the lot! Kill the lot!"'

Having at last achieved their objective, the Queen Mother and Anjou then quietly retired to her council chamber, where with their advisers they calmly proceeded to draw up a list of those Protestant princes and noblemen, headed by Henry of Navarre, Queen Marguerite's bridegroom of less than a week, whose lives should be spared as matter of policy. Charles IX, however, like certain wild animals, became physically violent at the sight of blood. As soon as the man-hunt was up, the King himself joined in it, taking pot-shots at his fleeing Huguenot subjects from one of the Palace windows.

Small wonder that with this Royal assent and example the Catholic Parisians also rose like savages against their victims. The gutters filled with blood; strangling, rape, murder, and loot- ing marked 24 August 1572 with a stain of infamy in the French calendar. The holocaust spread to the provinces. Yet this mas- sacre on a national scale was not a climax, but a precedent to all those on both sides that were to follow it.

The Prisoners in the Louvre

The annihilation of most of the supporters of the King of Navarre who were with him in Paris at the time of his wedding appeared to the Queen Mother to have wiped out any chances of peace between the two parties which Marguerite's marriage had been designed to achieve. Immediately after describing her harrowing experiences on that night of terror, the Queen of Navarre continued:

'Five or six days later, those who had begun this business, realizing that they had failed in their objective, which was aimed not so much at the Huguenots as at the Princes of the Blood, resented the fact that my husband and the Prince of Condé were spared. And, knowing that no one would dare to attack my husband, they decided to take another line, namely, to persuade the Queen my mother that I should divorce him.

'And having on a feast day gone to her *levée*, as we were about to attend Holy Communion, she asked me to swear to tell her the truth as to whether the King my husband was in fact virile. For if he was not, then it would be possible for her to arrange a divorce for me. I begged her to believe that I was not sufficiently experienced to be able to tell her what she wanted to know, but that in any case, since she had given me in marriage to him, I wished to remain his wife. For I had very little doubt that in trying to separate us they were planning to do him some harm. . . .'

In recording this interview with her mother, Marguerite, in retrospect rather than at the time, used one of her frequent analogies between her own case and an instance from classical history. She compared herself to a young Roman matron whose husband scolded her for not having told him that he was suffering from halitosis, to which the wife replied that not having known any other man she had simply assumed that all men had bad breath. This was undoubtedly an oblique disparagement of the King of Navarre. It would have been imprudent and tactless for his Queen to set down bluntly what she and everyone else knew, the fact that Henry did have an appalling halitosis. Yet with the physical repugnance she had always felt for him, and her irrepressible natural malice, Marguerite could not refrain from this classical analogy to the unpleasant defect of the first man with whom she had ever slept. But whatever she told her mother, she might have had some slight previous experience for comparison, by having exchanged a few secret kisses with Guise or even with one of her brothers, especially the youngest, the Duke of Alençon, who was beginning then to play an increasingly important part in her life.

Although most fortunately for France as well as himself, Navarre's life was spared, after St Bartholomew's Night he was politely but firmly held prisoner in the Louvre. The Queen Mother, not having succeeded in persuading her to agree to divorce him, also kept a strict eye on his young Queen. Marriage did not free Margot from those maternal shackles for a very long time still.

When Marguerite told her mother that having married the King of Navarre she intended to remain loyal to him, Catherine soon realized that this was indeed her daughter's intention. Yet although the Queen Mother dropped her scheme for seeking an annulment of the marriage on the grounds of non-consummation, the Queen of Navarre's relationship with her young King was not of the conventional kind.

In his furious blood-lust on St Bartholomew's Night, Charles IX was prepared to execute with his own hands the Huguenot leaders and princes of the Blood, Henry of Navarre and his cousin, Condé. Brantôme believed that Navarre owed his life to the passionate pleading of his young Queen—'for he was proscribed and his name was on the red list; but the said Queen threw herself on her knees before King Charles to beg him to spare her husband's life. The King reluctantly granted it to her, although she was his own sister.' Condé was also spared, owing to the pleas of the Duke of Nevers.

Charles insisted, nevertheless, that the two young princes abjured their Protestantism and reverted to the Catholic faith. Henry of Navarre was still under twenty, but already showed his exceptional capacity to remain unruffled in times of dire crisis. For the first but not the last time he decided to change his religion and keep his life. Whether or not he had an inkling of how glorious that life was to become, he found it precious.

His situation was and continued for some considerable time to be a highly dangerous one. He was treated little better at Court than any young page or officer; nevertheless, he kept his temper and his head. He was naturally as gay and witty as he was brave; time and again when in a difficult corner he would make some spontaneous merry quip that brought a smile even to the Queen Mother's grim lips. And his most able supporter was his own young Queen.

Marguerite was her husband's senior by only seven months, but in many ways she was far more mature. She possessed to the full from bitter personal experience the knowledge and understanding of his dangerous new in-laws that were essential if he was to avoid the constant pitfalls confronting him; the elaborate and often base intrigues of the Court were no secret to her. They very quickly established a good understanding. Each of them allowed the other all the sexual freedom they might desire. Marguerite's attitude to Henry was almost maternal, certainly wholly protective as far as lay within her power.

As both she and Henri of Guise were now suitably married, there was no longer any political impediment to an affair between them; Catherine had prevented the alliance between the Lorraines and her own House that would have given them too much power, but a mere intrigue presented no danger to her schemes.

Brantôme told a rather curious anecdote referring to such a possible liaison. Anjou, who at that stage was not yet the reigning quean he was in a few years to become, had fallen madly in love with Condé's beautiful wife, Marie of Cleves, who was giving the handsome young hero, victor of Jarnac, every encouragement. Their clandestine meetings took place in the Salle de Bourbon. Brantôme wrapped up the identities of those involved by presenting an incident as a comedy entitled *Love's Paradise*. It was performed privately, without an audience, but, wrote the chronicler, 'those who know the story will understand me'. There were only six actors in the cast, three men and three women—'one was a prince, whose lady was tall . . . yet he loved her dearly; another was a lord and played opposite a great lady; the third was a gentleman who subsequently married his partner . . .'. The characters in question were clearly identifiable as Anjou and Marie, Guise and Marguerite, and a couple of their attendants.

In another account, the Court poet, Philippe Desportes, referred to the Queen of Navarre as 'Fleur de Lys'—the lilies being the flower of France—who had been taken to the rendezvous by her friend 'Olympe'. But as soon as Fleur de Lys saw the three men awaiting them, she stopped in surprise and annoyance, and, in spite of their protestations and Guise's attempt to detain her, she 'vanished', leaving the others to their flirtations.

Never again did Marguerite trust Henri of Anjou; even if it meant renouncing Guise, she was not willing to walk into any trap that treacherous brother might have set for her. And very soon her youngest brother, François, Duke of Alençon, was to become another of her responsibilities.

By dint of diplomatic manœuvring and the outpouring of vast sums of money in bribery, the Queen Mother succeeded in getting the Poles to accept Anjou as their king. He himself was most loath to leave Marie of Cleves and his own country for that Slavonic wilderness; yet a crown was a crown, and finally his mother persuaded him to accept it.

Charles IX never recovered from the horrors of St Bartholomew's Night and his own criminal participation in them. Night after night he awoke in cold sweats from horrible dreams of them; the sweats were also due to the tuberculosis that was gaining on him with dreadful speed. Nor were the affairs of his realm settled by that futile blood-bath.

Although so many of the great Huguenot leaders, Coligny at their head, had been massacred and the young Protestant princes, Navarre and Condé, were prisoners in the Louvre, the Reformationists gradually reorganized their forces. Condé was able to withdraw to his estates; other aristocratic survivors had emigrated to England and the Protestant dukedoms of Germany. But in isolated pockets of the country the Huguenot masses were stronger than ever, in certain fortified towns and places to which, under the leadership of the local gentry and the fanatically brave pastors, they managed to cling. Their headquarters was the great and splendid seaport city of La Rochelle, which they converted into an almost impregnable fortress, and where the English fleet was able to provision them with men, arms, money, and nourishment.

Poland was a Catholic country, yet the Polish Diet contained Reformationist members also. The Fourth War of Religion occurred at an awkward time for Catherine, who was then busily engaged in securing the throne of Poland for Henri. A chivalrous Protestant leader, who nevertheless remained loyal to the crown, La Noue, was given the mission of bringing his co-religionists in La Rochelle to terms. In spite of the fact that La Noue was and remained popular with the intrepid pastors and citizens, his mission failed. On 11 February 1573 Catherine was reluctantly compelled to place Anjou once again in command of the Catholic forces to besiege the seaport. On this occasion he was joined by his younger brother, Alençon, also avid to distinguish himself in battle. But the Catholics were badly paid, equipped, and led, and made no progress.

Anjou could not simultaneously be in two places so far apart as the Protestant stronghold and his future kingdom. On 9 May he was elected King of Poland; on 24 June the Treaty of La Rochelle was concluded, restoring to the Huguenots many of the rights and concessions for which thousands of them had given their lives during the previous Wars of Religion.

The Parisians, who so loved magnificence, were highly gratified when on 19 August the Polish ambassadors arrived in a superb cavalcade to escort their new King—*le roi malgré lui* the pamphleteers scathingly called him—back to his country. They were offered the usual extravagant entertainments at the Valois Court, including a pageant in which sixteen lovely girls appeared with appropriate symbols as the sixteen provinces of France.

But the Polish nobles were completely swept off their feet by the dazzling beauty and impressive erudition of their new King's sister, the Queen of Navarre. Brantôme reported this fresh success of his idol:

'She wore a gown of crimson Spanish velvet embroidered with sequins, and a headdress of similar velvet with sweeping plumes and many precious stones.' Marguerite, whose hair was naturally dark, also wore the wig of tight little blonde curls which she chose for such grand occasions. 'She looked so ravishing in this costume, as she was often told, that she frequently wore it afterwards and had herself painted in it. . . . The Poles found her so beautiful, so richly dressed and adorned, with so much majesty and grace that they were all lost in admiration of her', so much so that one member of their embassy, as he withdrew from her presence, was overheard by Brantôme to say that 'after such loveliness I do not wish to see anything else'.

Marguerite also impressed the Slavs by her astonishing learning:

'When the Poles went to pay their respects to her, Adam Konarski, the Bishop of Posen, addressed her on their behalf in Latin', whereupon 'She replied to him so pertinently and eloquently, without any notes, having perfectly well understood his speech, that they called her a second Minerva, or goddess of eloquence'.

Catherine de Medici had given all her children the best tutors in their youth. And in spite of their physical and moral deterioration, the Valois princes were no fools; all of them were capable of considerable intellectual efforts when they chose to make them. In her Memoirs Marguerite emphasized that in her girlhood she had been interested in little except frivolous amusements—hunting, parties, balls and dressing-up. But very soon after her marriage, during her subsequent long years of boredom and loneliness under her mother's surveillance in the Louvre, mitigated only by the love affairs on which her detractors were to lay so much stress, she set about the task of improving her mind. She read and wrote a great deal of poetry; she enjoyed the romances and lighter literature of her day. But most unusually for so lovely a young woman, and especially a Queen at all periods, she also assiduously studied sacred and profane, Biblical and classical literature and philosophy. The admiration of the Polish ambassadors for her knowledge and command of Latin was wholly justified.

In spite of his great reluctance to say farewell to his beloved Marie and his mother's equally great sorrow at having to part from him, the elected King of Poland was at last obliged to leave France for his kingdom. The entire Court accompanied him on the first part of his journey; Charles, delighted at his going, took farewell of Monsieur on his sickbed at Vitry; the Queen Mother and the Queen of Navarre escorted him a stage further:

'We accompanied the King of Poland', wrote Marguerite, 'as far as Blamont. A few months before leaving France he had tried by every means to make me forget his ingratitude and the bad turn he had done me, and to restore our former friendship to the perfection of our earlier years, by vows and promises in the name of God', which, however, left her unmoved. 'His departure from France and the illness of King Charles, which began at almost the same time, aroused both parties of the realm to concoct various schemes against the State.'

Both Alençon and Navarre were in the royal company that escorted the King of Poland to Blamont. A plot was organized whereby on the Court's homeward journey the two princes were to escape in Champagne and to join the Huguenot troops awaiting them there.

Marguerite's good offices were not only sought by members of her family. M. de Miossans, whose life she had saved on St Bartholomew's Night, was still in his cousin Navarre's service. He considered that this attempted evasion was too risky for his master to engage in and decided to confide the secret to his Queen. Marguerite agreed with Miossans and took an instant decision:

'I went to the King and the Queen my mother and told them I had something of great importance to tell them, but that I would never do so unless they first promised me that it would do no harm to those concerned, and that they would deal with the matter whilst appearing to know nothing about it. I then informed them that next day my brother and the King my husband were to join a troop of Huguenots ... because of the promise they had given on the death of the Admiral, which was very excusable owing to their youthfulness, and I begged that they might be forgiven and, without allowing them to realize the reason for it, be prevented from leaving. This they granted to me; the matter was so prudently dealt with that they never had a chance to escape, nor to know what had made it impossible for them to do so.'

Marguerite's revelations, however, caused the Queen Mother to keep an even stricter eye on her son-in-law and youngest son. Nor did she hesitate to employ as her tool and spy one of her ladies, the most attractive, submissive, and perfectly trained spy in her Flying Squadron of beauties, Charlotte de Sauves. Both princes were in love with her; she knew precisely how to divide her favours between them, how to play on their mutual jealousy and to report every word and gesture of her two admirers to her Royal mistress.

Charles being on his deathbed and Henri in Poland, Marguerite's youngest brother, François of Alençon, now made his bid for his dear sister's interest and affection. But whereas before her marriage she had been the victim of Catherine's and Charles's fear of the Lorraines and therefore forced into wedlock by their scheming; whereas Anjou had treacherously betrayed her affection, François, the most unattractive of her brothers, the dark, ugly, weak, and cringing Alençon, had a completely genuine adoration for his beautiful sister.

'We arrived at Saint-Germain', wrote Marguerite, 'where we made a long stay on account of the King's illness. During that time my brother Alençon did everything within his power to make himself agreeable to me and to win my friendship... for until then, as he had been brought up away from Court, we had seen very little of one another. At last, in view of his undoubted devotion and affection for me, I made up my mind to love him and to take up his cause. ...'

So the new alliance between Alençon and the King and Queen of Navarre was formed.

The Duke of Alençon was the most pitiable as well as the most despicable of Catherine's sons. He was her youngest surviving child, the only son destined not to fulfil Nostradamus's prophecy that they would all win thrones. Perhaps because she had her hands full enough in keeping the uneasy truce between Charles and Henri, the Queen Mother segregated François from Court throughout his boyhood and adolescence, leaving him alone for months at a time at one or another of her country palaces. Yet he was quite as ambitious as his two seniors and in his loneliness sustained himself with dreams of the brilliant future on which he was determined. In appearance he was singularly unprepossessing, a dark, puny little fellow, hideously pockmarked, with an enormous nose, lacking all the natural physical handsomeness of his father and brothers, their undoubtedly regal presence and Valois looks. Catherine had never given up hope of marrying one of the younger princes to Elizabeth of England. The effort to do so in Anjou's case having failed, she had not sufficient sense of the unsuitability of such a match to refrain from pressing that little royal runt, François, on the ageing spinster Queen.

Marguerite's affection for François was not as ingenuous or innocent as might have appeared from her own account. In her

Memoirs she never referred to her love affairs, yet, newly married, ravishingly attractive, with an unloving husband who showed no jealousy nor hardly even interest in his young Queen's emotions, inevitably she was avid for love, romance, happiness. François's favourite courtier and closest confidant became Margot's first accredited lover.

Joseph de Boniface de la Molle was a younger son of a not particularly aristocratic Provençal family, possessing all the charm, natural lyricism, gallantry and passion of the men of the south. When Alençon was attracted by his mother's scheme to wed him to Elizabeth I of England he despatched La Molle to the English Court to prepare for his own visit there. Elizabeth was more than agreeably surprised by the French prince's personal envoy, handsome, brave, and the best dancer at the Court of France, where the loveliest and most elegant ladies were only too willing to share their hearts and beds with him. Even at forty-four La Molle appeared to be the ideal lover of whom Margot was dreaming.

Inevitably his sexual successes aroused the bitter enmity of the husbands of those ladies whom he seduced with so little difficulty. But whilst pursuing his profane passions with inexhaustible enthusiasm, La Molle did not neglect sacred love either. He was deeply religious and never heard less than three or four and occasionally five or six Masses daily. 'The King often laughingly said that anyone who wished to keep a record of La Molle's debaucheries need only count up the number of daily Masses he was attending.'

But as superstitious as the Queen Mother herself, La Molle also dabbled in more sinister rites and rituals. Among Catherine's less reputable countrymen who were battening on the Valois Court was Cosimo Ruggieri, astrologer and alchemist, who prepared perfumes, potions and poisons for his exalted clients. Ruggieri was devoted to La Molle, who spent more time in his company than was wise, indulging with him in various spells and sorceries for the purpose of winning the love of Queen Marguerite.

The Queen Mother and the King of Poland disliked La Molle intensely, mainly for his loyalty to his master, Alençon. Before leaving for Poland, Henri had demanded that this upstart be driven from Court and killed. At first—since Henri's hatred of any courtier was bound to have the opposite effect on Charles's attitude—the King had favoured and protected La Molle. Navarre did not like him, yet did not, apparently, object to Marguerite's liaison with this southern charmer, who at forty-four was still more handsome and virile than many of his juniors.

Charles, however, reacted as violently to the situation as he had done before Marguerite's marriage to her flirtation with Guise, who at least was a great and aristocratic feudal chief. To the King it was intolerable that so soon after the union into which he had forced her his lovely sister should take as her accredited lover a man who in Valois eyes was not much more than a commoner. So he arranged to lie in wait one night for La Molle, on the dark staircase he would have to come down when passing from the apartments of the Duchess of Nevers, where he had been spending the evening, to those of his master, Alençon, on the ground floor of the palace. Accompanied by Guise and other gentlemen carrying cords with which to strangle the upstart, Charles awaited the intended victim, but in vain. For when La Molle left the Duchess he did not come down, but went upstairs, to pass a blissful night in the arms of his mistress—Margot.

During the last year of Charles IX's life the Huguenot leaders, the Montmorencys and Bourbons, gradually rebuilt their military organization. And another party had come into being, the Politicals, with a smaller secular minority known as the Malcontents. Neither of these two groups were primarily impassioned by religious fanaticism; their declared objective was the theoretically entirely laudable one of restoring some order to the country, ravaged and nearly ruined by the preceding civil wars. As Alençon had openly declared his detestation of the murder of Coligny, had taken no part in the massacre of St Bartholomew, and was more than willing to become their figurehead, he would give the Politicals the sanction of being led by a Son of France, thereby making it clear that their campaign was not one of treachery to the dynasty. The Flemish Protestants, in their struggle to throw off the cruel Spanish yoke, also invited the youngest Valois Prince to lead their troops, and, failing to bring off his match with the canny old Queen of England, François already saw himself as king of the Low Countries. The King and Queen of Navarre were both in favour of Alençon's ambitions; meanwhile, however, both young princes were still captives at Court, held on a very tight rein by Catherine, to whom Charlotte de Sauves was responsible for reporting every move they might make to the Queen Mother.

In order to effect their next attempted escape, a well-organized armed rising was plotted to take place on 14 March 1574. But at almost the last moment this plot was exposed by the craven young Prince for whose benefit the insurrection was to have irrupted. Charles's illness was in its final phase, and it was in his bedroom at Saint Germain that on the night of 27 February François, grovelling and weeping, made a full confession of the entire scheme to his dreaded mother and dying brother. Who had urged him to compromise so idiotically and wickedly all those loyal supporters? According to Marguerite's account, it was La Molle who persuaded his master into this craven confession:

'God granted that La Molle revealed it to the Queen Mother ... that the Huguenot troops were to arrive on that same day at Saint Germain.'

This information threw the Court into consternation and panic. Catherine, Charles, and the Catholic faction foresaw a St Bartholomew in reverse, with themselves as the intended victims:

'We were obliged to leave two hours after midnight, placing King Charles in a litter, to reach Paris, the Queen my mother taking my brother [Alençon] and the King my husband in her own coach, who this time were not so kindly treated as on the previous occasion.'

For greater safety, the dying King and his Court were installed after a few days in the castle of Vincennes, where Alençon and Navarre were closely confined and forbidden to leave.

Although Marguerite only referred in this impersonal manner to La Molle, it was generally believed at the time that it was she and not he who had persuaded François to his confession.

The Duke of Bouillon, at that time Viscount Turenne, was in the conspiracy. In his account of it he explained that 'in all these matters love affairs were involved, which caused most of the quarrels at Court, for almost nothing took place there in which women were not concerned and generally caused endless calamities to those who loved them and with whom they were in love'.

If Marguerite was indeed responsible for François's confession, it was certainly with no intention to harm him nor to lose her adorer, La Molle. When only a short while previously she herself had revealed Navarre's and Alençon's proposed evasion to Catherine and Charles she had begged that the princes might not be punished, but only prevented from escaping. And the Queen Mother, with Charles under her thumb, had carried out their side of the bargain. So Marguerite had some reason to assume that the same would happen again; but this time matters did not work out as she hoped.

The supporters of the two princes were still going ahead with their plans, and the conspiracy, if not promptly put down, might have threatened the throne. On 11 March Montgomery—the accidental killer of Henri II—arrived in Normandy from England. La Molle allegedly was the go-between who kept his master, at Vincennes, in touch with his would-be rescuers. His aide was the lover of the Duchess of Nevers, captain of Alençon's bodyguard, a handsome and engaging adventurer, superbly named Count Hannibal de Coconat.

April 8 was the new date fixed for the rescue of the two princes. Thanks, however, to the loyalty and efficiency of their mistress, Charlotte de Sauves, Catherine was informed in time, and once again she struck like a cobra to preserve her power from this menace.

The Duke of Alençon and the King of Navarre were arraigned before a special court to answer for their disloyalty, the Marshals Montgomery and Cossé were imprisoned at Vincennes, and at last Catherine was able to pounce on her and Henri's *bête noire*, François's favourite and her daughter's lover, La Molle, who with Coconat was arrested on a charge of treason. Ruggieri, her astrologer, was also put under arrest; when Catherine de Medici struck she neglected no one. The magician and La Molle were accused of making a waxen figure of Charles IX and sticking pins into it to hasten his death in order that Alençon might succeed to the throne.

'The King my husband', wrote Marguerite, 'having none of his councillors available, charged me to put his defence in writing, so that his evidence would harm neither himself nor anyone else. God granted that I did so to his complete satisfaction, and the members of the commission of investigation were astonished to find it so well done.'

This defensive memorial composed by Marguerite on her husband's behalf was a brilliantly written plea for Royal clemency. It was directed to the Queen Mother personally. It began by recalling his boyhood and emphasizing the fact that his parents, Jeanne of Albret and Antoine of Bourbon, had brought him up in loyal obedience to the Throne. It told how his mother had taken him to La Rochelle, after being warned by an envoy of the Prince of Condé that their enemies—the Lorraines—were plotting to destroy them and their followers; how, after peace had been made, Catherine and Jeanne had arranged his 'very happy' marriage with Marguerite; how, only a few days later, on St Bartholomew's Night, all those accompanying him to Paris had been massacred, although most of them had not even left their houses; how at Court he was obliged to witness the unfair favours shown to the Guises by the Queen Mother, King Charles, and the King of Poland—yet despite it all he continued loyally to serve the Throne. The memorial then pointed out how Henry had been obliged to endure further tribulations from the King of Poland's favourite, de Guast—Marguerite's old enemy—and others of the Catholic faction. It described in detail the ignominies and petty persecutions that he and the Duke of Alençon had to endure at Court, where 'every day the captains of the guard entered my room and the Duke's, looking under our beds to see if anyone was hidden there'; how, at the Queen Mother's orders, Navarre had only one valet to serve him, and when he called on her he was informed that she was with the King, when in fact Guise and his followers were with her; and how, when he attempted to see

His Majesty the Queen Mother had him publicly informed in the ante-chamber that King Charles did not wish to receive him, which was 'a matter of grave discomfiture' to him. The memoralist then pointed out that Navarre and Alençon, in view of all the tribulations and humiliations they were made to endure, were in fear of their lives, and for that reason and only that reason they decided that they must leave Court. All he himself wished to do was to return to his own realm.

'That is all, Madam, I know', the memorial concluded, 'and I very humbly beg you to consider whether I did not' [in those circumstances] 'have just and sufficient reasons for going away; and may it please yourself and the King in future to treat me as I am, having no other desire than to be your very humble, very faithful and very obedient servant.'

Navarre's only contribution to this remarkable document was his signature at the end of it, his name written in the English style he habitually used—Henry.

The memorial had its deserved success; nothing further was done either to Alençon or Navarre except to continue the close watch on them both. Catherine's vengeance was, however, fully unleashed on poor La Molle and Coconat.

When put to the torture before his execution, La Molle showed admirable courage and fortitude. When his nails were torn off and his limbs were crushed he uttered no word of betrayal of anyone else in the conspiracy, only moaning, 'Poor La Molle!' He went to his death with similar bravery, his beheading on the Place de Grève watched in floods of tears by all those lovely ladies whose favours he had so often enjoyed. Even Queen Elizabeth, through her Ambassador to France, Valentine Dale, tried to persuade Catherine to spare him. But the Queen Mother remained implacable. La Molle's last words on the scaffold were: 'God have mercy on my soul, and the Blessed Virgin! Commend me well to the good graces of the Queen of Navarre and the ladies!' Perhaps all those Masses he had heard in happier times did give him the strength to die so edifyingly.

Coconat's head fell next; during his interrogation he had not shown the same stoicism as La Molle, but died almost equally regretted by the gallant ladies. Ruggieri was imprisoned, but released in due course, since the Queen Mother might have further need of his black arts.

It was the usual practice after executions to place the heads of the victims on public exhibition in the execution square. But by nightfall those of the two great lovers had disappeared. It was said that they had been collected by the Queen of Navarre's chamberlain, Jacques d'Oradour; that their two loving and inconsolable mistresses had taken them in their own coach to be embalmed and buried in the Chapel of St Martin at Montmartre, and that Marguerite ordered a Court poet to write a set of obituary verses in honour of La Molle, bitterly mourned by his beloved, 'Hyacinth'.

6 *Prince of Lovers*

Charles IX died at Vincennes on 30 May 1574 in very great mental and physical agony, barely twenty-four years old. On his deathbed he was informed of the capture of Montgomery, but showed no pleasure on hearing of it.

'What, my son,' said the Queen Mother, 'are you not happy that the man who killed your father has been taken?' and when he replied that neither this event nor any other interested him at all, she knew that he was dying.

This did not, however, mar Catherine's own special satisfaction, and she made a point of personally witnessing the public execution and quartering of Montgomery, the Protestant leader who all those years ago had accidentally but fatally injured her husband, Henri II.

The Queen Mother's sorrow at the death of King Charles was considerably lightened by her unconcealed joy at the early return of her best-loved son, now Henri III. She sent him the news immediately, assuring him that until his arrival she, as Regent, would take good care of his kingdom.

The King-of-Poland-in-spite-of-himself secretly fled from his adopted country in the night of 18 June, vainly pursued by a posse of the Polish nobility whom he was abandoning, and to the general disgust of those who had briefly been his subjects. He travelled home via Catholic Austria and Italy, avoiding the Protestant German States. Having obtained this lucky freedom, he was in no hurry to shorten his holiday and take up his new responsibilities. Instead, he squandered on his hosts and hostesses in Venice and Savoy millions of francs raised for him by the French Treasury, even giving away portions of his territory with extravagant generosity. Catherine bombarded her beloved with letters and advice on how to become the ideal king she expected him to be, but with no effect. It was not until two months later, in the stifling August heat, that she and the entire Court proceeded to meet Henri III at Lyons.

To France's bitter cost, the new ruler turned out to be incurably and dramatically frivolous, excessive, and ludicrous, as much in his sudden fits of religious mania as in his social and sex life. His orgies, to which his doting mother pandered, made Nero's performance during the Roman fire seem like mere fiddling. Chateaubriand called him the French Heliogabolus. After his accession, he ostentatiously paraded his homosexuality, surrounding himself with a group of young men and youths scathingly referred to by his contemptuous subjects as his *mignons*—pets and fancy-boys. He and they were also transvestists, nothing delighting the King more than dressing and making-up as a woman, occasionally surrounded by Court ladies in male costume—or what little they wore of it. The Queen Mother gave one notorious banquet and party in his honour at Chenonceaux, at which her loveliest maids-in-waiting wore little more than transparent veils, whilst Henri and his favourites were heavily made-up, dressed in feminine silks and satin skirts, with earrings, necklaces, and girdles of precious stones. This occasion alone was 'of Roman decadence'; the country was again torn by civil war, the Exchequer was empty, and the money for Henri's debaucheries had to be borrowed from the Italian Court bankers at ruinous rates of usury.

The Parisian populace watched with contempt and disgust the King and his *mignons* prancing through the streets of the capital, wearing outrageous semi-feminine chemises of lace and ruffles, with long curls flowing from under their little girlish caps, publicly playing the favourite Royal game of cup-and-ball. Henri also delighted to play with his little performing dogs, tame apes, and monkeys; then, quite suddenly, he would have a violent revulsion from his habitual frivolity and in recurring bouts of religious mania would flog himself, walking barefooted in macabre religious processions, in monk's clothes, his head wrapped in a cowl, a rosary of small ivory skulls clinking at his waist. At such times he made several pilgrimages to Chartres on foot, to implore the Blessed Virgin there to grant him an heir. Yet in spite of his persistent depravity and frivolity King Henri did have sufficient intelligence, had he used it as his mother hoped, to have been a successful monarch; on the occasions when he brought himself to concentrate on matters of State he showed a surprising grasp of them; but these were only too rare.

After a long stay at Avignon, the Court proceeded to Reims, where Henri III was crowned and married. When the crown was placed on his head he complained that it hurt him; it nearly fell off during the sacrament, which was regarded as a bad omen.

His marriage took place the next day. On his way to Poland, when he was still madly in love with Marie of Cleves, Henri had met at Nancy the Princess Louise of Lorraine. On returning from Poland, his grief at learning that in his absence his beloved Marie had died was as dramatic as all his other gestures. He remembered then that Louise resembled her, sufficiently to be chosen as his Queen. Their marriage put an end to Catherine's ambitions for his union with some more exalted princess. But although, for obvious reasons, it was sterile, in other respects it turned out very successfully. Queen Louise apparently accepted all her husband's homosexual vagaries and his extravagant parade of his male favourites with perfect equanimity, possibly because at least she had no feminine rival in his affections. When the mood took him, he would play with her as if she were a doll, dressing her, making her up, and doing her hair.

The one member of his family—apart from his insignificant

Queen—who sincerely mourned Charles IX was Marguerite. His death, she wrote, was a disaster for France and for herself. She had good reason to do so, for her arch-enemy, the brother whom she loathed, was now in power, and from the beginning of his reign their mutual antagonism steadily increased until it deepened into a relentless enmity which nearly ruined her.

Marguerite ascribed all the trials and tribulations that began again to beset her to the machinations of her old enemy, de Guast, who was more firmly than ever in his royal master's favour. Of that mutual hatred there was no doubt at all; yet, naturally enough, in her accusations the Queen of Navarre omitted to give Henri III's case. Before he left for Poland he had tried in vain to regain her friendship and good offices. She had permanently transferred her affection and services to her youngest brother, Alençon, and this Henri could never overlook nor forgive. And he was justified in his fear that François might—as he did—become a real danger to the realm, since he was a natural point of focus for all those throughout the country, Catholics as well as Protestants, who were ready to unleash another civil war on the King whom nobody wanted.

Marguerite believed that God conferred a degree of second sight on certain royal favourites of Heaven, including her mother and herself. Whilst Catherine and Henri were embracing one another on their reunion in Lyons, 'although the weather was so hot that in the dense crowd present we were stifling', she felt herself trembling and shivering with a sense of impending misfortune.

The first intrigue against her occurred very soon afterwards. With several ladies, Marguerite went to visit a fashionable local convent. Two of the King's equerries, jokingly saying that they too wished to see those 'lovely nuns', jumped on the running board of her coach as it set off. Whilst they were there the Queen of Navarre's coach was parked in a nearby square, clearly recognizable, as it was very large, gilded, and lined with yellow velvet and silver brocade. Various gentlemen of the Court had lodgings in this square. The King, accompanied by Navarre, a courtier named François d'O, and the Marquess of Ruffec, went to call there on the Baron of Quelus, who was laid up.

King Henri 'turned to the King my husband and said, "Look, here is your wife's coach, and here is Bidé's lodging. . . . I bet that she's with him," and ordered fat Ruffec, a suitable instrument of such malice, for he was a friend of de Guast, to go and see. He found nobody there, but, not wanting this fact to impede the King's plan, said to him aloud, in front of the King my husband, "The birds have been there, but they've flown." '

Henri then attempted to arouse Navarre's jealousy, 'but my husband, showing the kindness and understanding which he always had, detested such malice and knew very well to what end it tended'.

Henri then took care to see the Queen Mother before Marguerite's return. Catherine was more credulous than her son-in-law and fell into a fury with her daughter. When Margot came back, quite unaware of this attempt to besmirch her, her husband burst out laughting and said to her: 'Go and see the Queen your mother; I bet you'll come back in a pretty temper!' He refused to tell her why, only adding that he did not believe a word of it: 'It's simply an attempt,' he said, 'to put you and me at loggerheads and in that way to break up my friendship with your brother.'

In Catherine's antechamber Marguerite met the Duke of Guise, who told her what he had heard from d'O of the story. Catherine was not in her apartment, but one of her ladies said to Marguerite:

'My God, Madam, the Queen your mother is so angry with you that I advise you not to see her.'

'I wouldn't do so,' Marguerite replied, 'if I had done what the King told her, but as I am completely innocent of it I must explain it to her.'

'I went into her cabinet, which was only separated from the rest of the room by a wooden partition, so that those outside it could easily hear everything that was said in it. As soon as she saw me she fell into a furious rage', and although Marguerite tried to tell her where she had been, with ten or twelve other people, the ladies in her coach and the two equerries who had insisted on joining them, Catherine 'had ears neither for truth nor

reason, either because she wanted to believe those lies or to please
that son whom from affection, duty, hope, and fear she idolized,
and never stopped shouting and threatening me, which everyone
in her room could hear'.

Next day Marguerite, with several other princesses and ladies,
was invited to a banquet in the town, 'and, having always retained the respect I had for the Queen my mother as long as I
lived with her, both before and after my marriage never going
anywhere without asking her permission, I met her returning from
mass . . . when she publicly refused my request, saying I might go
where I liked for all she cared'.

Henri III, however, with one of his characteristic sudden
changes of mood, admitted the truth to Catherine, 'so that I
should not remain his enemy, seeing that I had enough intelligence to avenge myself more effectively than he had in offending
me . . .'.

The Queen Mother then sent for Marguerite, saying that she
had learnt that her daughter had told her the truth and that the
groom of the chamber who supposedly had made this report to
her was a scoundrel and that she would dismiss him.

'But she could read on my face that I did not accept this story
and was still convinced that it was the King who had conferred
this boon on me. And finding that she could not change my
mind, the King then entered her cabinet and apologized pro-
fusely to me, saying that he had been made to believe it and
offering me every possible satisfaction and demonstration of
friendship.'

When the Court moved from Lyons to Avignon de Guast
changed his tactics and used Charlotte de Sauves as his instrument
in separating Navarre from Alençon and both of them from
Marguerite, with considerably greater success. Margot had every
reason to detest this wily coquette, with whom both her husband
and brother were besottedly in love.

'This woman persuaded the King my husband that I was
jealous of her', which Navarre unfortunately believed, whereas
in the past 'he had always spoken to me'—about his numerous
love affairs—'as freely as to a sister, knowing perfectly well

that I was not in the least jealous, but only wanted him to be happy'.

Whilst Navarre refused to speak to his wife any longer, spending all his time in his mistress's company, even her devoted François, 'who in everything else believed no one but me, was unable to control himself for his good and mine, so great were the enchantments of that Circe, aided by that diabolical de Guast, so that instead of listening to my warning he went and repeated to that woman everything I had said to him'. This was typical of that despicable Prince, but his devoted sister did not blame him, only sadly asking, 'What can one hide from the person with whom one is in love?' Yet her loyalty to François was again not entirely disinterested.

One of the guests at the grand ball given amongst all the other festivities at Lyons to welcome back Henri III was Elizabeth I's envoy, Lord North. Seated on the right of the Queen Mother (always anxious to remain on good terms with the Island Queen), he was dazzled and enchanted by the beauty of the Queen of Navarre, who opened the dancing partnered by her brother Alençon. She was still only twenty-three and her loveliness was famous throughout the courts of Europe. It was hardly surprising that she was willing to accept a new lover to console her for all the tribulations and affronts she was forced to endure from the King her brother and her own husband.

Among several courtiers who had transferred their allegiance from the King to the Duke of Alençon was Louis de Clermont, squire of Bussy d'Amboise, known simply as Bussy, one of the most glamorous and irresistible of all French lovers. His good looks and elegance were matched only by his insolence and daring; his duels and amorous conquests were the talk of the Court. Brantôme told of an occasion at the play when he had high words with another Court gallant, and was only persuaded to drop the quarrel by being ordered to do so 'by a lady who had a great deal of power over him and was afraid of a scandal which would be very unpleasant for her'; yet next day he pursued this enemy 'to his mistress's very room'. They and their supporters then drew swords and Bussy was wounded in a finger;

when he then challenged his enemy, Saint-Phal, to single combat, the King forbade the duel. With typical insolence, next day Bussy appeared at Court 'accompanied by more than two hundred gentlemen' which considerably annoyed the King, who said 'it really was too much for a Bussy'. Bussy 'had such a hold over the Duke of Alençon', wrote L'Estoile, another contemporary chronicler, 'that he openly boasted of being able to do anything he liked with him; he had the keys to his coffers and his money and helped himself freely to as much of it as he wished'.

Although in her Memoirs Marguerite only referred as cautiously as possible to this lover, even all those years later she was unable, as she wrote them, to conceal her obvious passion for him. The fact that she was seeing so much of Bussy she explained away by saying that 'in Paris ... he was always close to my brother, and consequently to me, as my brother and I were nearly always together', but primed, according to her, by de Guast, the King once again took this scandal story to the Queen Mother. On this occasion, however, Catherine took up her daughter's defence:

'I don't know,' she said to Henri, 'what gives you these fantastic ideas. My daughter is unlucky to be living in such a century. In my young days we spoke quite freely with everyone; all the honest gentlemen who served your father, and the Dauphin and the Duke of Orleans, your uncles, were usually in the apartments of your Aunt Marguerite and mine; no one thought it strange, nor had they any reason to. Bussy sees my daughter in front of you, her husband, and everyone else, not in secret nor behind closed doors. Bussy is a person of quality and your brother's first gentleman; so what is there to worry about?'

Catherine then reminded her son of the calumny on Marguerite he had reported to her at Lyons, which her daughter would never forget. When the King then said that he was only repeating what others had told him, his mother answered, 'What others, my son? Only those who want to make trouble between you and your own family,' and when the King had left her Catherine repeated the conversation to Marguerite, adding again, 'You were born into a miserable age.'

Whether those were indeed Catherine's words or whether Margot put them into the Queen Mother's mouth so long after her death, there was nevertheless little doubt that Bussy was her lover. None of his enemies doubted it and they decided to deal with him traditionally, by setting a trap for him one dark night when he was on his way home and killing him. Bussy's recent wound had not yet healed; he was therefore carrying no sword and his sword-arm was wrapped in a silvery-grey silken scarf embroidered in gold which almost certainly Marguerite had given him. He was, however, as usual accompanied by his own body-guard. In the street his assailants extinguished their torches and a fight ensued. According to Marguerite, Bussy's attackers were a troop of soldiers provided by de Guast, who was Captain of the Royal Guard. Among the friends who were seeing Bussy home that night was, very luckily for him, one who had also recently been wounded in the arm and was wearing a similar scarf over his hand, although, wrote Marguerite, 'not as richly embroidered as his master's'—a typically feminine touch in his mistress's account. His assailants had been looking out for a man with a scarf over his arm, and in the darkness and confusion they hurled themselves upon this unfortunate companion, leaving him, as they thought, dead in the gutter. Bussy, meanwhile, reached his lodgings safely.

But an Italian in his service, one of the first to have been wounded in the affray, rushed back to the Louvre, dripping with blood, to inform Alençon of this assault on his favourite. François rose from his bed in a fury, determined to rescue Bussy.

'By good luck', wrote Marguerite, 'I was not yet in bed, and my room was so near to my brother's that I heard this gentleman shouting the dreadful news. I rushed into his room to stop him from going out, and sent to beg the Queen my mother to prevent him from doing so, because, although he nearly always listened to me, he was so carried away by his rightful wrath that he would have faced any danger to exact vengeance. We had great difficulty in holding him back, the Queen my mother pointing out to him that "there was no point in his going out alone like that in the middle of the night, that the darkness would protect any evildoers, and that de Guast was wicked enough to have laid this plot on purpose so that he should go out and meet with some accident." ' And to make doubly sure, the Queen Mother ordered that the Palace doors should be shut and guarded to prevent Alençon from leaving.

'Bussy', Marguerite continued, 'whom God had so miraculously saved, was not in the least perturbed by his danger, for his soul was incapable of fear, he having been born to strike terror into his enemies, to the glory of his master and the hopes of his friends', and as soon as he reached his lodgings he sent word to the Prince of the whole affair. 'And when day broke, without a trace of fear of his enemies, Bussy returned to the Louvre as bravely and gaily as if this attempt on his life had been a mere incident in a journey.'

Marguerite's passion for this impudent charmer caused her to exaggerate the story of this attack on him; instead of a troop of soldiers, his assailants were only a dozen, and Bussy escaped by sheer luck. Having taken refuge from his enemies in a doorway in that dark street, he found the door by chance to be unlocked, so simply backed into the house behind him until his pursuers had passed. But he did return to Court next morning, understandably in the best of spirits, laughing off the whole affair.

Catherine already had enough trouble in keeping the peace between her two obstreperous sons and, in spite of the defence of her daughter which Marguerite alleged her mother made to the King, at heart she was far from tolerant of the Queen of Navarre's flaunted love affairs; not on moral grounds, for Catherine had no bourgeois prejudices, but they were too inextricably mixed up with the political intrigues so dangerous to Valois power. So the Queen Mother decided that in the circumstances the safest and simplest course was to dismiss Bussy from Court 'for a time'. She succeeded in persuading Alençon to agree to this measure; Marguerite, reluctant as she must have been to part from this superb lover, claimed to have seen the necessity of it also, and begged her brother to let Bussy go. Even his departure, wearing in his hat the favours of his lovely mistress and Queen, accompanied by 'the highest noblemen at Court in the service of my brother', was a flamboyant spectacle.

After Bussy left Court the King and Queen of Navarre were reconciled for a short time, owing, said Marguerite, to her devoted nursing of him one night when he suddenly collapsed and 'remained unconscious for a whole hour', due to the fact, in her opinion, that he had exhausted himself by too much love-making.

Very soon afterwards, however, Henri inflicted a new and distinctly mean penalty on her through her husband, a trick which he first played on his own Queen, who was 'very virtuous and good'. He obliged Louise to dismiss one of her maids-of-honour called Changy, and then persuaded Navarre to do the same in Marguerite's case, 'depriving me of the one I loved best, called Thorigny, with no other reason than that one should not leave in the service of young princesses girls for whom they had a particular affection'.

Whilst there was never any question of Queen Louise's fidelity, however, there was possibly in Henri's mind and also in Navarre's a suspicion that Mlle de Thorigny acted as Marguerite's intermediary in her affair with Bussy, whom they both detested. Nevertheless, 'I remained so offended by this indignity', she very naturally wrote, 'following on so many others, that, unable to resist my justified anger and casting all prudence aside, I simply could not force myself to see the King my husband, so that whilst de Guast and Mme de Sauves were estranging him from me and I myself was withdrawing from him, we no longer slept together nor even spoke to one another'.

Fortunately, before de Guast's and the King's plot to break off the alliance between Alençon and Navarre also succeeded, the two princes realized their danger. They decided to overcome their mutual jealousy, and at last to break out of their imprisonment at Court. Once again they needed Marguerite's help. François approached her on their joint behalf, telling her how very sorry Navarre was for his recent unkindness towards her and informing her of their plans for escape. Alençon was to leave first, Navarre following him a little later on the pretext of a hunting expedition.

They were deeply regretful that they were unable to include her also in their evasion but felt certain, he reassured her, that once they were free she would not be in any danger.

Until after the King's marriage and the Court's residence in Paris, the two princes had never been allowed abroad except together, travelling by coach, as Catherine had taken them with her on several occasions surrounded by a guard. But latterly they had been given a little more freedom.

Contemporary versions of Alençon's escape differ slightly in detail, but the main facts are clear. On 15 September 1575, on the pretext that he was merely going to visit a lady in the Rue Saint-Marceau, just before the Court's dinner-time, he put on a cloak and, muffled in its folds up to his nose, went out of the Louvre on foot, slipping unrecognized past the guards. Arriving at the house, by arrangement he found one of his attendants, Simier, waiting for him there in a coach at the back door; having entered it and then driven a short distance, he then met a mounted escort sent, according to some, by Bussy. Taking to horse and joined by a growing number of his supporters, Alençon then galloped away, passing through Meudon and finally arriving at one of his own fiefs, the town of Dreux.

'His departure was not discovered', wrote Marguerite, 'until nine o'clock in the evening. The King and the Queen my mother asked me why he had not come to supper with them, and if he were ill? I told them that I had not seen him since the afternoon. They sent to his room and were informed that he was not there. They then ordered him to be sought in the rooms of all the ladies whom he used to visit. They searched the Palace, they searched the town, but in vain. The alarm then heightened. The King grew angry, furious, threatening, sending for all the princes and lords at Court, and ordering them to take to horse and bring him back, dead or alive, saying that he had escaped in order to raise the State and make war against him, but that he would teach him the folly of attacking so powerful a monarch as himself.'

Certain of these lords, however, said Marguerite, refused to carry out such a hazardous commission, since, as they observed to their King, although they would lay down their lives for him, one day he might turn against them if they dared to attack his royal brother; and, pursuing her theme that François meant no harm to the realm, she placed this reassurance in their mouths: the King ought, they advised him, first to make contact with the fugitive, to find out what his motives had been for leaving Court. Henri's forebodings were in fact entirely justified and once again he was obliged to use the Queen Mother as his intermediary.

Catherine set out on 21 September to parley with her troublesome youngest son, but he evaded her time after time and the ageing Queen Mother was obliged to follow him from place to place whilst renewed bitter fighting was breaking out. During one of these battles between the King's men and the Prince's supporters, on 11 October, the Duke of Guise—Marguerite's former handsome young suitor—was badly wounded in the face and lost his left ear; as a result he was nicknamed Scarface II, the first having been his illustrious father, Guise the Great. François was so successful that on 20 November Catherine was compelled to conclude a truce between the warring brothers which was greatly in favour of the younger, the King, thoroughly mortified, having to cede to him Tours, Amboise, and Blois, as well as large financial indemnities.

In Paris, meanwhile, the King and Queen of Navarre were still held in the Louvre. It was not until 5 February 1576 that Henry of Navarre succeeded in escaping. Meanwhile, however, Marguerite had one great satisfaction: on 31 October, the Eve of All Saints' Day, her enemy de Guast was murdered. Marguerite's hatred for him was well-known and her enemies and libellers, both then and later, accused her of having planned his death. According to this story, she persuaded the Baron Viteaux to assassinate him. Viteaux had a strong grievance and motive, for, having killed one of Henri III's favourites in a duel, it was de Guast who persuaded the King to banish him from Court. He returned secretly to Paris, where he was hiding in an Augustine monastery. Marguerite allegedly visited him there one night and even allowed him to make love to her as the price for this murder.

Viteaux, disguised as one of de Guast's servants, went up to his room, where he was reading in bed whilst awaiting his mistress, and stabbed him to death, then, as he was leaving, met the lady who had come to keep their rendezvous, and 'was even cruel enough to wipe his bloody sword on her dress'. Viteaux escaped from Paris and joined the Duke of Alençon's army.

According to Brantôme, however, Marguerite had no part in or knowledge of de Guast's assassination. He was present on one occasion when de Guast had paid a visit to Marguerite, bringing her a letter from Henri III when that King was still in Poland. She did not hide her extreme displeasure and, when he handed her the letter, said to him: 'It's lucky for you, de Guast, that this letter from my brother is your safeguard, owing to the affection I have for him; otherwise I would teach you how to speak of a princess such as I am, the sister of your kings, sovereigns and masters.' De Guast answered her with outward humility that 'I would not, Madam, have come before you, knowing very well that you wish me no good, except on my master's instructions, and knowing that as you are both kind and generous you would allow me to address you,' and he then assured her that he had never spoken of the King's sister except with the deepest respect. 'But she remained his enemy until the day of his death.'

According to another version, this had been planned before François left Paris, for he also had good reason to hate de Guast, who on at least one occasion, meeting him in the street, impudently cut him dead, saying that 'he had no master but the King, and that if he ordered him to kill his own brother he would do so'. And L'Estoile's epitaph was that as de Guast had boasted of killing some of the Huguenots in their beds on St Bartholomew's Night, 'so he himself was killed'.

Marguerite, however, made no secret of her delight on learning of the death of this detested enemy, 'whose body', she wrote, 'was diseased as the result of his many villainies and was consigned to rot as it had been doing already, whilst his soul was claimed by the devils to whom he had paid homage by practising magic and all manner of wickedness'. She even added regretfully that the news of his death was brought to her whilst she was ill

Henri III of France. 16th-century French school

Henri of Lorraine, Duke of Guise, in 1585. School of Clouet

Admiral Gaspard de Coligny in 1570 by François Clouet

in bed, so that she was unable to celebrate it as she would otherwise have done. It was true, as her devoted Brantôme maintained,
that she was immensely kind, loyal, and generous to those whom
she loved and who loved her, but those lines were written by a
daughter of the Medici who could hate her enemies as passionately as she loved her friends.

The King of Navarre, meanwhile, was practising the cunning
diplomacy at which at the age of twenty-two he was already a
past-master, becoming on the most intimate terms with the King
and Guise so successfully that the most fanatical Catholics were
convinced of his sincerity. In January he wrote to his cousin, M.
de Miossans, ironically and with tongue well in cheek, summing
up his situation:

'I was very pleased to have your news and to know how
matters are going. I hope that with God's help they will soon
go even better. This Court is the strangest you have ever seen. We
are all of us ready to cut one another's throats, carrying daggers
and wearing coats of mail even under our clothes. . . . The King
is in as much danger as myself and loves me more than ever. You
cannot imagine how successful I am; in this Court of friends I
outstrip them all. The entire Court would like to see me dead for
my love of Monsieur, and for the third time my mistress has been
forbidden to speak to me and hardly dares to look at me. I am
only waiting for the moment to launch my own little war, for
they are threatening to kill me, but I intend to get my blow in
first.'

So the sly and debonair young King of Navarre was allowed to
go hunting with Guise in the Forest of Senlis, 'where, having
shaken off his guards and spies, at one bold leap he crossed the
Seine near Poissy, reached Châteauneuf-en-Timeraye, then
Alençon, where in a full Protestant service he renounced the
Catholic faith, and then proceeded to Maine and Anjou'.
Navarre, wrote L'Estoile, 'never spoke a word until he had
crossed the Loire, but then, giving a sigh of relief and raising his
eyes to the heavens, he said, "Thanks be to God for my deliverance. They caused my mother to die in Paris; they killed the

Admiral and all my best servants there, and would have done the same for me had God not delivered me from them. Never will I be dragged back there!"; then, reverting to his usual jocular manner, he added that he only regretted Paris for two reasons—one was the Mass and the other his wife. Regarding the former, he would try to do without it, but as for the latter he could not do without her, and very much wished to see her again.

Never were truer words spoken in jest. Navarre did not join in the renewed civil war led by Condé and François against the King, but went straight home and remained there. He had been absent from his small kingdom for more than four years and his first concern was to resume his rulership. It was also his considered policy to remain on good terms with the King of France and to keep in touch with the Court. For that purpose, Marguerite's continued presence there was indispensable to him. It was in that sense that he could not do without her, and even had he been able to take her with him he might well not have done so.

Although in her Memoirs Marguerite made the mistake of advancing her husband's escape by more than four months, she seems very clearly to have remembered the events immediately preceding it:

'The day after my brother left', she wrote, 'I cried so hard all night that half my face was swollen by a dreadful cold, and with a high fever and much pain I was in bed for several days.' It might well have been during this illness that she learned of de Guast's death, although she did not then refer to it. 'Whether my husband', she continued, 'was busy planning his escape or wanted to spend the short time remaining to him in the voluptuous presence of his mistress, Mme de Sauves, my husband never had time to come and visit me. He came back to bed as usual at one or two o'clock in the morning, and as we slept in separate beds I did not hear him come in. And as he got up before I was awake, in order to attend the levée of the Queen with Mme de Sauves, as I have already said, he did not remember to speak to me as he had promised my brother he would, and left without even saying A Dieu to me.'

7 A Diplomatic Cure

In spite of the reassurances given to Marguerite by her brother and husband, Henri III promptly vented his fury at their evasion on his defenceless sister, whom he not unreasonably suspected of having organized both escapes, which she had certainly abetted. Had the Queen Mother not restrained him, she wrote, her life might have been in danger. And even Catherine could not deter the King from ordering that she be confined to her room and closely guarded.

He also plotted a singularly mean act of revenge on her. When describing it in her Memoirs, Marguerite attributed this plot to the villainy of de Guast—who by then was dead. It was apparently on his instigation that, shortly before, the King had insisted on Navarre banishing from Court Gilonne de Thorigny, Marguerite's favourite lady-in-waiting. Writing so long afterwards, her hatred for the late favourite no doubt caused her to link the two incidents together.

Mlle de Thorigny was staying at the country house of her cousin, M. de Chastellas. Suddenly a posse of the King's men arrived there under the pretext of taking her back to Court, but in fact with orders to drown the poor girl in a nearby river. They bound her and locked her in her room, but before carrying her off proceeded to gorge themselves on their helpless host's food and drink, after which they began to loot the premises and beat up the retainers. Some of these, rushing out to escape, very luckily encountered two of Monsieur's supporters, MM. La Ferté and Avantigny, who with 200 horsemen were on their way to join him. Hearing from one of the valets whom La Ferté recognized of the attempted kidnapping of Mlle de Thorigny, they decided, wrote Marguerite, 'to do me the favour of rescuing her, thanking God for this chance to prove to me the affection they had for me'. The rescuers arrived just as the villains were hoisting the unfortunate girl on to a horse to bear her off, 'crying, "Stop, you murderers! If you touch her you're all dead men!"' Mlle de Thorigny, 'first thanking God for her deliverance, as overjoyed as she had been petrified by fear', was then escorted in her cousin's coach to François, who for love of his sister looked after her with the greatest kindness.

Meanwhile, the Queen Mother, knowing nothing of this despicable trick, went to visit her daughter, who was suffering from a feverish cold and not yet dressed.

'Please do not be angry,' Catherine begged her, 'at what I am going to say to you,' and then proceeded as tactfully as possible ('you are intelligent and will therefore understand me') to explain the King's motives and suspicions to Marguerite and to ask her to put up for the time being with her confinement, which by God's will should not last long. 'And don't be angry, either,' Catherine concluded, 'If I myself don't come to see you too often in order not to arouse the King's suspicions, but believe me that I will not allow any harm to come to you, and that I will do my utmost to make peace between your brothers.'

'After she left me,' Marguerite wrote, 'I remained thus for several months, without anyone, even my best friends, daring to visit me, afraid that if they did so they would be ruined. At Court one is always alone in adversity, whereas when all goes well one is surrounded by people. Persecution breaks up the best and most intimate friendships.' Only one courtier, 'that good Crillon', in contemptuous defiance of the King's orders and the risk of disfavour, visited her five or six times, 'and the Cerberuses guarding my door were so surprised by his doing so that they neither dared to report him nor refused to let him in'.

During those months of imprisonment Marguerite was certainly unhappy, but she was neither idle nor bored. Whilst her detractors laid so much emphasis on her love affairs during her days of success and freedom, even most of her admirers did not sufficiently emphasize the great reserves of intelligence and culture on which she was always able to draw in times of adversity. Thanks to good fortune and Divine Providence, she said, she was able to spend her enforced leisure in reading and religious devotions. And in her love of literature and philosophy she was completely sincere; her Memoirs contain constant allusions to or quotations from Biblical and classical sources with which she was thoroughly familiar.

An even greater consolation, however, was her highly secret but successful correspondence with her husband. The fact that she was forbidden by the King to receive or write any letters was in itself an incentive to her to do so, and 'aided by necessity, the mother of invention', she wrote gaily, they did exchange several; by what means she did not reveal.

Very soon after arriving home, in Béarn, Navarre was anxious for news of Monsieur in Champagne. His method of getting in touch with him was to write Marguerite 'a very nice letter', in which he begged her to forget the past and to believe that he did want to love her and wished to prove it to her. No doubt her captivity inclined Margot to accept Henry's excuses; in her state of ostracism it would have been natural for any kind words to touch her heart and, generous as she was, she was only too ready to forgive him. But Navarre's motive was obvious—'to keep him informed of the state of affairs where I was [at Court] and with regard to my brother'. As far as he was concerned, she was of more use to him in Paris than by his side. It was not to her husband but to her brother, that Marguerite owed her release.

The King's situation was becoming daily more desperate. Condé had raised an army of German mercenaries who were devastating the country; the Protestants and Politicals disposed of more than 50,000 men, including, Marguerite wrote, 'the bravest and most gallant nobility, and since my brother's departure neither by commands nor threats had the King been able to persuade anyone to horse against my brother, all the princes and noblemen of France rightly afraid of getting their fingers caught between two stones'. Henri, lacking both the troops and the money to finance this new civil war, had only, as so often in the past, his old mother's glib tongue as a defensive weapon. But when Catherine set out once again to reason with her youngest son she found him adamant: unless Marguerite were immediately released and brought to him by their mother, he refused to treat with her or the King. Very reluctantly Henri was then persuaded by Catherine to agree to François's terms.

The Queen Mother sent for Marguerite to inform her of her release, begging her not to desire vengeance for her imprisonment, for which the King was extremely contrite; she had seen him shed tears on account of it and now he would give her every satisfaction. 'I answered her that I would never prefer my own good to the welfare of my brothers and the State, to which I was ready to sacrifice myself; that I wanted nothing more than peace, and would do all in my power to bring it about.'

Henri then joined them and begged Marguerite's forgiveness, which she granted him, she wrote—still with implacable antagonism to him—more to show her contempt for his treatment of her than to give him satisfaction. He then asked her to use her good offices with François to bring an end to the civil war.

The peace treaty between the King and the rebels concluded in 1576 became known as the Treaty of Monsieur, for its conditions were a triumph for François and so harsh for the King that he shed bitter tears of mortification on signing it.

The Edict of Beaulieu, confirming this Treaty on 7 May 1576, did nothing to unite the country; on the contrary, its clauses established two-party parliaments and repudiated the entire attempt to wipe out the Huguenots on St Bartholomew's Night, even including the rehabilitation of the late Admiral, of Montgomery, and for full measure exonerating La Molle and Coconat.

All three of the rebel leaders received enormous territorial concessions: Anjou, Touraine and Berry passed to Monsieur, Condé was appointed Governor of Picardy, and Navarre, although on his escape he had formally renounced Catholicism, was proclaimed Protector of the associated Reformed and Catholic Churches. The Count Palatinate, who had provided the rebels with those savage German Reiters against a promise of 4 million florins, refused to withdraw them until the Crown paid him an indemnity of 300,000 *livres*.

This ignominious Royal defeat naturally enough infuriated the Catholic party. Henri of Guise, who remained the idol of the Parisians, had founded the Catholic League in the previous year; it now developed rapidly over the whole country, which was soon more deeply divided than ever by religious schism and implacable enmity.

When Monsieur achieved these territorial and financial advantages for himself, he endeavoured to include his sister in them, since neither Charles IX nor Henri III had ever implemented Marguerite's marriage settlements. The Queen Mother, however, begged her daughter not at that moment to insist on her rights, saying that it would be preferable for her to receive her endowments from the King and herself.

Marguerite, meanwhile, had had several increasingly affectionate letters from Navarre, begging her to rejoin him as soon as peace was concluded. Her hatred of Henri and her vivid memories of her recent imprisonment made her anxious to do so, and she asked her mother's leave to go to him instead of returning to Paris. But Catherine, 'with tears in her eyes, said that if I did not return with her I would ruin her, as the King would believe that she had persuaded me not to do so, that she had promised him to bring me back and arrange that I would remain there until my brother returned, which he would soon do, when she would see that the King allowed me to leave'.

Marguerite had no illusions about the King's motives in wanting Monsieur back: 'as soon as he had my brother at Court again he would find some excuse for making war on the Huguenots, in order that they should not enjoy what with bitter regrets and by force he had been compelled to grant them. . . . Shortly afterwards he arrived at Court accompanied by all the Catholic nobility who had been on his side, the King receiving them with great cordiality, including Bussy, who was there also, since de Guast [Bussy's arch-enemy] was by then dead, killed by Divine Judgment.'

Nevertheless, Marguerite was still insisting on joining her husband, who had sent M. de Duras, his Court chamberlain, to escort her to his kingdom. Henri hypocritically told his sister that he could not bear to part with her until the last possible moment, 'owing to his great affection for me and the glamour my presence gave to his Court'. In due course, he said, he would himself escort her as far as Poitiers. With that assurance M. de Duras was sent back to his master without his Queen.

Henri, meanwhile, pressed ahead with his preparations for making war on the Huguenots, including the King of Navarre. 'Nothing else was being discussed from Paris to Blois, where the King had convoked the States-general.'

This convocation opened on 6 December 1576. On its eve the King summoned Monsieur to his cabinet, where in the Queen Mother's presence he proceeded to explain to his brother that the Catholic League 'was of the greatest importance to his own authority and the realm; that the Catholics were right to complain; that his own duty and conscience compelled him to take sides with them rather than with the Huguenots; and he begged and conjured my brother, as a Son of France and a good Catholic, to assist him in this matter, in which his Crown and the Catholic religion were at stake'. Henri then further informed François of his decision to head the League in order to prevent its members from electing another chief, and demanded that Monsieur and all the Catholic nobles who had been supporting him should sign its roll after himself.

By thus setting his signature to the League's proclamation, Henri III broke with the sacred tradition of the French monarchy, according to which the King was above all parties and political feuds. But by violating the dynastic code and creating yet another faction, the King's party, he simply added to the troubles besetting him.

Marguerite explained that in the circumstances Monsieur could do no less than offer his services to His Majesty and the Catholic cause. Once again he changed sides, abandoning his former allies; at last Henri III had achieved his design of depriving them of a Son of France as their figurehead. Marguerite found no word of blame for François' defection, although she herself was still determined to rejoin her husband before war again broke out.

The States of Blois opened on the following day. The King, heavily guarded by several thousand troops, had only one objective in addressing them: to raise the funds necessary to pursue his plan to exterminate the Huguenots.

The Queen Mother and the Queen of Navarre were present. Marguerite's regal beauty made a deep impression on the lower orders—parliamentarians and civil servants—privileged to gaze at her during the King's Speech.

'She was dressed', wrote Brantôme, 'in a gown of orange and black, the black part of which was covered in shimmering embroidery, and was wearing the great veil of majesty.'

Catherine and Henri III shrewdly put the dazzlingly lovely Queen of Navarre on show on such State occasions; the King had not been altogether insincere when he told his sister that her beauty and glamour were one of the reasons why he wished to keep her at Court.

All the Huguenot leaders, including Danville, Condé and Navarre, refused to negotiate with the King's envoys; he therefore publicly revoked the concessions made to them in the previous May and declared a new war on them. He had great difficulty in raising the necessary funds from his reluctant Catholic subjects, including even the clergy, and to supplement them had to revert once again to his Italian bankers for a further 100,000 *livres*.

Navarre, meanwhile, sent yet another envoy to Paris to bring his Queen home. This time Henri made no glib or polite promises

to his brother-in-law's representative, but 'rudely and threateningly told him that he had given his sister to a Catholic, not a
Huguenot, and that if the King my husband wished to have me
back he should first become a Catholic'.

'Genissac', Marguerite continued, 'having come to tell me of
his rough dismissal by the King, I thereupon went straightaway
to the cabinet of the Queen my mother, where the King then
was.'

Throwing all caution aside and wasting no time on preliminary
politenesses, Margot reminded Henri of his previous prevarica-
tions and delays in giving her leave to rejoin Navarre.

'I told him that I had not pleased myself in getting married,
but had done so under the will and authority of King Charles,
the Queen Mother, and himself; that as they had given him to me
they could not prevent me form sharing his fortunes; that I
wanted to go to him, and that if they still refused to allow me to
go, I would run away and do so somehow, even at the risk of my
life.'

'The King answered me, "This is not the moment, sister, to
press me for my permission. I admit what you have said, that I
did deliberately put off your departure intending to prevent it
altogether, because since the King of Navarre has again become
a Huguenot I never thought it a good thing that you should
join him. What we are doing, the Queen Mother and myself, is
for your own good. I am going to make war on the Huguenots
and exterminate that miserable religion that has done us all so
much harm, and there is no question of you, a Catholic and my
sister, being in their hands as a hostage. And who knows whether,
in order to harm me irreparably, they might not take your life in
revenge for the harm I shall do them? No, no, you will not go;
and if you try to run away, as you said, be sure that I myself
and the Queen Mother will be your bitterest enemies and will do
all in our power to make you feel it, so that you would do your
husband's position more harm than good."

'After this cruel sentence, which made me extremely angry',
Marguerite decided to ask the advice of her most intimate men
and women friends at Court as to the next step she should take.

'They said that it would make a very bad impression for me to remain there, amongst the open enemies of the King my husband,
and advised me to leave Court for the duration of the war, and
that it might be even better if I left the country on some pretext or
another, either on a pilgrimage or to visit relations.'

Marguerite had invited both François and her most intimate
woman friend at that time, the Princess of La Roche-sur-Yon,
to this informal conference. This Princess was about to leave
France to take a cure at Spa, the Belgian watering-place. With
Monsieur was a diplomat, M. de Mondoucet, who was the
French King's representative in Flanders.

Throughout his life François had only one ambition, a
kingship in his own right. At heart he cared neither for the
Catholic nor the Protestant cause, but only for his own ambitions.
He became the most ridiculous aspirant ever for the hand of that
middle-aged virgin, Elizabeth I of England; he was even prepared to marry a Spanish Infanta to achieve his goal, but so far
none of his attempts to do so had been successful. Now, however, a
new opportunity had arisen whereby he might yet achieve power.

Marguerite wrote that M. de Mondoucet had recently arrived
from Flanders in order to inform the King of the sufferings of
the Flemish people under Spanish domination; that several noblemen and civic leaders had requested him to assure the King of
their loyalty and love of France and to ask for his assistance in
their attempt to resist this cruel Spanish colonialism.

'Mondoucet, realizing the King's indifference, since he had
then nothing else in mind except the Huguenots, whom he wished
to punish for having supported my brother, made no attempt to
put their case to him, but instead turned to my brother, who like
Pyrrhus [the ambitious character mentioned by Plutarch, whom
she had read] only enjoyed great and dangerous enterprises, having
been born to conquer rather than to hold on to his possessions.'

As a woman, Marguerite was excluded from pursuing similar
enterprises directly, but as Catherine de Medici's daughter she
had her own full share of secret ambition, which she gratified
vicariously by her unfailing support of François's schemes.

'He decided', she continued, 'to take up this cause, which

appealed to him all the more since he saw that he would be committing no injustice by doing so, but only intending to restore to France what had been usurped from her by Spain.' And, as she refrained from adding, winning himself at least a ducal crown by doing so. 'For this reason Mondoucet had entered my brother's service, who was sending him back to Flanders allegedly in order to accompany the Princess of La Roche-sur-Yon to take the waters at Spa; but in fact to assure the Flemish nobility of Monsieur's willingness to place himself at their head in their resistance to Spain. Mondoucet listened as Marguerite's friends were discussing various pretexts for enabling her to leave France during the coming war, 'some of them suggesting that I might go to Savoy or Lorraine, or to Sainte-Claude, or on a pilgrimage to Notre-Dame-de-Lorette' when the diplomat suddenly whispered to her brother:

'Monsieur, if the Queen of Navarre could pretend to have some ailment that needed a cure at Spa, where the Princess of La Roche-sur-Yon is going, this would be most helpful to your plans regarding Flanders, where she would make a tremendous impression.'

'My brother thought this an excellent suggestion, and said to me out loud: "My dear Queen, you need look no further; you must go with the Princess to take the waters at Spa. I saw some time ago that you had a rash of erysipelas on your arm; you must say that the doctors had then prescribed this cure for you, but that it was the wrong season; now is the right one, and you must request the King to allow you to go there.'

'My brother refrained from saying in this company why he wished me to go, because the Cardinal of Bourbon, who was on the side of the Guises and the Spaniards, was present, but I knew that it was on account of the Flanders question, of which Mondoucet had already spoken to both of us.'

All her friends strongly approved of Monsieur's suggestion, however, and the Princess was delighted, saying that she would accompany Marguerite when she visited the Queen Mother to discuss it with her, and persuade Her Majesty to agree to this plan.

Next day Marguerite visited Catherine and put the suggestion to her, reminding her of the King's refusal to let her join her husband, who, she said, would think that by not doing so she was deserting him and his cause, and that between the King and Navarre her position was a dangerous and even impossible one. She then repeated the story of the alleged erysipelas that François had suggested to her and begged her mother to persuade the King to give her permission to go to Spa for treatment.

For some time past Catherine has been deeply grieved by Henri III's attitude towards her, and profoundly annoyed by his ruthlessly taking out of her hands the authority she had so long wielded. Henri was in the hands of the Jesuits and the most bigoted Catholic bishops, who were egging him on in this war against the Huguenots. With her considerable intelligence and long experience in matters of State, she fully realized the implications of the step the King had taken when he placed himself at the head of the League. When the States of Blois showed signs of refusing the King the credits he needed for his coming war, Catherine, knowing that Henri was resolved to make it anyway, personally addressed them, reminding them that she herself was as good a Catholic as any, which her fatal mistake on St Bartholomew's Night had unfortunately proved to be true. Nevertheless, in that very same month of December the Queen Mother had sent personal messages to her son-in-law, Navarre. Both of them were equally cunning and astute; neither of them liked one another, yet did not neglect the possibilities of a future alliance between them. Both of them, moreover, had in common a genuine love of France and detestation of the civil wars that were devastating the realm. Whilst the Queen Mother did undoubtedly agree with the King that this was not the moment to allow Marguerite to rejoin her husband, she was in the right mood to favour her request to leave the country, and promised to speak to the King about it.

Henri III, busy as he was with his preparations for war, no doubt considered that in this situation his sister's beauty and glamour would not be of much immediate use to him. He had attained his immediate objective, to detach Monsieur from his own enemies. Pending the outcome of his negotiations with the

Flemish nobility, François, who had succeeded to the title of Duke of Anjou, was to command one of the Royal armies against the Protestants. There was no longer any danger of Marguerite acting as intermediary between her brother and husband.

'The King spoke to me about the matter [her wish to take the waters at Spa] without appearing to be annoyed by it, being sufficiently satisfied at having prevented me from rejoining the King my husband, whom he then hated more than anyone else on earth, and ordered that a courier should be sent to Don Juan of Austria, who was then the King of Spain's commander in Flanders, requesting him to provide me with the necessary passports to travel freely through the territory under his command, in order to take the waters at Spa, which was in the bishopric of Liège.'

8 Ambassadress-Royal

This mission to Flanders was the second turning-point in Marguerite's life.

She was twenty-four, famous throughout Europe for her beauty, intelligence, and erudition. After she was forced into her loveless marriage, she had had at least two passionate affairs, yet in spite of them she had known very little genuine happiness. Nor was she given an opportunity to use her natural talents or to be a queen in anything but name. Until then too, from the moment she arrived at Court from St Germain, she had spent hardly a day or night when she was not under the Queen Mother's vigilant eye; yet Catherine had done little for her youngest daughter except to protect her from the worst effects of Charles IX's and Henri III's spite. Nor, after her marriage, did she have either the household or even appurtenances of her own to which her rank entitled her—a grievance of which she was keenly conscious.

Now, everything suddenly changed. With the King's consent and the Queen Mother's approval, the Queen of Navarre was to travel abroad in the style befitting a Daughter of France. Her delight in this reversal of her previous ill-fortune shines through every line of her retrospective description of the magnificence in which she set out on this cure and her secret embassy for Monsieur.

Whilst the preparations for her trip were being made, her brother briefed her in further detail regarding the situation in Flanders and her diplomatic task on his behalf when she would meet the Catholic Flemish nobility.

Philip II had given the sadistic Duke of Alba, Governor of the Low Countries, special orders to crush the northern Calvinists by cruelty and terror and to subdue the southern Catholic nobility by hardly less unjust methods. The Calvinist leader was Prince William of Orange, the 'Silent' and crafty; the southern Catholics were led by Counts Horn and Egmont. In spite of their irreconcilable religious differences, these two parties formed a compact front against Alba's terrorism.

Lamoral, Count of Egmont, was originally in the service of Spain. In 1554 Philip II had sent him to England to ask the hand of Queen Mary—'Bloody Mary'—Elizabeth I's half-sister and predecessor, and Egmont was present at their wedding in Winchester. But in 1558 the Count incurred the envy and personal hatred of Alba. He became the leading patriot amongst the Flemish nobility and was the idol of the people. In 1565 he made a special journey to Spain to lay the Netherlands case before Philip, the only tragic result of which was his fall from that bigoted monarch's favour. Three years later, with the King's approval, Alba's 'Court of Blood' seized Counts Horn and Egmont and several of their followers; they were condemned for alleged treason and executed in Brussels on 5 June 1568. To his countrymen Egmont thenceforward became a martyr as well as a hero; more than two centuries later his fate inspired Goethe to his famous tragedy and Beethoven to a musical setting of it, of which the overture is still constantly performed.

The Lowlanders, Calvinists and Catholics alike, put up a magnificent resistance to Spanish colonialist oppression. In 1573 they finally succeeded in throwing Alba out. He left Brussels and returned to Spain, the everlasting stain of his name on Netherlands history being all that remained there of him.

Philip II then decided to adopt a less harsh policy towards the brave Netherlanders, and appointed his bastard brother, Don Juan of Austria, as Governor and pacificator. Although not comparable to Egmont, Don Juan was also a romantic figure. In 1571, when he was only twenty-six, he won great fame by defeating the Turks in the Battle of Lepanto; he was as handsome and amiable as he was brave. Yet the Flemish were still unwilling to accept the Spanish yoke.

William of Orange had escaped Alba's fury by retreating to his German estates. But on his return to Brussels ten years later the Catholic leaders of the southern nobility were not prepared to follow this rigid Calvinist, and it was then that they thought of turning to the King of France for help; it was on their behalf that Mondoucet had visited the French Court, where François, eagerly grasping at the chance to become their ruler, took him into his service.

Marguerite's secret and congenial mission, as her brother then explained it to her, was to foster by her charms and diplomacy the desire of these Flemish nobles to invite Monsieur to lead them against Spain.

The King and the Queen Mother had already left for Poitiers, in order to be closer to the Duke of Mayenne, Guise's able brother, who was besieging Brouage, six miles south of La Rochelle, before entering Gascony to make war on Henry of Navarre.

After Catherine's last attempt to reconcile her sons had succeeded, François, in this Sixth War of Religion, was given command of the army that was moving against his former Huguenot allies in the Puy-de-dôme. On 28 May he captured and sacked Issoire, committing atrocities similar to and as vile as any on St Bartholomew's Night.

The Queen of Navarre, on leaving Paris shortly afterwards, was accompanied by a large retinue of ladies: the Princess of La Roche-sur-Yon, Madame de Tournon, her personal lady-in-waiting, and her daughter Hélène, with several other women and maids-of-honour. The Cardinal of Lenoncourt, the Bishop of Langres, gentlemen-in-waiting and her household staff—'my first *maître d'hôtel*, my first Master of Horse, and other members of my suite', attended her.

'I travelled', Marguerite wrote, 'in my litter lined with scarlet Spanish velvet embroidered in gold and various shades of silk; my coat-of-arms and forty different other shields emblazoned on it with lettering in Spanish and Italian. . . .' This sumptuous equipage was followed by the litters of the Princess and Madame de Tournon and by ten young ladies-in-waiting on horseback, accompanied by their chaperon, as well as six coaches containing female attendants and servants.

'I travelled through Picardy', she continued, 'where the cities had been commanded by the King to receive me with the honours due to me as his sister, which they did to my complete satisfaction.' And she added that her splendid and colourful procession gave so much pleasure to all the foreigners who beheld it that their admiration for France was greatly increased.

Marguerite's last stop on French soil, on 14 July, was at Le Châtelet, a small fortified town on the Picardy frontier, where she spent the night at the local hostelry. She herself made no mention of the incident said to have occurred there, and as it was not reported until more than a century later it may well never have happened at all. According to this account, by a curious and obviously contrived 'coincidence', on that very same morning another traveller had arrived at the same hostelry. His features were swathed in scarves and almost invisible, the excuse being that he was suffering from an outbreak of erysipelas on his face. This mysterious stranger was no less a person than the Duke of Guise—Scarface—disguised under this pretext to avoid recognition. The Queen of Navarre, obviously knowing who he was, and even expecting him, admitted him to her room, where he spent most of the night. Margot's detractors, who were always increasing the number of her love affairs, immediately assumed that she had given her former suitor this rendezvous; serious historians who accept the tale as true at least give it a more plausible interpretation. According to this, they were not making love at all, but having a very serious political conversation, which Monsieur had asked his sister to have privately with Guise. Preparing for his own invasion of the Low Countries, François was particularly anxious that Don Juan should not have foreign mercenaries at his disposal with which to repel him. Guise, the acknowledged leader of the French Catholics, did have such troops at his disposal; as ever, the Lorraines were also intriguing with Spain against France. It was therefore to Henri III's interest, as well as Monsieur's, that Marguerite should try to persuade the Duke not to provide Don Juan with these troops. Whether or not this incident occurred—and if it did, Margot failed completely to influence her former adorer—Guise did later on supply Don Juan with 5,000 or 6,000 men, much to the annoyance of the King of France.

The first important Flemish town on Marguerite's royal progress was Cambrai, a Spanish citadel under the governorship of Archbishop Barlemont, who paid his distinguished and lovely guest 'the very highest honour and Spanish ceremonies'. She noted that his entourage wore the clothes and had the appearance of 'real Flemings, and in that district they are very coarse people'. From the moment of her arrival Marguerite looked about her, observed, and recorded her impressions like the keenest tourist:

'I found this town of Cambrai, although not built of such good materials as our French towns, much more agreeable, for the streets and squares were much better proportioned, and the churches very large and beautiful, a common feature of all the cities of Flanders.' She also admired the citadel built by the Emperor Charles V, 'one of the best built and most beautiful in all Christendom'.

Marguerite was equally favourably impressed by the Governor, M. d'Inchy, a nephew of the late Count Egmont and the first of the Flemish noblemen with whom she made contact on her brother's behalf: 'In charm, appearance, and everything necessary to a perfect cavalier, he was the equal of our most polished courtiers, having not the least touch of the bumpkin, a natural trait of most of the Flemish.'

The Archbishop gave a banquet and ball in Marguerite's honour, at which M. d'Inchy, quite clearly immediately captivated by her, was present throughout—'imprudently, it seemed to me, since he was in charge of the citadel'.

'My brother never being far from my thoughts, since I had no greater affection than for him, I remembered the instructions he had given me, and saw my chance to do him a good turn in Flanders, since that town and citadel were the very keys to it, so I used all the wits God had given me to win over M. d'Inchy.' And she succeeded so well that he insisted on accompanying her to Namur, where Don Juan was awaiting her, saying that he wished to witness the triumphs she would have on arrival there.

During the journey, which lasted ten or twelve days, Marguerite continued the good work she had begun on M. d'Inchy at Cambrai, although she thought it unwise of his superior, the Archbishop, to have given the citadel's guardian permission to leave his post.

Her next conquest was at Valenciennes, where she was met at the border between that town and Cambrésis by 300 local landowners led by the Count of Lalain, Governor and Captain-General of the province of Hainault, and M. de Montigny, his brother. At Valenciennes the royal tourist was particularly impressed by the fountains and musical clocks, like those of Germany, with all kinds of amusing clockwork figures on them.

Lalain 'claimed to be related to the King my husband, and was a man of great authority and wealth, to whom the Spanish domination had always been odious; he was particularly outraged by the execution of the Count of Egmont, who was a close relative of his. And although he had maintained his authority without entering into the League of the Prince of Orange and the Huguenots, as he was a very Catholic lord, yet he would never meet Don Juan, nor allow him or anyone connected with Spain to enter his territory. Don Juan did not dare to force him to do so, fearing that if he were attacked the League of Catholics of Flanders, known as the States, would join the Prince of Orange and the Huguenots. . . .'

The Count could not have honoured the Queen of Navarre

more highly had she been his own sovereign. He escorted her to his residence at Mons, where she was to stay, and where she found nearly 100 of the local ladies assembled in the courtyard to welcome her, headed by the Countess of Lalain, 'not like a foreign princess, but as if I were their own mistress, for the Flemish are naturally informal and jovial'. The Countess was also intelligent, which gave Marguerite the idea of making an intimate friend of her in order to further her brother's plans, since the Count was very much under his wife's influence. The Lalains insisted on the Queen of Navarre remaining their guest for more than a week, and Marguerite found their Flemish candour and informality both amusing and slightly touching:

'She was breast-feeding her baby son'—which impressed Marguerite because a Frenchwoman of similar rank would never have done so in public if at all,—'and next day at the banquet, sitting quite close to me at table, where in this country they have the habit of talking to one another most freely, she was arrayed and covered in jewels and embroidery, wearing a Spanish-style dress of gold brocade, with gold and silver trimmings and a silver-white jacket embroidered in gold with large diamond buttons (a costume highly suitable for a wet-nurse). They brought her baby son to her there, as richly attired in his swaddling-clothes as his wet-nurse was to feed him. She placed him on the table between us and without more ado unbuttoned her jacket, offering him her nipple, which in anyone else would have been regarded as a lack of politeness; but she did this, like everything else, with so much grace and *naïveté* that she received as much praise from the company as they had entertainment from watching her.'

Marguerite's comment in parenthesis reveals how diverting she herself found the Countess's performance. Her brief yet masterly description of the scene recalls those great Flemish paintings of unbuttoned jolly banquets, the hearty appetites and flushed faces of the guests, the tables loaded with gold and silver-ware, flesh, fowl, and wines.

'When the tables had been cleared the ball began in that same hall in which we were sitting, when, as we were close to one another, I told her again how pleased I was to be in her company, but was almost sorry to have met her for the sadness I would feel in leaving her; that it was one of the sorrows of my life that Heaven had prevented us from being born in the same country; which I said deliberately in order to lead her up to a discussion that might be of use to my brother.'

The Countess replied, as Marguerite hoped she would, that since the deaths of the Counts of Egmont, Horn, Montigny and others who were their close relatives, the Flemish nobility hated no one more than their Spanish oppressors and longed for nothing more than to free themselves from their tyranny, but that their religious differences had prevented it; were the country united they would soon throw out the Spaniards, but it was weakened by religious divisions. And she ended by saying: 'Might it please God that the King your brother would wish to reconquer this country, which is his by ancient right! We would all welcome him with open arms!'

This, of course, gave Marguerite the opportunity she had been so laboriously seeking. She explained to the Countess that the King was unable to undertake any foreign wars, since he was entirely preoccupied in dealing with the French Huguenots, but that her brother, 'M. d'Alençon, who in valour, prudence, and goodness is in no degree inferior to the kings my father and brothers, would wish them well and would have no less means than King Henri to come to their aid'. And she continued to sing François's praise to the naïve young Countess, who, she saw, was taking great pleasure in their conversation, of which she eagerly promised to inform her husband.

'When the ball was over we went to hear vespers in a convent for the daughters of good families, an institution such as we do not have in France. These girls are placed there until they are old enough to be married. They do not sleep in dormitories, but in separate houses, although all in one enclosure like those of the nuns; in each house there are from three to six young girls with an older one, and a certain number of these, like the Abbess, do not get married. They only wear religious habits in the morning during divine service and after dinner, at vespers. As soon as the services are over they change from their habits into dresses like those of other marriageable girls, going to parties and balls as freely as the rest, so that they change their clothes four times daily. Every day they were at the banquets and balls and danced like everyone else.'

In the course of that evening Mme de Lalain had carried out her promise and reported everything Marguerite had told her to her husband. Next day the Count assured the Queen of Navarre how gladly he would welcome the Duke of Alençon's arrival in Flanders. He suggested that she should also win over M. d'Inchy, who was still in her company, but 'I did not wish to inform him that I had already spoken to him about it, but asked him to do so, which he could do better than myself, since he was his neighbour and friend. I then assured him that for his great services he would be rewarded by the friendship and protection of my brother. We agreed that on my return I would stay at my property, La Fère, where my brother would join me, and where the Count of Lalain's brother, M. de Montigny, would meet us in order to discuss the matter in further detail.' La Fère, an estate belonging to the House of Bourbon, had been part of Marguerite's marriage settlement by Navarre.

Her account of this conversation with Lalain, and her suggestion to him that he himself should speak to M. d'Inchy, not wanting him to know that she had already approached and won over that gentleman, reveals how seriously Marguerite was taking her secret mission, and the professionalism with which she was setting about it. In handling these Flemish aristocrats she showed herself to possess a considerable share of her mother's guile and love of intrigue.

On parting with her Flemish friends, Marguerite presented the young Countess with a casket of jewels and the Count with a bejewelled necklace. M. de Lalain accompanied her for a couple of miles outside his own territory, until they saw in the distance the procession of Don Juan of Austria riding to welcome her; he then turned back, since he refused to meet the Spanish overlord. M. d'Inchy, however, remained with her, as they had previously arranged.

Brantôme wrote of Don Juan, whom he had known in Spain,

in lyrical terms. He also told a romantic story of the Austrian gallant's first sight of Marguerite. When Don Juan was travelling from Milan to Flanders he broke his journey in Paris on purpose to see her dancing at Court with her brother. He had declared that he placed her 'above both Italian and Spanish beauties, although her beauty, more divine than human, was more likely to damn men's souls than to save them'—in view of the misfortunes that tended to befall Marguerite's lovers, an uncannily accurate appraisal. This appearance of Don Juan's at the French Court was, however, incognito: he had attended one of Catherine's famous masked balls disguised as a Moor and had not made his presence known to the Queen Mother, much to her regret.

Now, accompanied by a large suite, Don Juan welcomed the Queen of Navarre with full regal honours. With her usual acute observation, however, she noted that with the exception of one courtier, Ludovico of Gonzaga, 'the rest of his servants were of no account and poor appearance, and did not include any of the Flemish nobility'.

'He dismounted to salute me in my litter, which was raised up and wide open. . . . After a few words he remounted, continuing to talk to me until we reached the town, where we did not arrive until evening, because the ladies of Mons had detained me as long as they could. . . . Nevertheless, Namur was so beautifully laid out (the Spaniards being excellent at this kind of thing) and the town so well illuminated that the windows and shops were fully lit up, and it looked almost as if a new day were shining.'

Don Juan, tactfully assuming that the Queen of Navarre and her suite would wish to rest after their journey rather than immediately be given a banquet, conducted her straight to her lodging, which, said Marguerite, contained 'the most beautiful, rich, and superb furniture I ever remembered having seen . . .'.

The Cardinal of Lenoncourt remarked to the Duke of Arscot, one of Don Juan's courtiers, that this setting was more appropriate to a great king rather than a young bachelor prince like Don Juan, whereupon the Duke told him how the Don had acquired it. These priceless materials of gold, silver, and silk, which he had had made up in Milan, had been presented to him by a Turkish pasha whose children he had taken prisoner and then returned to their father without demanding any ransom for them. 'And as a reminder of how he came to receive them, he had the bed coverings and walls of the Queen's room hung with tapestries representing the naval battle and glorious victory [Lepanto] he had won over the Turks.'

'Next morning Don Juan arranged for me to hear a Spanish Mass with music—violins and cornets.' The usual banquet and ball followed. Don Juan told Marguerite that she reminded him of her late sister, his former Queen, Elisabeth, the eldest Valois princess, who was Philip II's third wife and died in childbirth in 1568.

The next stage of Marguerite's journey was to be down the River Meuse from Namur to Liège, but as her boats were not yet ready she was obliged to remain overnight. Next morning, after seeing her to the boat he had provided for her, Don Juan took leave of her and so, at last, did M. d'Inchy, 'who had no permission from his master to accompany me any further, and left me with as many regrets as assurances that he would forever be the humble servant of myself and my brother'.

But now Marguerite's luck suddenly changed:

'The envious and treacherous goddess of fortune, unable to bear the success that until now has been mine during this journey, gave me two sinister hints of the trials she was preparing for me on my return. The first of these was that as soon as the boat moved off Mlle de Tournon, a virtuous and charming girl of whom I was very fond, was suddenly taken so violently ill that she screamed with pain. This was apparently due to a heart attack, of which the doctors were unable to prevent her from dying a few days after I arrived in Liège. I shall in due course tell her sad and extraordinary story.'

The second stroke of misfortune was a minor although unpleasant one. They had arrived at Huy, a town clustering on one of the steep hills leading down to the valley of the Meuse, of which the last houses were on the river's edge. Owing to a heavy rainfall, a torrent of water swept down the mountainside just as they were about to land. The river rose so rapidly that they barely had time to jump ashore, and 'although we ran as fast as we could to the top of the hill, the river rose almost as quickly to the highest street, near to my lodgings. That evening we had to make do with what the householder was able to provide, as it was impossible to land either my staff or my belongings, or to set foot in the town, which was nearly submerged by the deluge; from which it was, however, almost miraculously as quickly freed, for when day broke the waters had withdrawn completely.'

Next morning they were able to re-embark and duly arrived in Liège: 'The town is larger than Lyons and almost on the same plan, the River Meuse cutting through its centre; very well built, every canon's house almost as fine as a palace; the streets broad and wide; the squares beautiful, containing very fine fountains; the churches decorated with so much marble (which is quarried near there) that they appear almost built of it; the clock-towers in the German style, all with carillons, reproducing every kind of music, with amusing clockwork figures. The Bishop, who received me as I stepped from my boat, led me to his magnificent palace, which he had vacated for me, one of the handsomest and most comfortable town houses one could wish for, with very fine fountains, gardens, and galleries, painted and gilded and containing so much marble that there is nothing more splendid and delightful.

'As the wells of Spa were only two or three miles from there, and there was only a hamlet of three or four drab little houses nearby, the Princess of La Roche-sur-Yon was advised to remain in Liège and have the waters brought there to her at night, before sunrise, so that their strength would be unimpaired. This was most agreeable to me, since it would mean spending our stay more conveniently and in good company.'

Marguerite then gave a list of the Austrian, German, and other aristocrats who, hearing of her arrival, had come specially to Liège to meet her. All would have been most pleasant had it not been for the extraordinary and unfortunate death of Mlle de Tournon, the story of which she then told:

'Mme de Tournon, my lady-in-waiting, had several daughters,

the eldest of whom had married M. de Balançon, Governor of the county of Burgundy. She asked her mother to allow her sister to come and live with her, as she would be so far away from all her relatives. Her mother agreed to let her sister go. She lived there for some years, endearing herself to everyone (although she was not exactly beautiful, her chief attractions being her virtue and charm). The Marquess of Varembon, who at that time was destined to enter Holy Orders, living in his brother's, M. de Balançon's, house, and therefore seeing so much of Mlle de Tournon, fell in love with her and, not as yet having entered the Church, wished to marry her. He spoke of this both to his own and her relatives; her family agreed to the match, but M. de Balançon, considering that his brother would be more useful to him as a priest, did everything he could to prevent it, insisting that he should become one.

'Mme de Tournon, a very wise and prudent woman, annoyed by this attitude of his, removed her daughter from her sister's house and took her home. But as she had a somewhat rough and terrifying tongue, paying no attention to the fact that her daughter was grown-up and deserved to be treated more kindly, she scolded and shouted at her incessantly, so that the poor girl's eyes were hardly ever dry, although she never did anything that was not praiseworthy; but that was her mother's manner.

'Longing for nothing more than to be freed from this parental tyranny, when she heard that I was travelling to Flanders she was extremely happy, expecting that the Marquess of Varembon would be there, as was the case; and that having given up Holy Orders, being able to get married, he would ask her mother for her hand, and that by this marriage she would be freed from her bullying.

'Varembon and his brother, the younger Balançon, were both at Namur. There young Balançon, who was not much pleasanter than the elder one, paid the girl much attention, but during our whole stay at Namur Varembon did not once so much as look at her. So long as he was present she pretended not to care about him, but as soon as they had said goodbye and left the boat her heart was so filled with despair, regret, and frustration that she was unable to breathe for crying, and in mortal pain. As she was otherwise young and healthy, her youth held out for eight or ten days, but death, armed by despair, was finally victorious, snatching her from her mother and myself, who mourned her with equal sorrow, for although her mother had such a harsh tongue, she did truly love her.

'Her funeral was as magnificent as possible, since she belonged to a great House and was even in the service of the Queen my mother'—Catherine had lent Mme de Tournon and her daughter to Marguerite for this trip—'and four of my gentlemen were appointed as pall-bearers to carry her coffin. One of these was La Boessière, who during her lifetime had adored her without ever having dared to disclose his feelings to her, owing partly to her virtue and partly to their social inequality, and who now, as he bore her mortal remains to her grave, felt his love for her dying a thousand deaths.

'The sad procession was in the middle of the street leading to the church when the Marquess of Varembon arrived in Liège. A few days after my departure from Namur he suddenly repented of his cruelty to her. His former passion, that had not been fanned by her presence, was (strangely enough!) rekindled by her absence. He decided to ask her mother for her hand, trusting, in my opinion, to his good fortune with all the women whom he desired, as has since been shown when he married that big girl [Dorothy, widow of the Duke of Brunswick] against her parents's wishes. . . .

'He therefore asked Don Juan to give him a message for me, and he arrived by coach just as the corpse of that unfortunate and innocent girl, in her glorious virginity, was in the middle of the street. The funeral procession made it impossible for him to go any further. He looked to see what was holding him up. From afar, in the middle of a group of people in mourning, he saw a white cloth covered in wreaths. He asked what was happening and someone told him it was a funeral. With too much curiosity, he pressed forward, trying to find out whose it was. Oh, fatal reply! Love, thus avenging his faithless ingratitude, made him then feel the suffering he had caused his former loved one. The person whom he addressed all unknowingly informed him that it was the funeral of Mlle de Tournon, whereupon he fainted and fell from his horse. He was carried to a nearby lodging, where he lay as if dead, or as if joined in death to her whom he had spurned when she was still alive. I think his soul may have visited her tomb to ask her forgiveness, leaving him for a time to all appearances lifeless, and when it returned brought him back to consciousness in order that he might again suffer from her death, for by doing so only once he was insufficiently punished for his ingratitude.'

This romantic and sentimental story of Mlle de Tournon was based on fact, although Marguerite may have embroidered on it for her own amusement and Brantôme's. It was later turned into a novel by Mme de Souza and published in 1821.

Once this sad event was over, Marguerite thoroughly enjoyed the remainder of her stay in Liège:

'And although the doctor who had advised me to take this cure was my brother, it nevertheless did me good, for I had no further eruption of erysipelas on my arm for the next six or seven years.'

But whilst she had been amusing herself being fêted, playing the diplomat, and sipping the waters, she had not kept in touch with current events, either in Flanders or at home. So it was a rude shock to her when Mme d'Havrach, one of her Flemish women friends, came to inform her of recent events in Namur. The country was once again in a state of ferment and insurrection. Almost immediately after seeing her off, Don Juan had treacherously seized the city's citadel, in contravention of his agreement with the States.

In order to leave Liège, Marguerite was obliged to apply to Prince William of Orange for the necessary papers, and sent him one of her gentlemen, Mondoucet, to do so; but the Prince returned neither the messenger nor the necessary authorization.

To her even greater anxiety, meanwhile, she received a messenger from her brother, who brought her still more disagreeable news. He wrote to her that since her departure, and after winning several victories against the Huguenots, he had rejoined the King and Court at Poitiers, where to his bitter surprise 'as little notice was taken of him as if he had done nothing for the King; that

Bussy'—who had served Henri III equally well—'whom he had previously favoured, was now out of favour and as much persecuted by the envious as in the time of de Guast; that they were both of them insulted day after day'. François had also learnt from a reliable source that 'the King very much regretted having allowed me to make this journey to Flanders, and that on my return I would be victimized, either on his account, either by the Spaniards (who had been informed that I was negotiating in Flanders on his behalf), or by the Huguenots, avenging themselves for his having made war on them after they had assisted him.'

This startling and unpleasant change in Anjou's and Marguerite's fortunes was due to the Peace of Bergerac with the Protestant leaders, which Henri III signed on 17 September 1577, and which ended the Sixth War of Religion. Satisfied at having re-established his authority, he once again turned to blunting, if he could not altogether pluck out, that thorn in his regal flesh, his over-ambitious younger brother, and as the war between himself and Navarre was over—largely on account of that astute Bourbon's diplomatic relations with his mother-in-law—there was no longer any reason why the Queen of Navarre should not return to France.

But far from being a triumphal progress, that return was more of a retreat, with one or two moments of comical unpleasantness and even of danger. Perhaps the most sinister aspect of Marguerite's problem was that some of the men in her suite were also disaffected, favouring either the Spaniards or the Huguenots:

'I could confide only in the Princess of La Roche-sur-Yon and Mme de Tournon, who, realizing our danger and knowing that it would take us five or six days to reach La Fère, with tears in their eyes replied to me that only God could protect us. . . .'

After a wait of two or three days the Prince of Orange had still not supplied her with the necessary papers. Both the Cardinal of Lenoncourt and her Master of Horse, Salviati, urged her not to leave without them, but Marguerite did not trust their advice and resolved to do so nevertheless:

'Whereupon Salviati, conspiring with my Treasurer, who was

also a secret Huguenot sympathizer, informed me that I had run out of money'—which on arriving at La Fère she found entirely untrue—'and had my horses removed, adding this public insult to my danger.'

From this dilemma Marguerite was rescued by the devoted Princess, who lent her the necessary funds. And having presented a diamond worth 3,000 *écus* to the Bishop of Liège and golden chains and rings to his staff, she set out for Huy, 'my only passport being my trust in Almighty God':

'This city belonged to the Diocese of Liège, but it was mutinous and rebellious (as all the people felt themselves part of the general revolt of the Netherlands), and no longer willing to acknowledge its Bishop, since he was neutral and the town was on the side of the States. Having heard that as I was passing through Namur Don Juan had seized the citadel, they refused to recognize the authority of the Bishop's representative, who was accompanying me. As soon as we had settled down, they rang the tocsin and began dragging artillery through the streets, hanging chains across them so that we might not meet, keeping us in suspense all night, with no one in authority with whom we might parley, since they were only a stupid and brutal rabble. In the morning, having placed armed men all along our route, they allowed us to leave.

'The following night we slept at Dinant. Unfortunately, there they had been holding local elections and there was general debauchery; they were all drunk, there were no magistrates in authority—briefly, everything was chaos. And just to make matters worse for us, in the past the Bishop's representative had made war on them and they looked on him as their mortal enemy.

'When they are in their senses, this town is on the side of the States, but at that moment they were all under the domination of Bacchus, not even on their own side and recognizing nobody. As soon as they saw a convoy as large as mine approaching they became alarmed, laid down their glasses and reached for their arms, and instead of opening up for us they closed the barriers. I had sent a gentleman with two other male servants ahead, asking that they should make way for us, but I found them all still shouting in vain, unable to make themselves heard.

'Finally, I stood up in my litter, removed my travelling-mask, and beckoned to the nearest citizen that I wished to speak to him. When he came up to me I begged him to obtain a little silence, so that I might be heard. This having been done after a good deal of trouble, I told them who I was and the reason for my journey; that, far from wishing them any harm, I would not like them to have the least suspicion of such a thing; and I begged them to allow me, my women, and as few of my attendants as they might decide to enter the town for this one night, whilst the rest remained in the suburbs. This they agreed to.

'I then entered the town with leaders of my party, amongst whom was the Bishop's representative. Unfortunately, just as I was entering my lodging, accompanied by all this armed and drunken rabble, they recognized him. They began to insult him and were about to attack him, a venerable old man of over eighty, with a white beard nearly down to his waist. I insisted that he should enter my lodging, where those drunkards then began battering their halberds against the walls, which were only made of lath and plaster. Hearing this disturbance, I asked for the house-owner, who, fortunately, was there. I asked him to go to the window and arrange for me to speak to the nearest of them, which, after a great deal of trouble, he was able to do.

'After further shouting through the window, the town councillors came to speak to me, but they were so drunk they did not know what they were saying. However, I managed to explain to them that I did not know the Bishop's representative was their enemy, and I made them realize the gravity of offending a person of my quality, who was a friend of all the leading noblemen belonging to the States, and that I was certain that M. de Lalain and the other heads would be extremely annoyed to hear of the reception they were giving me.

'As soon as I mentioned M. de Lalain everything changed; they showed as much respect for him as they could have done for all the kings to whom I was related. Smiling and stuttering, the oldest of them asked me if I were a friend of the Count of Lalain? Seeing that being related to him would be of more use to me than my connections with all the potentates of Christianity, I replied

Henry IV of France by Franz Pourbus

Marie de Medici by Rubens

to him, "Yes, I am his friend, and his relative also." They thereupon bowed to me and kissed my hand, showing me as much respect as they had previously been insolent, begging me to forgive them and promising that they would do no harm to the Bishop's representative, and would let him leave with me.

'Next morning, as I was about to attend Mass, the King's agent to Don Juan, Du Bois, who was very pro-Spanish, arrived, telling me that he had orders from the King to find me and conduct me home safely, and that for this purpose he had asked Don Juan to lend him Barlemont, with a troop of cavalry, to escort me safely back to Namur. He said I must ask the local leaders to allow M. de Barlemont, who was their overlord, to enter, together with his troop, to accompany me. But this was for two purposes—on the one hand to take the town for Don Juan and the other so that I would fall into the hands of the Spaniards.

'This put me in a very great difficulty. I discussed the situation with the Cardinal of Lenoncourt, who no more wanted to be held by the Spaniards than I did. We decided to find out from the citizens if there were not another way out of the town by which I might avoid de Barlemont's troop. Leaving Du Bois, that little agent, chatting with M. de Lenoncourt, I went into another room, where I sent for the townsfolk. I told them that if they let in M. de Barlemont's troop they were lost; that their town would be seized for Don Juan. I advised them to arm themselves and mount guard at their gates, like people who refused to be taken unawares; that they should only admit M. de Barlemont, and no one else.

'As they were by then sober, they took my point and believed me, offering to devote their lives to my service and to give me a guide to show me the way by which I might put the river between those troops of Don Juan and myself, going always by ways and towns belonging to the States.

'Having decided on this with them, I had them send for M. de Barlemont alone, who tried to persuade them to allow his troop in as well. But at that they mutinied and were almost on the point of massacring him, telling him that if he did not withdraw his troop they would open up their artillery fire.

'M. de Barlemont and the agent Du Bois did all they could to persuade me to go to Namur, where Don Juan was awaiting me. I pretended to accept their advice, and having heard mass and had a short meal I left my lodgings, accompanied by 200 or 300 of the townsfolk, all armed.

'I continued talking to M. de Barlemont and the agent Du Bois as I went on my way, straight to the city gate on the riverside, completely opposite to the Namur road, on which M. de Barlemont's troop was waiting. Realizing this, they told me that I was on the wrong road, but, continuing to keep them in conversation, I arrived at the city gate.

'From there, accompanied by a considerable number of the people, I hurried towards the river and entered my boat, ordering all my suite and attendants to follow me as quickly as possible. From the bank M. de Barlemont and the agent Du Bois kept on shouting to me that I was doing the wrong thing—that it was the King's intention that I should travel via Namur. In spite of their shouting, we embarked promptly. Whilst our litters and horses were being put on board in two or three trips the townsfolk, in order to give me more time, were deliberately annoying M. de Barlemont and the agent Du Bois with a thousand and one complaints: pointing out to them in their patois how wrong Don Juan was to have betrayed his word to the States and broken the peace, harking back to the old quarrels of the time of the death of Count Egmont, and still threatening that if his troop came near the town they would train their guns on it. In that way they gave me time to get away, guided by God and the man they had lent me for the purpose.'

Yet a further comical misunderstanding occurred on that evening, when she was to lodge in a fortified castle called Fleurines, 'belonging to a gentleman of the States party, whom I had met with the Count of Lalain. Unfortunately, he was not there; only his wife was at home. As soon as we entered the yard, which was wide open, she became alarmed, and fled to the keep, lifting up the drawbridge over the moat, determined not to let us in, whatever we might say.

'Meanwhile, a company of 300 infantrymen sent by Don Juan

to cut us off and take this castle of Fleurines, knowing that I was intending to stay there, appeared on a little hill not 1,000 paces away. Having from that vantage-point seen us enter the court-yard, they assumed that we had gone on into the keep, and re-mained in a nearby village, intending to catch me next morning.

'The courtyard was enclosed only by a flimsy wall and a door which might easily have been broken open. As we were in this predicament, still arguing with the lady of the castle, who re-mained quite impervious to our requests, by the grace of God her husband, M. de Fleurines, arrived at nightfall and immediately let us into his castle, extremely annoyed with his wife for her in-civility towards us.

'This M. de Fleurines had come after us on the orders of the Count of Lalain, to assist me in passing without any further trouble through the towns loyal to the States, as M. de Lalain, head of their army, could not leave it to accompany me himself.'

At Château-Cambrésis her guides left her; two of them had been sent by her friend, the Countess of Lalain, and when they returned Marguerite gave them for her one of her own dresses which the Countess had admired when she had worn it at Mons: 'It was of black satin embroidered in gold and had cost 1,200 *écus*.'

Even her final stage to La Fère was not without danger:

'On arrival at Château-Cambrésis I learned that certain Huguenot forces were intending to attack me between the Flemish and French frontiers. Having told this to only a very few of my suite, I was ready an hour before daybreak. In sending for our litters and horses, the Chevalier Salviati was procrastinating again, as he had done at Liège. Knowing that he was doing so on purpose, I decided to leave my litter. Mounting my horse, all those who were ready following me, I arrived at Châtelet at ten o'clock in the morning, having by the grace of God escaped all the ambushes and traps of my enemies.'

9 *White Lie*

At La Fère, Marguerite found a messenger awaiting her with a letter from her brother. Peace having been made, the King was returning to Paris. But Monsieur complained bitterly that his own situation was becoming more and more intolerable:

'Every day he and his adherents were insulted and offended; every day there were quarrels and provocations against Bussy and his other honest followers, which was why he was awaiting my return to La Fère with the greatest impatience, so that he could join me there.'

As soon as François' messenger brought him back news of Marguerite's arrival, he hastened to send Bussy and all but fifteen or twenty of his men to Angers, and with these few he joined her:

'It was one of the greatest satisfactions of my life to have with me someone I so loved and honoured, and I did everything I could to make this visit agreeable to him, so that with St Peter he might have said, "Let us here build our tabernacles," had it not been for the fact that his royal courage and generosity of soul were spurring him on.

'The peacefulness of our Court, after the turmoil of the one from which he had come, was such a joy to him that he could not refrain from constantly telling me: "Oh, my Queen, how delightful it is here with you! My God, it's a paradise filled with every kind of delight, but the one I've just left is a hell, full of furies and torments.'"

This visit of Monsieur's to his beloved sister lasted for two months, during which she informed him in detail of the results of her mission to Flanders. As had been arranged, M. de Montigny, the Count of Lalain's brother, arrived with four or five other leading Catholics of Hainault; the Count promised to hand over the whole of Hainault and Artois to the French Prince on his arrival there. M. d'Inchy also kept his word to Marguerite, offering his personal services to her brother and, more important still, the precious citadel of Cambrai.

Well satisfied with these assurances, Monsieur sent back the Flemish gentlemen with many gifts, including two gold medallions on which were the portraits of himself and the Queen of Navarre. He then prepared to return to Paris in order to obtain the necessary funds for his expedition from the King.

Their obvious happiness together and mutual love gave rise to the legend, avidly spread by Margot's calumniators, that she and François had an incestuous passion for one another. No libels were too gross for her detractors to print about her. Later historians, including even her most admiring biographers, repeated these, although the more serious of them discussed them with some scepticism.

Incontestably, the Duke of Anjou worshipped and adored his sister above all other women. Yet so did Brantôme and others at Court. Marguerite's devotion to her youngest brother was also beyond doubt: in her Memoirs she invariably referred to him and his supposed virtues in superlatives, with obvious exaggeration. When she wrote them, François had been dead for years. During his lifetime she was always prepared to fight his battles for and with him, sometimes at the peril of her own life. But in order to explain this devotion, is it necessary to postulate that she was actually in love with François?

From childhood onwards their mother never showed any

particular affection for her youngest daughter, although after Marguerite's marriage she found her beauty, intelligence, and superlative dress-sense an asset at Court: Catherine never hesitated to use Marguerite to influence those men whom she attracted. For her youngest son, the Queen Mother quite frankly felt contemptuous dislike rather than maternal love, although she was constantly intriguing to bring about his marriage with some useful foreign princess, especially Elizabeth of England. There was undoubtedly an incestuous streak in Catherine's passion for Henri III, who absorbed all the genuine emotion that, with her hard and ruthlessly ambitious nature, she was able to bestow on any human being. Both Marguerite and François bitterly resented this situation and this grievance was one of their closest bonds. And the orgies in which the Queen Mother encouraged the King and even staged for his amusement, pandering to his worst vices, were not likely to cause any sexual inhibitions in her other children, who were obliged to take part in them.

Marguerite certainly did have her full share of Valois sensuality. Although in her Memoirs she quite understandably refrained from any direct references to her many affairs, she could never quite disguise her admiration for men like La Molle and Bussy, nor the attraction they had for her. She proclaimed with absolute sincerity that she worshipped beauty as fervently as the classical authors whom she was so fond of quoting, and the men with whom she did have affairs were all extremely handsome and glamorous males. No one could have been less so than her poor younger brother, hideous to repulsiveness.

The Duke of Bouillon described François as having been 'of medium height, dark, with high colouring, with very handsome and agreeable features. . . . But after a virulent attack of smallpox he became almost unrecognizable: his features all crumpled, his nose swollen to the point of actual deformity, his eyes sunken and red-rimmed, so much so that, having been so handsome, he became one the ugliest of men; nor was he any longer as intelligent as he had been.' His nose was so deformed that it appeared to be split in two, on which subject, at the time of his Flanders invasion, some cruel doggerel was written: 'Flemings, do not be sur-

prised to find that François has two noses, for according to
reason and custom a two-faced person needs two noses.'

It is scarcely surprising that this physical affliction had a de-
plorable effect on Anjou's character; he became a cowardly,
cringing, whining double-dealer, deceitful, untrustworthy, and
incompetent, consistent only in his obstinacy and ambition to win
himself a throne. No prince in history, probably, had fewer
admirers, and none a more devoted and loyal sister. But might
not Marguerite's love for François have been inspired by pity and
maternal affection for this unfortunate little runt of a brother?
To suggest that it went beyond such pure emotions seems oddly
inconsistent with her character and passion for physical and
spiritual beauty.

During their enforced periods of residence in the Louvre,
François undoubtedly knew of Marguerite's liaison with Bussy.
Whether or not he was jealous of him, it was to his own interest
to encourage it, since Bussy's adoration of the glamorous Queen
of Navarre was an additional incentive for him to remain in
Monsieur's service.

From a merely speculative point of view, it might have been
that Marguerite would never have developed such extraordinary
devotion and loyalty to her younger brother had the elder
Henri not so bitterly frustrated her girlish affection for him. She
was just as good a hater as she was a lover; like all the Valois, she
was almost absurdly attached to her friends and implacable towards her enemies, such as de Guast, at whose death she rejoiced; of those enemies the King had become the chief. Very
shortly their antagonism was to be revived, when he showed his
usual instability in dealing with his sister and brother. At first all
went well, but not for long.

Marguerite was still determined not to return to Court, but to rejoin her husband. After François left La Fère, 'I, intending to
travel to Gascony and having prepared everything in order to do
so, went back to Paris. My brother met me at one day's journey
from there; the King, the Queen my mother, Queen Louise and the
whole Court did me the honour of meeting me at Saint-Denis,

where they received me with great splendour and banqueting, taking pleasure in hearing me tell them of the honours and magnificences of my journey and visit to Liège, and my adventures on returning home.

'Continuing these pleasant conversations, we arrived in Paris in the coach of the Queen my mother. After supper and the ball were over, as the King and the Queen my mother were together, I went to them and begged them not to be displeased if I asked their permission to join the King my husband. As peace was made, it could not longer seem harmful to them, but it would be extremely prejudicial and harmful to me if I delayed my departure any longer.

'They both appeared to think this a good plan, and the Queen my mother said that she would go with me, as it was necessary for her to do so on the King's behalf; she also asked him to provide the funds for my journey, which he willingly agreed to do.

'Not wishing to remain at Court on any account once my brother had left for Flanders, I begged the Queen my mother to remember that she had promised me that once the war was over she would have the lands which formed part of my dowry assigned to me. She remembered this. The King also thought it very reasonable and promised me that it would be done. I begged them to arrange it all as speedily as possible, because if it pleased them I wished to leave at the beginning of the next month. This was immediately agreed to, but in the manner of the Court'—she wrote with bitter irony—'for although I asked them every day to expedite matters, they kept me waiting another five or six months. They did the same to my brother, who was also urging that he might leave for Flanders. . . .'

There ensued perhaps the worst period that Marguerite and François spent during their years of semi-imprisonment in the Louvre. For it was then that Henri III's *mignons*, his bedmates and play-fellows, began to assume such power over him that, with his tacit approval, their licence knew no restraint. The King's favourites at that time were, like himself, often dressed up, made up, and perfumed like women. Some were genuinely homosexual, some perhaps only pretended to be so to win his patronage. Yet in spite of their outward effeminacy they were all of them proficient swordsmen, extremely quarrelsome and violent.

The *mignons'* arch-enemy was Bussy d'Amboise, as brave, reckless, and impudent as ever. On Twelfth Night, 1578, when the King and his suite, arrayed in dazzling costumes, their hair curled, scented and falling over their open lace collars on to the *décolleté* revealing their necks and bosoms, went in procession from the Louvre to hear Mass in the Bourbon Chapel, Bussy, in attendance on Monsieur, arrived 'dressed in the simplest and most modest manner, but followed by six pages in cloth-of gold', loudly remarking that 'it was the season when the least important were most nobly arrayed'.

Although the King himself disapproved of it and quite ineffectively forbade it, there was constant duelling and fighting between his *mignons* and Monsieur's followers. Several on both sides were killed and on more than one occasion even Bussy only narrowly escaped being murdered by his enemies.

'My brother, considering that these episodes were not furthering his expedition to Flanders, wishing to appease the King rather than to irritate him, and thinking that Bussy might be employed in drilling the troops for his army, sent him to his estates for this purpose. But Bussy having gone, this did not end the persecution of my brother ... and after he left, they [the *mignons*] tormented and harassed my brother with such open contempt that everyone was aware of it. . . .'

At this time Lord Saint-Luc, one of the King's chief favourites, was married in great pomp and circumstance to Jeanne of Cossé. According to L'Estoile, the poor little bride was 'humpbacked, ugly, and deformed'.

Monsieur firmly refused to attend the wedding, nor, accordingly, did Marguerite. The Queen Mother, fearing that Monsieur's refusal would lead to some further harm being done to him, persuaded the King to allow her take them both to dinner during the marriage ceremony to one of her country seats, St Maur. Although Marguerite did not mention it until later, on the way home from there Bussy secretly rejoined his master:

'We returned that evening. All day my mother had been preaching so hard to my brother that she finally made him promise to attend the ball that night in order to please the King. But instead of this mending matters, it only made things worse, for Maugiron and others of his clique being there, they began to taunt him so rudely that anyone of much lower rank would have been offended, saying that "he had wasted his time in dressing-up again; that he had not been present at dinner, but had waited until dark, because the dark suited him much better", and attacking him on account of his ugliness and small stature. All this was said in the presence of the bride, loudly enough to be overheard by her. My brother, clearly realizing that it was being done on purpose to provoke him and to set the King against him, left, so enraged and infuriated that he could no longer bear it.

'After conferring with M. de la Châtre, he decided to leave for a few days' hunting, thinking by his absence to cool down those young men's animosity and to deal more easily with the King over the army he needed to go to Flanders.

'He went to see the Queen my mother, who was undressing, and told her what had happened at the ball, which annoyed her intensely. She thought his decision excellent and said that she would obtain the King's agreement to it. . . .'

Catherine then sent one of her courtiers to advise the King of Monsieur's plan.

'My brother retired to his room, assuming that his leave was granted, and telling all his attendants to be ready next morning to go hunting at St Germain. . . .'

M. de Villequier, Catherine's messenger, obtained the King's leave for Monsieur to leave Court during the next few days. But as soon as he left, the five or six young *mignons* with the King immediately renewed their mischief-making, 'and put him in such a state of apprehension that they made him commit one of the greatest follies of our day, which was to imprison my brother and all his principal servants'.

It was never very difficult to set one Valois brother against another. Whilst Henri did not suffer from Charles IX's attacks of maniacal rage, he was in his way just as unstable and had the same hatred for his younger brother and heir as Charles had had for him. There was not the slightest indication that on this occasion Monsieur was plotting against him; quite the reverse, since he had set his heart on the Flanders expedition, which he could not possibly undertake without the King's consent and aid.

'Suddenly the King, snatching up his dressing-gown, went off to the Queen my mother, as much excited as if there had been a public alarm and the enemy were at the gates.

' "Madam!" he exclaimed to her, "how could you possibly have asked me to let my brother go? If he does so, don't you see the danger in which this will place my realm? Undoubtedly there is some sinister plot behind this alleged hunting-party. I am going to arrest him and all his followers, and I shall have his coffers searched; I'm sure we shall discover a lot of things there!"

'With him were the Captain of the Guard, M. de Losse, and some of the Scottish archers. When the Queen my mother noticed them, she feared that he was plotting some attempt against my brother's life, and, all undressed as she was, putting on only her night-cloak, she followed him upstairs to my brother's room. Here the King knocked roughly on the door, calling out that it was himself, and to open up.

'My brother awoke with a start, and, knowing that he had done nothing wrong, told Cangé, his valet, to let him in. The King, entering in a fury, began to shout at him that "he would never cease to plot against his realm, and that he would teach him what it meant to attack his king". Whereupon he ordered the archers to take away the coffers and to drag his valets out of the room. He himself then began to search his brother's bed, where he thought he might find some hidden papers.

'My brother had in his hand a letter from Mme de Sauves, which he had received from her that evening. He tried to hide it, whilst the King was struggling to take it from him. The more he begged and implored him with clasped hands not to read it, the more the King insisted on doing so, thinking that it would incriminate him.

'Finally, when he did read it, in my mother's presence, they were both as embarrassed as Cato, when in the Senate, having forced Caesar to reveal a paper he had received, on the grounds that it referred to the welfare of the Republic, he found it to be a love-letter from his own sister.

'Instead of allaying the King's anger, the shame of this discovery heightened it. He refused to listen to my brother, who kept on asking him of what he was being accused, and why he was being treated like this, and finally gave him into the custody of M. de Losse and the Scots, ordering them not to allow him to speak to anyone. This was about an hour after midnight.

'My brother was more worried about me than himself, thinking that the same had been done to me, and that so violent and unjust a beginning could not have any but a sinister ending. Seeing that M. de Losse had tears in his eyes—but unable to speak to him openly on account of the archers who were there—he only asked him what had happened to me? M. de Losse told him that so far I had been asked nothing. My brother then said: "It's a great comfort to me to know that my sister is free, but I know that she loves me so much that she would rather share my captivity than live at liberty without me", and he requested him to go and beg the Queen my mother to allow me to join him, which she did.'

Marguerite was deeply moved by François' faith in her love and loyalty, to which she immediately responded. At daybreak the Prince asked M. de Losse to send one of his Scottish archers to bring her to his room.

'This archer, entering mine, found me still asleep, without knowing anything that had happened. He drew my curtain and in his own manner of speech said: "Good morning, Madam. Your brother is asking for you."

'Still half asleep, I looked at the man, thinking I was dreaming. Then, recognizing him, I asked him if he were not one of the Scots Guard? When he confirmed this, I said: "What has happened? Has my brother no other messenger to send to me?"

'He said no, that all his servants had been withdrawn from him, but that my brother had been allowed to have me share his imprisonment. And, seeing that I was extremely upset, he came close to me, whispering: ''Don't be angry. I can save your brother and will do so, but I shall have to leave with him." I told him we would reward him well, and, hurriedly dressing, I went all alone with him to my brother's room.

'I was obliged to cross the whole court, full of people who normally ran to see and honour me, but as fortune had now turned against me they all pretended not to recognize me.

'When I entered my brother's room I found him as imperturbable and calm as usual: "Cease weeping, my Queen, I beg you! Your unhappiness is the only thing that could upset me in my present condition, for my innocence and honest intentions give me no reason to fear the accusations of my enemies."'

And, according to his devoted reporter, presenting him as usual as part saint and part hero, François then made an unctuous declaration to her of his good intentions and resolution in the face of death, which only caused her to weep the more as she assured him that 'if he were taken away and I were separated from him I would kill myself in his presence'.

Whilst they were consoling one another with these lofty sentiments an incident occurred of which they only learned later.

It was then morning, and the palace gates were opened.

'An indiscreet young man, who was in Bussy's service, was recognized by the guard and arrested; they asked him where he was going? Surprised, he replied that he was going to join his master. When this was reported to the King, he suspected immediately that he [Bussy] was in the Louvre, where my brother had brought him back amongst the troop accompanying him the previous evening.'

Orders were given to the Captain of the Guard, M. de l'Archant, to arrest Bussy and another of Monsieur's adherents, Simié, if he could find them. It happened that this elderly officer was a very dear and intimate friend of Bussy's, so much so that he called him 'his son'. He found M. Simié in his room, and promptly arrested him, but made only a perfunctory search for Bussy, relieved not to find him. But Bussy was hidden in the bed and 'had no intention of being left behind, to be discovered perhaps by his enemies.

'As he was of a gay and humorous disposition, and however great his danger, fear was unknown to him', wrote Marguerite, slightly contradicting her previous sentence—'as l'Archant was about to leave with Simié, he put his head through the bed-curtains, calling out to him, "Hi, Papa! You're not leaving without me, surely?" to which M. de l'Archant sorrowfully replied, "My son, would to God I had lost an arm rather than find you here!" But Bussy retorted happily, "Papa, it's an omen that my luck is in!" and he laughingly made fun of poor Simié, who was quaking with terror.'

M. de l'Archant then regretfully put them under arrest whilst he took M. de la Châtre, another of Monsieur's intimates, to the Bastille.

The Queen Mother, however, was thoroughly alarmed by Henri's sudden and unprovoked attack on François, and this time really feared for her youngest son's life. Monsieur was, after all, heir to the throne, and could not be allowed to die as the result of a spiteful Court intrigue by the *mignons*. In order to stress the political gravity of the occasion, Catherine therefore hastily summoned all the leading statesmen and councillors to her chamber and herself led them in deputation to the King.

By morning Henri's sudden nocturnal fury had apparently spent itself. None of his favourites were with him and, after quietly listening to these old advisers, he gave in completely, as usual requesting his mother to patch up matters with his brother on his behalf. He also agreed to release Bussy and Monsieur's other followers, on condition that they showed no resentment towards his *mignons* and that Bussy should publicly make his peace with Quélus, the arch-favourite of the moment, whom he had previously openly referred to with maximum contempt as the 'royal bed-*mignon*'.

All Monsieur's guards were then immediately withdrawn and the Queen Mother came up to his room, where at first she did not find it easy to appease François, and especially his guardian angel, Marguerite, for the King's outrageous treatment of him. But with her usual tact and patience she at last succeeded in outwardly doing so. She then persuaded the King to receive his brother with full honours for their official reconciliation.

'For this purpose he came to the Queen my mother's chamber,

with all the princes, lords, and other members of his Council, and then sent M. de Villequier for us—my brother and myself. As we were on our way to His Majesty we found all the halls and rooms through which we had to pass filled with people who looked at us with tears in their eyes, thanking God to see us out of danger.'

After her two sons had made appropriate speeches of regret on the one hand and loyalty on the other, the old Queen took them both by the hand and made them embrace one another.

'Suddenly the King ordered that Bussy be sent for to be reconciled with Quélus.'

Bussy entered the royal presence with his usual arrogance and panache—'the delightful manner that was natural to him'— and when the King ordered him to embrace Quélus as a sign of their reconciliation, Bussy replied, 'No more than that, Sire? If you would like me to kiss him I am perfectly willing to do so,' and promptly accompanying the words with the deed, Bussy put his arms round the prinked and perfumed young *mignon*, kissing him loudly and several times '*à la Pantalonne*', so that even the King and everyone else there could not help laughing. Marguerite's admiration for this incorrigibly gay and audacious lover was hardly surprising. But matters could obviously not remain for long on this uneasy footing, this royal reconciliation *à la commedia dell'arte*.

'That having been done, the King and the Queen my mother, coming over to me, told me that I was to make sure that my brother would retain no rancour that might impair the obedience and affection he owed the King. I replied that my brother was so prudent and devoted to his service that he did not need to be reminded of it by myself or anyone else, but that he never had received, nor would receive, any advice from me that would not conform to their will and his duty.

'As it was then three o'clock in the afternoon and no one had yet dined, the Queen my mother wished us all to have dinner together, and ordered my brother and myself to go and change our clothes, which were suitable to the sad state from which we had just emerged, and to dress ourselves more appropriately to appear at the King's supper and ball. As far as our clothes went, which were easily taken off and put on, we obeyed her. But when it came to the expression on our faces, it was a different matter, for the face is the mirror of the soul, and our justified resentment was as obvious on ours as if it had been engraved there, with all the passionate and rightful disgust we felt for the successive acts of this tragicomedy.'

Among the courtiers present was the Chevalier de Seurre, a diplomat whom the Queen Mother had assigned during this crisis to sleep in Monsieur's room, 'and liked occasionally to gossip with, because he was of a dryly philosophical and cynical turn of mind. Finding him near her [during this ball] she asked him, "Well, M. de Seurre, what do you think of all this?" "It's too little," he answered her, "to have been done to good effect, and too much if it were merely meant as a joke," and turning to me so that she was unable to overhear him, he said to me: "I do not believe that this is the last act of this play; I would be very much mistaken in our man"—meaning my brother—"if he left it at that." '

And the harm, as Marguerite correctly pointed out, was only superficially repaired, since her own and her brother's resentment was as bitter as ever, and the King, forgetting the former bad advice of his *mignons* and the grave mistake into which it had led him, listened to them again as they still relentlessly pursued their vendetta against the Duke of Anjou. Almost immediately he gave strict orders that all Monsieur's attendants should leave the Louvre every night, with the sole exception of those valets who according to custom actually slept in his bedroom and dressing-room.

After three days of this treatment, Monsieur could no longer put up with it, and decided for better or worse to leave Court and to continue his preparations for his Flanders expedition on his own estates. When he informed Marguerite of this decision she, of course, wholeheartedly approved of it. But how was he to escape?

'He could not go out through the gates of the Louvre, which were so closely guarded that the faces of everyone passing through them were carefully scrutinized. There was no other way except through the window of my room, which was on the second floor, overlooking the dry moat. He therefore asked me to provide him with a strong rope of the necessary length, which I did on that same day, by arranging that a groom who was devoted to me should take out one of my trunks, on the pretext of having it repaired; a few hours later he brought it back, containing the rope we needed.'

Bussy, meanwhile, was making the necessary arrangements for his master's escape from Paris, once he had succeeded in leaving the Louvre.

Marguerite described the scheme as if it had been entirely her brother's invention. Yet it seems more probable that it was her own quickwittedness and natural talent for intrigue that were responsible for it.

The King was fasting on that evening, so Marguerite went to dine alone with the Queen Mother. When they rose from table, her brother came up to her, whispering that he would be waiting for her in her room, and begging her to come up there as soon as possible. Unfortunately, M. de Matignon, one of Monsieur's enemies, noticed their hurried conversation and informed Catherine of it, saying that '"no doubt my brother was intending to leave; that he would no longer be there next day, and that she had best take steps to prevent it".

'I saw that this news had upset her, which increased my fears that our plan might be discovered. When we entered her cabinet, she took me aside and asked me, "Did you hear what Matignon said to me?" To which I replied, "I did not hear it, Madam, but I saw that it was causing you anxiety." "Yes," she said, "very much so, for you know that I am responsible to the King for seeing that your brother does not leave, and Matignon told me that he will not be here tomorrow."'

Marguerite then described very disingenuously how she lied to her mother in order not to break her promise to her brother; even using God's name to justify her deceit: 'His divine goodness being operative in saving my brother, I arranged my features and my words in such a way that she had no inkling of my intentions, and I offended neither my soul nor my conscience by a false oath.'

This peculiar sophistry was apparently quite satisfactory to her religious principles; so long as she did not *swear* to the lie she was telling her mother she was committing no sin. And having decided on this policy Marguerite had no hesitation in making her lie sound thoroughly convincing:

'I thereupon asked her whether she did not know how much M. de Matignon hated my brother; he was a mischief-maker, who could not bear to see us all on good terms with one another; that if my brother left, I would answer for him with my life, and that I was convinced that if he intended doing so he would have told me of it.

'I said this, knowing that once my brother was safe I would not come to any harm, and if it came to the worst and we were discovered, I would rather have lost my life than offend my conscience by a false oath and put my brother's life in danger.'

Catherine, still suspicious, admonished her daughter to "think well about what you are saying, for you may have to answer for it with your life". Marguerite smilingly replied that that was her intention, then, wishing her mother good-night as soon as was possible, she went up to her room, where 'I quickly undressed and went to bed, in order to be rid of my ladies-in-waiting. When I was alone with my maids, my brother came in, with Simié and Cangé.

'I then got up, and we fixed the rope to the window, and having looked out to see that there was no one in the moat, helped only by my women and the groom who had brought me the rope, we first let down my brother, who was laughing and joking fearlessly, although it was from a very great height; then Simié, pale and trembling, so frightened that he could barely stand up; and finally Cangé, my brother's valet. With God's protection my brother safely reached [the monastery of] Sainte-Geneviève, where Bussy was awaiting him. With the Abbot's consent Bussy had made a breach in the adjacent city wall there, through which he slipped out, and finding horses ready for him he arrived at Angers with no further trouble.

'But as we had been letting down Cangé, who was last, a man

arose from the moat and began running towards the lodging near the tennis court, on the way to the guardroom.'

This threw Marguerite and her women into a panic. Fearing that Monsieur had been betrayed and arrested, she ordered them to throw the rope on the fire, so that if her room were searched it would not be found. It was a very thick and long rope, however, and as it was burning the chimney caught fire. The smoke and flames were seen from below by the archers on duty outside, who immediately rushed up to Marguerite's door and loudly banging on it demanded that it be opened. In spite of her terror she just managed to keep her head:

'Seeing that the rope was still only half-burnt, I told my women to go quietly to the door and ask what they wanted, speaking in a whisper, as if I were asleep. The archers replied that the chimney was alight and they had come to put out the fire. My women told them it was nothing, that they would deal with it themselves, and that on no account must I be awakened. So they left.

'That alarm being over, two hours later M. de Losse came to fetch me to the King and the Queen my mother, to explain my brother's evasion to them. They had been informed of his escape by the Abbot of Sainte-Geneviève, who, in order not to be involved, and with my brother's consent—as soon as he should be far enough away not to be recaptured—came to tell the King of it, saying that he had kept them locked up, but during that time they had breached the wall, and that was why he had been unable to inform the King of it sooner.

'He [M. de Losse] found me in bed, for it was night, and as I was putting on my night-cloak one of my women lost her head and grabbed hold of it, crying out loud that I should never come back! Pushing her away, M. de Losse whispered to me, "If that woman had behaved like this in front of someone who was not your devoted servant, as I am, it might have been very awkward for you, but do not fear, and praise God, for your brother is safe."

'Those words were a very necessary consolation to me and gave me the strength I needed to face the threats and intimidation I had to suffer from the King, who was sitting at the bedside of the Queen my mother, in such a fury that I think he would have vented it on me if his fear of my brother's successful escape and the Queen my mother's presence had not restrained him.

'Both of them reminded me that I had assured them that my brother would not leave, and that I had given them my word on it. I agreed. But I said that he had deceived me in the matter as much as he had them, and I assured them on my life that his departure would make no difference to his loyalty to the King; that he was only returning home in order to do what was necessary for his Flanders expedition. This satisfied the King to some extent, and he allowed me to return to my room.

'He soon had news from my brother, confirming what I had told him. As the result of it, his complaints against him ceased, but not his dislike of him. He appeared to be willing to help him, but in fact underhandedly impeded his preparations for Flanders.'

10 Marriage of Inconvenience

The King's reluctance in supporting Monsieur's Flanders expedition was not altogether due to perfidy. He was harassed by the Spanish Ambassador, who was constantly conveying his monarch's threats of war with France should his Christian brother dispute his hegemony over the Netherlands. The Lorraines were also intriguing as deeply as ever with Philip II, and as the Duke of Guise's League became more and more popular and powerful, they presented another danger of which the Queen Mother and the King were acutely aware.

Henri would have given much to rid himself of his brother, as Charles IX had done in his own case, but no convenient Polish crown was at hand. Catherine again tried to divert her youngest son's ambitions by proposing various marriages to him, and he was still hoping for the Virgin Queen's hand. As one commentator nicely put it, he was determined either to marry the Netherlands or the Queen of England. In neither case was he to succeed, for as soon as François lost the benefit of his devoted sister's guidance and the courage and energy with which she set about promoting his aims, he shrank back into his usual incompetence and insignificance. The Flanders expedition was to end in ignominious failure.

Immediately after his escape, his mother set out for Angers in the hope of bringing him back to Paris. François, still smarting under his recent mean treatment at Court, this time sulked to some effect. He pretended to have sprained a muscle in his leg, and sent Bussy and La Châtre to receive the Queen Mother in his place. When she arrived at the castle she was obliged, to her natural and considerable displeasure, to enter by the postern gate, and her son was carried downstairs in a chair to meet her. As she completely failed to move him, Catherine was compelled to turn once again to Marguerite to do so. The Queen Mother lacked her usual astuteness this time, since Marguerite was every bit as wholeheartedly committed to the Flanders project as her brother. When they visited him at Alençon, it was, according to her, merely to wish him goodbye before he set out for Flanders, and she to rejoin her husband.

Catherine had at last kept her promise to Margot and persuaded the King to allow the Queen of Navarre to travel to her husband's Court. She herself would conduct her daughter there, for she had serious business of her own in the south.

In finally, however reluctantly, allowing his brother's departure for Flanders, the King was as usual closely advised by his mother. The southern half of the realm was by no means completely pacified by the Treaty of Bergerac. According to its provisions, certain lands, cities and strongholds had been assigned to either side. But the local Catholics and Huguenots, whether great lords or mere town councillors and mayors, were still forever feuding and making raids on one another's preserves; one night the Catholics, the next the Huguenots would be carrying out some minor foray or other.

To Catherine and Henri III the risks of a war with Spain over Flanders seemed the lesser evil when balanced against the horrors of yet another civil war. But it needed the supreme authority of the dynasty, and Catherine's personal exercise of it on behalf of the monarch, so she thought, to implement the King's peace.

Nor was Henry of Navarre's situation at all a stable one. To his Puritan subjects his reconversion to The Religion did not cancel out his previous lapse from it sufficiently to allay their doubts of him completely, and they frowned on his marriage to Marguerite of Valois, followed by the horrors of St. Bartholomew's Night. His chief personal grievance was that, although he himself was titular Governor of Guyenne, the King's Marshal, Biron, was the military commander. A fervent Catholic, he was constantly impinging on the authority of the Huguenot King of Navarre, and their mutual enmity and dislike of one another seemed unshakeable.

As Henri III was obviously going to leave no heir behind him, and François, already showing symptoms of the tuberculosis that had killed his brother, Charles IX, was equally unlikely to do so, the Queen Mother was acutely aware—as was Navarre himself—that he, Henry of Bourbon, was the next legitimate heir to the throne of France. They had a certain amount in common, for they were both realists and intellectually enlightened in the best Renaissance tradition. Catherine, whilst paying lip-service to Catholicism, was almost an agnostic. Navarre, a born Catholic, was brought up as a Huguenot by his fanatically Calvinist mother, Jeanne of Albret. Under duress in the Louvre after St Bartholomew, he had become a Catholic, almost at the point of the King's sword, and after his escape reverted to Protestantism in order to regain his kingdom. At his Court, however, he employed aristocratic adherents of both faiths, and in 1577 he had written that 'those who honestly follow their consciences belong to my religion, and I belong to the faith of all who are brave and good'. If he nevertheless blew now hot, now cold, and in due course changed back to Catholicism allegedly because 'Paris was well worth a Mass', this was again dictated by the unavoidable expediency of statesmanship. Unlike the Valois, Henry of Bourbon had his feet firmly planted on the ground, and his head was never in the clouds.

Even at this time Catherine did not despair of winning him back to France's traditional religion. Although it was yet too early, she knew that the French people as a whole would never accept as their king an apostate from the faith of St Louis. Her proposed tool for carrying this plan to success was her daughter, the Queen of Navarre.

As she had been from childhood, Marguerite was fervently and sincerely Catholic. She was also ambitious and, being unable to follow her mother's example and rule France in all but name, she devoted herself to the cause of her brother and dreamed of doing the same for her husband, by whose side she might yet one day become Queen of France. Now that Monsieur had left the Court, it was genuinely abhorrent to her and she was more than ever determined to rejoin Navarre.

At last her wish was to be granted, since the moment had come when her own desires fitted in with the policy that the Queen Mother had persuaded Henri III to adopt. In his usual impulsive way, once he was committed to it, the King went about the matter wholeheartedly, even more generously than he had fitted out his sister for her visit to Liège. Catherine had a hand in this also, for she was determined that the royal progress of the two Queens should be of such splendour as to dazzle the aristocracy, the masses who should witness it, and the King of Navarre himself.

Marguerite was as suspicious as ever regarding her detested brother's motives in suddenly showing her so much kindness and generosity. He did so, she wrote, because, as he could no longer prevent her from joining her husband, he was anxious that she should not leave him on bad terms and also, 'longing to undermine my affection for my brother . . . he assigned to me the lands forming part of my dowry, as well as certain other benefices. And in addition to the allowances he made me, such as the Daughters of France are entitled to, he even gave me money from his privy purse, taking the trouble to visit me every morning, telling me "how useful his friendship might be to me, that my brother's would lead me to ruin, but that his would make me happy, and a thousand other reasons of the sort".' As usual, Henri's attempts to win her away from François met with her unshakeable resistance. She merely assured him that 'he might be sure that when I rejoined my husband I would not in any way fail to obey his commands, and would work at nothing else but to maintain the King my husband in his fealty'.

Henri III personally saw the two Queens off from his estate at Ollainville on 8 August 1578.

With her love of pomp and splendour, Marguerite would no doubt have rejoiced in describing to her friend Brantôme the magnificent state in which she travelled south. But in fact he went with the Queens on this journey and, an eye-witness of his adored royal lady's triumphs, himself chronicled them.

Marguerite's establishment comprised several hundred persons. According to her household accounts for that year, they included her 'ladies-in-waiting, maids-of-honour, chambermaids, washerwomen; *maître d'hôtel*, bakers, wine-waiters, grooms and stablemen; her almoners, confessor, chaplains, clerks of the chapel; doctors, apothecaries, surgeons, and grooms-of-the chamber, amongst whom were several violinists and other musicians; the masters and valets of the wardrobe, various footmen and porters, upholsterers and their mates, and the grooms in attendance on the maids-of-honour. The list then mentions her Chancellor—Pibrac, who was to play an important part in her life at that stage—her Treasurer, members of her Council, several secretaries, controllers, and quartermasters, and a list of another forty or so individuals, including all those involved in transport, such as littermen, coachmen, a saddler and spurrier, and even a barber for dressing the pages' hair.

The Queen Mother was accompanied by the Cardinal of Bourbon, Navarre's cousin, her old friend and confidant, the Duchess of Uzès, and an even larger suite than her daughter's, so that they could not have been followed by less than 500 and possibly more persons.

As this cavalcade slowly progressed through some of the most famous cities of France, including Orleans and Tours, remaining for several days at a time at one or another of Catherine's superlative castles, such as Chenonceaux, wherever it arrived they were welcomed—the Queen of Navarre in particular—by sumptuous receptions and a thrilled populace.

One cannot dismiss Brantôme's superlatives as merely the fulsome adulation of a courtier, for they were so obviously sincere. When the Queen of Navarre arrived at Cognac on 28 August, 'she was received by many grand, lovely, and distinguished ladies of the district . . . who were all enchanted by the beauty of

Queen Marguerite, and could not praise her enough to the Queen her mother, who was delighted. For this reason, one day she asked her daughter to wear her most magnificent dresses, such as she wore at Court, to please these ladies. . . . She appeared in a superb robe of silver brocade . . . with such majesty and grace that one would have thought that she was a goddess from Heaven rather than a queen on earth. . . .

'The Queen Mother then said to her, "My daughter, you look splendid," to which she replied, "Madam, I am already wearing the dresses and ornaments I brought with me from Court, for when I return there I shall not take them back with me, but I shall simply arrive with scissors and materials which I shall have made up in the current fashion." The Queen Mother answered her, "Why do you say that, my daughter? For it is you who invent and set the fashions, and wherever you are, the Court will copy them from you, not you from the Court."'

At Bordeaux Marguerite had another of her dual successes. Dressed in brilliant orange-gold—according to Brantôme, her favourite colour—she entered the city on a white palfrey, and was welcomed there officially by the King's representative, Marshal Biron, with the head of the clergy and the President of the Law Court.

'To all of them she replied', wrote Brantôme, 'one after the other (which I myself heard, since by her orders I was close to her on the platform) so eloquently, wisely, and spontaneously, with such grace and majesty . . . that the same evening the said President came up to me in the Queen Mother's chamber, telling me that he had never heard better speeches in his life, although he had often had the honour of hearing her predecessors, the Queens Marguerite and Jeanne of Albret, but that in eloquence they were no match at all for this Queen Marguerite, who was truly her mother's daughter', to which Catherine, when Brantôme reported it to her, answered that 'even though she was her own daughter, she could honestly say that she was the most accomplished princess in the world'.

She was then twenty-five, at the height of her beauty. Her flawlessly white skin, perfect neck and bosom—which the *décolletée* gowns she designed for herself showed off deliberately, were especially admired. Yet had Marguerite been as ugly and deformed as Jeanne of Cossé, she could hardly have taken greater pains to prepare herself for her reunion with her husband. According to a letter from the Duchess of Uzès to the King, she spent hours hidden away in her room, soaking in perfumed baths, being massaged by her tiring-women, who also plucked her eyebrows to the fashionable shape. Her hair was dark and luxurious, and she wore it off her forehead, again setting a fashion, when she was not for a change wearing one of her dozens of little blonde wigs with tight curls.

No doubt after a separation of two and a half years she was anxious to arouse his admiration, yet her motive was not merely to reconquer Navarre sexually. He was notoriously one of the most lascivious men of his time, and Marguerite, who never loved him physically, neither hoped nor expected him to be faithful to her. She did, however, want to make herself indispensable to him—to his career if not to his heart—for it was indispensable to herself to win this success over him.

For in spite of her outward triumphs Marguerite's position was an unstable one. The thought of returning to Court was a nightmare to her, yet if her husband would not receive her as his Queen, she would have no other choice. And her welcome was still by no means certain.

Catherine had taken a deliberate risk when she set out with her daughter, calculating that Navarre would not dare offer such a public affront to the King of France as to repudiate his sister. But, following her compatriot Machiavelli's precept that the end justified the means—her laudable end being the prevention of renewed civil war—she unhesitatingly prepared to play on her son-in-law's known weakness by including in her train the most seductive young women of her Flying Squadron—amongst them Charlotte de Sauves, with whom the young Navarre had been so madly in love, as well as a great Spanish beauty, Victoria de Ayala, known as Dayelle.

The first difficulty on both sides was to find an appropriate meeting-place, for the fanatically Catholic cities, such as

Bordeaux and Toulouse, were barred to the apostate Henry of
Bourbon. Their bitterness towards him, however, was more than
equalled by the repulsion felt by the narrow-minded Puritans of
his own small kingdom towards his wife, this Papist temptress of
known loose morals, in whom they saw a reincarnation, not of a
goddess, but of the Whore of Babylon.

In spite of their resistance, Navarre fully realized his responsibilities and future opportunities as the potential King of
France, showing great tact and willingness to deal with his
mother-in-law. In Guyenne Marguerite wrote, under his government, 'I was received officially everywhere'. And their first meeting went off very well.

'He came to meet the Queen my mother as far as La Réolle, a
town held by those of The Religion, the antagonism which still
existed (peace not yet having been properly established) not per-
mitting him to come any further.'

Catherine was keeping Henri III informed of her progress in
a series of detailed personal letters. In one of these she told him
how she and Marguerite met the King of Navarre on 2 October
at a manor house called Casteras, between Saint-Macaire and
La Réolle, and that he welcomed them 'with very good grace
and what appeared to be great affection . . .' bringing with him in
their honour 600 of his gentlemen, including several Catholics
who were his friends. But his most intimate companion was the
young Viscount of Turenne, who, although a convert to The
Religion, had spent considerable time at Court.

The King of Navarre respectfully greeted his mother-in-law,
affectionately embraced his wife twice, and then took his seat in
the Queen Mother's coach, opposite to them, to accompany them
to La Réolle.

Very soon, however, it came to the first clash between the
domineering old Queen and her determined son-in-law.
Catherine was most anxious to reconcile Navarre with Biron, the
King's general in Guyenne, but Navarre lost his temper and she
could not influence him at all. Marguerite immediately showed
her value to her mother's policies by tactfully inducing her husband, all the same, to meet Biron on 8 October, but with little

success, for when they were face to face they simply glared at one another and might even have done worse had Marguerite not again persuasively intervened.

Shortly afterwards the couple, so recently reunited, parted again. Marguerite was due to make another of her triumphal entries, into the town of Agen, which was part of her endowment, but Navarre was unacceptable there as well. However, he met the Queens again in the middle of October and also at the beginning of November, which they spent at Toulouse, an ardently Catholic and anti-Huguenot city.

Catherine was now getting down to the political business for which she had made this tiring trip: the arranging of a conference between southern Catholic and Protestant representatives and delegates, to implement the Treaty of Bergerac. There was more difficulty in finding a meeting-place for these crucial discussions. Finally it was agreed that it should be the King of Navarre's capital, Nérac, although reluctantly on the Catholic side, since this town was also a Huguenot stronghold.

Yet in spite of all the tricky problems raised by the religious wrangling, Marguerite and her husband appeared to be on excellent terms, although no more in love with one another than before. Navarre and his 600 gentlemen had cast appraising and highly approving eyes on the beauties of the Flying Squadron and were in no hurry to lose such delightful feminine company:

'The Queen my mother had intended to remain only a short time, but there were so many incidents, some provoked by the Huguenots, others by the Catholics, that she was obliged to remain for eighteen months. As this annoyed her, she sometimes said that her departure was being deliberately delayed in order that her ladies-in-waiting might remain. The King my husband had fallen deeply in love with Dayelle'—no longer interested, in his fickle manner, in Charlotte de Sauves—'and M. de Turenne with La Vergne', a situation that Catherine, having deliberately planned it, should not have complained of.

But Navarre's passion for the Spanish beauty did not diminish his renewed affection for his wife:

'In spite of it, he treated me with great honour and friendship, as much as I could have wished. From our very first meeting he told me of all the tricks that had been played on him at Court in order that we should be on bad terms. He realized that this had been done solely in order to disrupt the friendship between my brother and himself, and to ruin all three of us, and he showed great pleasure that we were together again.'

The Queen Mother was chiefly delayed owing to the intransigence of the stiff-necked pastors, who would only implement the Nérac Convention after weeks of haggling, during which they wrung further concessions from the King. The Conference, which had opened on 4 February 1579, lasted nearly the entire month. Finally, the Convention was signed on the 28th, and ratified by Henri III on 14 March.

When the time came for Catherine's return to Paris, the King and Queen of Navarre, to her contentment on such excellent terms, conducted her and, no doubt to the King's great regret, the lovely Dayelle in her service as far as Castelnaudary. They themselves did not travel from there to Nérac but to Pau, which Marguerite contemptuously referred to as 'that little Geneva' and where her first bitter personal encounter with the fanatical Calvinists took place. She was by then very conscious of her exalted position as Queen Consort and, with her Valois pride and courage, loyally supported her own co-religionists against the ceaseless persecution they were forced to endure:

'As the Catholic religion was proscribed there, I was only allowed to hear Mass in a little chapel barely three or four feet long and very narrow, so that when seven or eight of us were inside it was quite full. When it was time for Mass to be said, the drawbridge of the castle was pulled up, for fear that the local Catholics, who were unable to practise their religion, might hear it, for they were infinitely anxious to take part in Holy Communion, of which they had been deprived for several years past. Urged by this sacred and righteous longing, some of the inhabitants of Pau found a means of entering the castle before the bridge was withdrawn, and managed to slip into the chapel, where they were not discovered until nearly the end of Mass, when the door was half-opened for one of my people. A Huguenot spy, discover-

ing them there, went and told Pin, my husband's secretary, who
had great authority in his household, and was in charge of all
religious affairs. He sent some of my husband's guards down,
who in my presence dragged them out of there, beating them up,
and threw them into jail, where they remained a long time, paying heavy fines.'

The Queen, of course, immediately went off in a fine fury to
complain of this high-handed and brutal action to her husband.
But she found Pin with him, and 'without allowing his master
to answer me, he told me that I would not budge my husband in
this matter, and that whatever I said, so it would remain; they
had well deserved what they had got, and I should be well satisfied that I was allowed to have Mass said for myself, and those of
my own people whom I took there.

'I was deeply offended by such a statement from a man of his
quality, and I begged my husband that if I was fortunate enough
to find favour in his eyes he would make it clear that he resented
the indignity I had suffered from that little man'—which was indeed an outrageous impudence from a mere secretary towards the
King's wife and the King of France's sister.

This molehill of an incident, typical in the mutual hatred it expressed, threatened to become a mountain of contention between
the King and Queen of Navarre. He would gladly have given way
to her, but to release the Catholic prisoners directly was too risky
even for him to authorize. Henry tried to pacify Marguerite by
promising that he would consult the Councillors of the Pau Parliament as to what could be done for them. But Marguerite still
insisted that he should dismiss the insolent secretary, who was unpopular even with his co-religionists for his high-handed manner.
Some of his advisers pointed out to Navarre that 'he should
not offend me for the sake of a man like that, who had so insulted me, and that if it came to the knowledge of the King and
the Queen my mother, they would think it very bad of him to
have retained him in his service'.

So Marguerite won her point: Pin was dismissed, but her husband, she said, sulked with her for some time afterwards.

'According to what he later told me, M. de Pibrac had been

playing a double game, advising me that I should not suffer being
defied by anyone so insignificant, and that whatever happened I
must have him dismissed; but saying to the King my husband
that I should not be allowed to deprive him of so valuable a
servant, which M. de Pibrac did in order to oblige me, owing to
my great displeasure, to return to France, where he himself wished
to resume his post as Counsellor to the King's Council!'

Marguerite never forgave Pibrac for this alleged double-dealing,
although he vehemently denied it. Their relationship was a peculiar one. Pibrac, who was then fifty-nine, was one of the most
respected public servants of his day. He had accompanied Henri
III to Poland and remained in service to the Valois ever since.
He was rich, respectable, and happily married, with three sons
and a daughter. But when he was appointed Chancellor of the
Queen of Navarre's household, this dignified and learned elder
statesman fell madly in love with his glamorous employer. Marguerite treated him very badly, taking umbrage at the fact that he
had apparently dared to raise his eyes to one so far above him in
station, but particularly accusing him of intriguing behind her
back to compel her to return to Paris and the Court, 'ruining'
her in the process. The Pau incident was the beginning of her
resentment against him; in 1581 she wrote him two particularly
cruel and angry letters which nearly broke the devoted old
courtier's heart; he died three years later. It was said that Marguerite had not hesitated to borrow so much money from him,
which was never returned, that she reduced him to penury.

Navarre soon consoled himself for the loss of Dayelle with one of Marguerite's maids-of-honour called Rebours. But 'Rebours was a malicious girl who disliked me, and did me all the disservices she possibly could'. When, to Marguerite's great relief, they left Pau, that hated 'little Geneva', Rebours fell ill and stayed behind. Brantôme told of a later occasion, when she was dying at Chenonceaux. Marguerite visited her on her deathbed. 'This poor girl is suffering a great deal,' she said, 'but she also did a great deal of harm. May God forgive her as I forgive her.'

Henry's amours were temporarily curtailed when 'at a little town called Eause, the night we arrived there my husband fell ill of a severe fever, with violent headaches, which lasted seventeen days, during which he had no rest night or day and had constantly to be moved from one bed to another.' During this illness Marguerite nursed him with unswerving devotion, 'without undressing, never leaving him for a moment', for which on his recovery he was genuinely grateful.

Very soon afterwards he found a successor to Rebours, Françoise de Montmorency, fifth daughter of the Baron of Fosseux, who was known at Court as Fosseuse, and who was barely in her

teens. Although Navarre himself was still only twenty-five, he behaved over this pretty little girl like a besotted elderly man. At
first he merely petted and played with her, taking her on his lap
and feeding her sweets and comfits. 'At that time she was a mere
child, and very good', but as she grew into adolescence and the
King in due course had her virginity, she was to become a real
problem to Marguerite.

They continued their journey to Nérac, about twenty miles
from Agen, the small capital of Navarre's small kingdom. There,
for the next four or five years, Marguerite enjoyed one of those
rare periods in her life when she knew real pleasure and freedom.
She was no longer at the beck and call of her awesome mother,
nor at the mercy of her detested brother Henri's changes of mood:

'Our Court was so delightful and agreeable that we did not
envy that of France. We had with us the Princess of Navarre, his
sister'—Catherine, who, when her mother had taken her to Paris
as a child, had so admired her lovely young future sister-in-law—
'and a number of my ladies and maids-in-waiting. The King my
husband had in his service a fine company of lords and gentlemen, as accomplished as any I had known at Court; there was
nothing to cavil at about them except that they were Huguenots.
But there were never any arguments about religion. On their side
the King and his sister went to hear their preachers, and I and my
suite to Mass in a chapel in the park; and when we came out
we all went for walks together, either in a very beautiful garden
with long avenues of laurels and cypresses, or in the park I had
made, of avenues 3,000 feet long by the river-bank.'

The castle was an ancient fortress which Marguerite embellished with luxurious furniture, pictures, tapestries and other
works of art with her usual Valois-Medici extravagance, disdain-
ful of expense, spending far more than she could afford, and
when short of money either raising it on her estates or, when
hard-pressed, borrowing it from her unfortunate Chancellor,
Pibrac.

'The rest of the day was spent in all manner of harmless
pleasures, the ball as a rule taking place after dinner and in the
evening.'

This Court of Nérac, Marguerite's own particular creation and delight, appears to have been a kind of Rabelaisian Abbey of Thelemis or a Cytherea, where life was one perpetual round of love-making and dancing. Marguerite deliberately defied the austerity to which Jeanne of Albret's Puritan rule had reduced the naturally joyous Gascons, including her husband. And there was something more than merely seductive in the highly civilized manner—centuries ahead of her time, as Marguerite was in so much else—in which Protestants and Catholics at Nérac, headed by their King and Queen, went about their respective religious duties in perfect accord and amity.

Inevitably the pastors were shocked and horrified. At the Synod of La Rochelle on 27 June 1581 they denounced 'make-up, split skirts, exposed bosoms and other diabolical inventions', sternly forbidding these sinful fashions set by the Queen of Navarre to the female faithful.

Agrippa d'Aubigné, a Huguenot courtier and literary man who hated Marguerite and whom she thoroughly disliked, wrote that 'the Queen of Navarre taught the King her husband that a cavalier had no soul if he were not in love, and her own practice of it was not in any way concealed, for she claimed that to make love openly was virtuous, but to do it in secret was vicious'.

All her detractors and even some of her admirers regarded her as a lascivious adulteress. From their point of view she un-doubtedly was so, but nothing could be more scantly true. In her theories on love and amorous friendship Marguerite was also a pioneer of that sex equality that women in her day might only practise secretly, but not publicly uphold.

Amongst her favourite bed-books at Nérac was Plato's *Banquet*, in a Christianized French adaptation from the Italian by Guy de la Boderie, which he dedicated to her in 1578. Marguerite worshipped physical beauty as much as any Platonist; she was also entranced by the ideal of Platonic love. Her creed was that the physical beauty of the body must be matched by and reflect the spiritual beauty of the mind; only in such a combina-tion could ideal perfection be attained. And nothing gave her greater intellectual pleasure than to discuss such theories with the poets and philosophers with whom she loved to surround herself.

For Nérac was not merely a rendezvous for the young and flighty. In the tradition of the Kings of France since the time of her glorious grandfather, François I, the Queen of Navarre entertained at Nérac a distinguished group of contemporaneous poets and scholars. The greatest of them all, Montaigne, who in his youth had been a gallant courtier and knew her well, described her as being 'like one of those divine, supernatural and extraordinary beauties that one sometimes sees shining like stars through the veils of an earthly body'. Unfortunately, she was temperamentally unable to follow the sage's advice in the Preface to the first edition of his *Essays*, which was dedicated to her, to practise moderation in all things and not to seek after novelty or strange experiences. For to a feminist innovator like Marguerite these were the spice of life.

So famous was the Court of Navarre, with its lovers, poets, and grave men of learning, that across the Channel an actor-manager, Will Shakespeare, was inspired by it to write what is thought to have been his first play, *Love's Labour's Lost*. The setting is the 'kingdom of Navarre' where the young King, Ferdinand, persuades three of his courtiers to renounce with him for three years all feminine society and to devote themselves to the study of philosophy. But at that moment the 'Princess of France' arrives with her beautiful female attendants on a mission from the King, her father. The result of this visitation is obvious; King and courtiers fall in love with beautiful Princess and maids-of-honour. The plot also includes a satirical portrait of a schoolmaster, a pedantic intellectual, and much bawdy humour.

The earliest known edition is that of 1598, 'corrected and augmented' from an earlier edition thought by some scholars to have been written eight or nine years previously. It was 'presented before her Highness the last Christmas'—that Princess being Queen Elizabeth I, for whom it was performed in 1597, later eliciting this enchanting comment from Dr Johnson:

'It must be confessed that there are many passages in this play mean, childish, and vulgar; and some which ought not to have been exhibited, as we are told they were, to a maiden queen.' But the maiden in question was then sixty-four years of age, and of a ruder period than the learned Doctor's.

The character of the Princess of France, whose beauty is equalled by her intelligence, wit, and courage, bears distinct resemblances to Margot's. Her reply to the flattery of her lord-in-waiting, Boyet, might have been made by Marguerite to Pibrac:

> My beauty, though but mean,
> Needs not the painted flourish of your praise:
> Beauty is bought by judgment of the eye,
> Not utter'd by base sale of chapmen's tongues.
> I am less proud to hear you tell my worth
> Than you much willing to be counted wise
> In spending your wit in the praise of mine.

Navarre, wrote Marguerite, 'continued to serve Fosseuse' who, 'at that time entirely dependent on me, behaved so honourably and virtuously that had she continued to do so she would not have fallen into the subsequent disgrace that brought so much unhappiness to her and to myself as well'.

At that time the Queen herself, with her husband's tacit consent, took a serving cavalier. In spite of her approval of his 600 gallant gentlemen, there was only one amongst them whom she considered worthy of her own favour. She was never in love with Turenne, but he was of high birth and breeding, brave, cultured, versed in the traditions of the Court of France, and more than willing—for a short time—to become her accredited lover. He was, however, a Huguenot, and when it came to a conflict between his love for his mistress and loyalty to his master's cause, he unhesitatingly chose to serve the latter. Their brief affair finally came to an end on 3 March 1580, when Turenne left Nérac to take over the Huguenot command in Languedoc, for all over the country the Huguenots were again marching to war.

No calumny on Marguerite is more untrue than that she was responsible for the 'Lovers' War', as Aubigné wittily and spitefully called it, which broke out in 1579. He alleged that her motives for egging on Navarre against Valois were jealousy of

her husband and hatred of her brother. The allusion was to the
fact that the lovers at the Court of Nérac deserted the lure of
Eros to follow the call of Mars. They unquestionably did so for
a short time, but their motives were political and religious.

When Catherine de Medici had persuaded the Huguenots to
sign the Peace of Nérac, the strongholds they demanded had
been ceded to them only temporarily, for a period of six months.
At the Assembly of Montauban, in June 1579, they decided to
hold on to them. On 29 November Condé, acting independently
of Navarre, captured La Fère, whereupon Henry of Bourbon
wrote apologetically to the King of France that he had been unable to prevent this incident. But at the same time he reiterated
his personal grievances against Biron.

Nothing could have been less to Marguerite's own interests
than this war. She was and wished to remain on good terms with
her husband, but also with her mother and the King her brother,
since financially she was dependent on them. She found herself
then between the devil and the deep blue sea:

'In spite of all my efforts, to my very great regret, I was unable to prevent the conflict from spreading . . . which was the one
thing I feared, since I had linked my fortunes to those of the King
my husband, and in consequence would find myself in a party
opposed to that of the King and my religion. I discussed it with
my husband and all the members of his Council, trying to prevent
it, pointing out to them what little profit this war would bring
them. . . . But . . . although the King my husband did me the
honour of placing a great deal of faith and confidence in me, and
the leaders of The Religion admitted that I had a certain amount
of commonsense, I still could not persuade them to what, in due
course, at their own expense they had to admit was the truth.
There was no preventing the torrent sweeping over them, when
experience taught them that I had been right in my predic-
tions. . . .

'But long before then, seeing how matters stood, I had several
times informed the King and the Queen my mother of the situation, asking them to improve it by giving some satisfaction to the
King my husband; but they had taken no notice, apparently con-

vinced by the late Marshal Biron that he would be able to bring the Huguenots to their knees. As my advice was ignored, matters went from bad to worse, until it came to fighting. But those of the so-called Religion were very much mistaken with regard to the strength of their forces, the King my husband's being much weaker than Marshal Biron's, and all their attacks failed except that of Cahors ... where they fought for two or three days in street after street and from house to house, and where the King my husband revealed his leadership and valour, not as a Prince of the Blood, but as an able and brave captain. ...'

War was declared by the Huguenots on 20 April 1580, and although Navarre wrote his wife most apologetically and affectionately on 10 April he could not keep out of it. For if there was one thing Henry of Bourbon enjoyed more than making love, it was making war.

'My dear', he wrote, 'as we are so closely united that our hearts and wills are but one ... I feel I owe it to you to ask you not to think it strange of me to have been compelled to come to a decision without having told you anything of it. But as you will inevitably learn of it, I may say, my dear, that it is with extreme regret that instead of the contentment I hoped to give you, as well as a certain amount of pleasure in this country, precisely the opposite is the case, and you have the displeasure of seeing me in such an unfortunate situation. God knows who is to blame. ...'

Navarre continued by setting out his complaints and his case, and ended: 'Do not grieve; it is enough that one of us should be unhappy. I kiss your hands a million times.'

There is something more than slightly disingenuous about this letter, which Henry might even have written at his wife's suggestion, to protect her against her brother the King of France's wrath when he learned of the capture of Cahors by Navarre on 31 May. As was to be expected, he was furious, not so much with his brother-in-law as with his unfortunate sister, for the Catholic town of Cahors, like Agen, was part of Marguerite's marriage settlement and the King chose to hold her responsible for it. Her Chancellor, Pibrac, had meanwhile returned to Paris. As the King was going to Mass, he unexpectedly met him in one of the courts of the Louvre, when he publicly poured scorn and fury on that unlucky official's head.

'Didn't you know,' the King bawled at him, 'that Cahors has been taken and sacked, all the inhabitants massacred, and the loot from the churches publicly sold to Nérac?'

Pibrac had previously assured the King of Marguerite's fidelity and had not yet heard this news.

'The officers', the King went on, 'appointed by your Queen have betrayed the city and received the enemy in it. She shall no longer have this power to harm me, and this morning I am ordering my Procurator-General to invalidate the documents assigning it to her; as for you, I forbid you to use her seal or to seal any documents whatever!'

At that moment Catherine was ill in bed. Nevertheless, the faithful Chancellor sought an audience with her and begged her to have his mistress's rights restored, since the Queen of Navarre was in no way responsible for the sack of Cahors by her husband. In due course this was done.

Yet Pibrac received no gratitude from Marguerite for this act of devotion. He was already in her bad books over a fantastic incident that had occurred earlier in the year.

An Italian astrologer in Paris had predicted that during the Lenten period, between 21 and 29 March, the Queen of Navarre would be murdered by her husband. The lovesick Chancellor consulted with the King and the Queen Mother as to whether he should inform Margot of this prophecy, and was advised by them to do so. Henri was well informed about the Court of Nérac and his sister's liaison with Turenne; perhaps he thought such a warning might do her good, a singular misreading of her character. When Marguerite received Pibrac's letter, begging her to perform her Easter duties elsewhere, she was, not unnaturally, extremely angry. For she had never been on better terms with her husband. Not only was the prophecy untrue; it was, as she saw it, a plot to disrupt their marriage. In the first of two long, bitter, and reproachful letters she wrote to Pibrac in the following year:

'You may also remember the warning you gave me in March a year ago', she reminded him, 'when you informed me (in such moving terms that you said you were writing with tears in your eyes) that in view of our horoscopes you realized that during that month he would kill me with his own hands, and you advised and begged me to retire to Agen or some other town loyal to me. If I had done so, when he was being so much kinder to me, I could not have hoped ever to be reconciled to him for the rest of my life.' And she added at the end of this letter:

'I forgot to mention that I know you told several people when you sent me that fine warning in March that I had written to you that I had had a dream in which I was being murdered, from which I awoke in apprehension and fear. I was astonished that you should have invented this, for you know it is not true, and yet you gave it currency.' And she signed herself: 'Your best and least obliged friend, M.'

In her second letter, replying to those he had sent her attempting to defend himself—for Pibrac was as superstitious as Catherine de Medici and had sincerely believed the astrologer's forecast to be true—Marguerite ordered him to return her seals, since he was ill, he had said, and she did not wish his peace of mind and health to be affected by his responsibilities any longer, as hers had been by his conduct.

In the early summer of 1580 Biron was drawing nearer and nearer to Nérac:

'I therefore wrote to the King and the Queen my mother, begging them, if they would not order a cease-fire in view of the danger in which I stood, as least to order Marshal Biron to declare Nérac, where I was living, a neutral city, and not to make war within three miles of it, whilst I would persuade my husband to do the same on behalf of the party of The Religion. The King agreed to this, on condition that the King my husband was not in Nérac; his presence there would annul this neutrality.'

At first both sides observed it, 'but this did not prevent my husband'—the arch-lover of this Lovers' War—'from coming often to Nérac where his sister and I were, it being natural to him to enjoy himself in feminine society and he then being very much in love with Fosseuse . . . and for that reason the King my husband continued to live with me in such friendship as if I were his sister, seeing that I wished for nothing more than to please him.'

Biron, on learning that Navarre had broken the pact of neutrality and was in Nérac, attacked the town with cannon, of which one ball actually hit the castle. But this was done as a warning, and he retired, sending an ensign to apologize to the Queen—his co-religionist and his King's sister—for the necessity.

'On all other occasions Marshal Biron had shown me much respect and friendliness, for when during the fighting some of my letters fell into his hands, he had returned them to me with the seals unbroken, and all those who said they were my people were well and honourably treated by him.'

Biron's envoy explained to Marguerite that had she been alone he would not have attacked the castle for anything in the world, but that he had orders from the King to fight Navarre wherever he might find him.

'I replied to his ensign that I well knew that the Marshal was only doing his soldier's duty by the King, but that a prudent man, such as he was, might well satisfy one side and the other without offending his friends; that he might have granted me the pleasure of those three days that my husband was spending at Nérac; that he could not attack him without attacking me as well, and that I was extremely offended and would complain to the King about it.'

But the King was in no mood to listen to his sister's complaints. He still chose to blame her for not preventing the war and for the loss of Cahors, and took a particularly mean revenge for her alleged plotting against him. In the following September Henri saw fit to write to his brother-in-law that Turenne was 'caressing' his wife. Turenne had left Nérac six months previously, and at that time Navarre was particularly grateful to Marguerite for allowing him to 'caress' Fosseuse, so he shrugged off the King's belated warning with a laugh and complete indifference. It was nevertheless a straw in the wind pointing to the great harm Henri in due course did his sister, largely brought on herself by her own pride and the unabashed publicity with which she conducted her love affairs.

After the incident of the shelling of Nérac, Marguerite proceeded, without a break, to describe the campaign of her brother François in Flanders. On his return to France the King sent him south, but with Bellièvre and Villeroy, two of his own most trusted councillors, to keep an eye on him, whilst he negotiated a treaty between Navarre and the Huguenots and the Catholics who had been fighting them.

According to Marguerite's account, Monsieur was unable to prevent the Spaniards from besieging Cambrai (which the faithful M. d'Inchy had handed over to him) because most of his men had joined the King's forces under Biron to fight in Gascony:

'The King accepted his offer to mediate and make peace between the parties because by doing so he hoped to turn him away from his Flanders enterprise, which he had never favoured.' This was true. But Monsieur had had next to no success in Flanders, whilst his officers and men, Bussy at their head, had ruthlessly and cynically enriched themselves by looting the unfortunate Flemish people.

The Duke of Anjou left Flanders on 8 January 1579, resolved to return there to relieve Cambrai as soon as he should have raised the necessary funds and men. The Queen Mother persuaded Henri III to a reconciliation with his brother, who welcomed him with relief and apparent affection. The bait then dangled before François to keep him out of further mischief in the Netherlands was his proposed marriage to Elizabeth I, who at that stage appeared favourably inclined towards it, so much so that in the following August Monsieur crossed from Boulogne to England 'under the safe-conduct of the Queen, by whom he was joyously and magnificently received in one of her castles about two miles from the city of London, where they remained together for a week, during their interviews and discussions of their marriage'.

The Virgin Queen, then forty-six, appeared to be much entertained by her young French suitor, half her age. She flirted with him, even kissed him, gave him a ring, and with playful affection called him her little 'frog'. (For centuries afterwards the English, when at war or loggerheads with the French, would contemptuously thus refer to them.) But Elizabeth would still not definitely commit herself to the alliance.

Before leaving for England, François had made certain that his former favourite, Bussy d'Amboise, would not be welcoming him on his return. Bussy had accompanied him back to Alençon, and there he committed the mistake unforgivable to a courtier: he told him the truth. By then he was undoubtedly in far too good conceit with himself; his audacities had won him so much success that it went to his head. They were amusing themselves by playing the Truth Game. Monsieur ordered Bussy to speak out as frankly as if he were talking to himself. This might have been said in jest, or it might have been a deliberate trap set him by François, with the cruel cunning of the Valois. If that was the case, Bussy rashly fell into it and told him that his master was 'so ugly that he would not employ him to feed his dogs'. Monsieur was not amused. Bussy had already opposed his return to France; this was the last straw. Without informing him of his plans, the Duke of Anjou left for the Louvre two days later.

To amuse his brother the King, with whom he was then again

on such affectionate terms, he showed him a letter from Bussy, in which he gaily boasted that 'he was about to entrap in his nets the doe of the Master of the Hunt'. This lady was the wife of the Count of Montsoreau, to whom Monsieur had given the post at Bussy's request, perhaps to gain favour with the Countess.

After all the insults, including the mock-embracing of his favourite *mignon*, young Quélus, that Henri III had suffered from Bussy, he saw his chance to avenge himself on that impudent lady-killer. Undoubtedly with Monsieur's connivance, he kept the letter and gleefully showed it to the cuckolded husband. Montsoreau then took a fiendish revenge on his wife and her lover. Either he would kill her or she would invite Bussy to a rendezvous in her room, where he would be assassinated by the Count's minions. On 19 August 1578 Bussy walked into the ambush with his usual nonchalance:

'This gentleman', wrote L'Estoile, 'finding himself so treacherously betrayed, nevertheless defended himself to the bitter end, proving that fear, as he had so often said, never had any place in his heart. But so long as a scrap of his sword remained in his hand he fought on to the very hilt; then, throwing tables, chairs, benches and stools at them, he wounded three or four of his enemies until, overcome by their numbers and bereft of all means of defence, he was killed and thrown from a window out of which he was about to jump.' But he was not yet dead; he landed on some spiked railings and expired there miserably.

All the world loves a brave and handsome lover, such as Bussy had been. Brantôme and others wrote of him admiringly and respectfully.

What did his death mean to Marguerite, who had been his most illustrious conquest? From her veiled references to him in her Memoirs, it is clear that she had adored him for his courage, inimitable wit and gaiety, and good looks. Their relationship was in a sense a triangular one: whilst it lasted she was deeply involved with her brother François' problems, helping him to resist the harassments to which he and she were constantly subjected by the King. The three of them time and again found means of countering these. 'Audacity, more audacity, and always audacity' was their response to them, and for audacity Bussy had no equal. There was always a spice of danger in her liaison with him, and during those constant crises Marguerite's relief from the tension was the sexual pleasure that Bussy gave her. In arranging the escape of François from the Louvre, they collaborated for the last time—she within the palace, he in Paris. She knew that soon afterwards Bussy would be leaving for Flanders with Monsieur, and the thought of remaining at Court without him might well have been her real reason for constantly pressing the Queen Mother to allow her to rejoin a husband of whose welcome she was not at all certain.

When she travelled south she knew that they might never meet again, and even if they did so she had no illusions that meanwhile he would have remained faithful to her. The sixteenth century was not an age of constancy. Life was cheap. Men were killed in their youth, either in battles or duels; women died in childbirth at the height of their beauty. Those in love had little time to grieve; over all their lives lay the shadow of 'Here today, gone tomorrow'. The sensible thing was to enjoy the present, forgetting the tragedies of the past and stifling fears of the future.

Marguerite herself was always faithful to the lover of the moment, but after her separation from Bussy she did not hesitate to take Turenne as her cavalier, although he meant very little to her emotionally. On hearing of Bussy's horrible death, no doubt she did feel real grief, although it was possibly mitigated by the fact that he had died when about to make love to another woman. She had a set of verses composed in his honour. But when shortly afterwards his successor appeared, there remained neither in her heart nor her thoughts any room for the late lamented Louis de Clermont, Lord Bussy of Amboise.

In the whole of her Memoirs Marguerite never once mentions the name of Jacques de Harlay, Marquess of Chanvallon, with whom she fell madly in love—so madly that she was never again the same woman, and through this passion drew on herself all the misfortunes she was to suffer for the rest of her life.

In our language we have no exactly fitting expression to

describe a woman who is a great lover—*une grande amoureuse*. To become one is a matter of circumstances, temperament, and personality. Such a woman, of whom Queen Margot was the incarnation, is in love with love, as she remained throughout her life, and that ideal emotion seemed to her to justify her constant search for it.

At this period, when she was nearly thirty, no longer a girl, but a woman, Margot's heart was empty, filled only with dreams and longing, ready for the *coup de foudre*, the lightning-flash of a grand passion that truly and completely swept her off her feet, wholly possessing both her body and her mind. Frequently the principal outward sign of such an utter surrender to erotic emotion is that the woman tends to throw off all discretion—even the caution necessary for self-preservation. Marguerite was badly in need of some such protective caution: her reputation was already tarnished. Both the King and the King her husband were aware of her past adulteries; both were to demand retribution from her for them in due course. But at this crucial period, and from then onwards, she lost all self-restraint. Her behaviour inevitably recalls the famous line from Racine's *Phèdre*, written almost exactly a century later: '*C'est Vénus toute entière à sa proie attachée.*'

Jacques de Harlay, Marquess of Chanvallon, belonged to a distinguished but not rich family. His father was the squire of Césy; his mother, Louisa Stuart of Carr, was related to the Scottish Royal Family. He had been in the King's service before passing into Monsieur's. Whilst not the most famous swordsman of his time, he was sufficiently brave and able to be mentioned as one of them by Brantôme.

But what distinguished young Chanvallon—he was a year or two younger than Marguerite—setting him above all the men of his day in that respect, was his physical perfection. By general consent, he was not merely the most handsome but the most beautiful man of his generation. His beauty was that of a young Greek god. Since in her letters Marguerite called him her Narcissus, he must have been aware of it. Perhaps that was why, in his adolescence and early manhood, he was shy and self-conscious in the presence of women. For he did not make a great impression on Marguerite when they met during her two months' stay at La Fère on her return from Flanders. Possibly his beauty had not then matured, or she might still have been in love with Bussy and paid no attention to her brother's other numerous gentlemen, including his Master of Horse.

Chanvallon was intelligent as well as beautiful; a lover and reader of poetry and even a minor poet himself. So that he seemed to possess that physical and spiritual perfection which Marguerite always maintained was the supreme height of human personality.

Monsieur, accompanied by Bellièvre and Villeroy, as well as his numerous suite, arrived in Gascony on 12 September 1580. His sister was delighted, his brother-in-law relieved. Moreover, Navarre at last got his way: Marshal Biron, his personal enemy, was deprived of his command, which was taken over by Marshal Matignon, whilst Biron was fobbed off by being appointed Commander-in-Chief of Monsieur's Flanders armies, when he should have assembled them.

The Treaty of Fleix—called after the old castle in the Dordogne where they were all staying at the time—ended the Lovers' War. For Marguerite, however, it was not a happy ending:

'As fame and happiness always arouse envy, the King took no pleasure in it, nor in the seven months that my brother and I remained in Gascony, negotiating the peace. In order to justify his ire, he chose to imagine that it was I who was responsible for this war, having pushed my husband into it (who can certainly testify to the contrary) in order to give my brother the distinction of bringing about the peace, which, if it had depended on me, would have been made at the expense of far less time and trouble; for his business in Flanders and Cambrai received a serious setback from the delay. Well, people's eyes are blinded by envy and hatred and in consequence they cannot look facts in the face.

'On this false foundation the King built up his deadly hatred of myself, and, reviving past events in his memory (that when he was in Poland and after his return I had always devoted myself more to my brother's interests than to his) and putting all these things together, he swore to ruin me and my brother. . . .'

This complaint of Marguerite's was quite justified. Even Bellièvre wrote to the King and the Queen Mother that they were being unfair to her. But they possibly had other reasons for taking such a harsh view of her conduct.

It was during those seven months that Marguerite began her passionate affair with Chanvallon, and it was not long before they heard of it. After leaving Fleix, the parties spent some time at Coutras in the Gironde. Henry of Navarre left them there. Brother and sister went on to Bordeaux and then spent two months of the early spring at the nearby castle of Cadillac—the perfect season in the south for romance, for walking and riding, secret meetings in woodland glades and groves, stolen kisses and caresses. It was here that Marguerite and Chanvallon became lovers.

But a new complication soon arose, which caused her the greatest anxiety:

'It happened that during the seven months my brother spent in Gascony my bad luck would have it that he fell in love with Fosseuse. . . . The King my husband blamed me for this, considering that I was encouraging my brother's suit against his. Realizing this, I begged my brother to cease his attentions to her, which were causing me such unhappiness, and as my peace of mind was more important to him than his own happiness, he suppressed his passion for her and did not speak to her any more.

'But having put this right, Fortune (unappeased by the first blow which one had been able to parry) prepared another much more dangerous snare for me. Fosseuse, who was very much in love with the King my husband, had nevertheless not allowed him more privileges until then than an honest girl might. But now, in order to appease his jealousy of my brother, and to prove to him that she loved only him, she allowed him everything he asked for, with the unfortunate consequence that she became pregnant. When she knew this was so, her whole behaviour towards myself changed completely. . . . She began to hide away from me, and to do me as many bad turns as good ones in the past. She had so much influence over my husband that in a short time he too changed completely towards me. He became estranged from me, withdrew from me, and no longer found my company as agreeable as he had done during the four or five happy years I spent with him in Gascony whilst Fosseuse was behaving honourably.'

As he had done when in love with Dayelle, Navarre returned at frequent intervals, not to see his wife, but Fosseuse. Being so acutely aware of Henri III's enmity, Marguerite clung more than ever to her good relationship with him. It was therefore more than indiscreet of her—rash to the last degree—to make no secret of her infatuation with Chanvallon.

Agrippa d'Aubigné was still in Navarre's service. A glance at his portrait shows an intelligent but thoroughly mean face: beady, sharp black eyes, a jutting nose and thin lips stretched in a sneering smile. He was the grandfather of Mme de Maintenon. He impudently faked his own pedigree, claiming to be of far nobler birth than he was. Both his son and grandson were scoundrels. His hatred for the Catholic Queen of Navarre had not lessened. Whether he himself spied on her or was merely retailing gossip, in his *Histoire Universelle*, published as late as 1616, he saw fit to tell how she was discovered 'in her privacy' with Chanvallon. But no doubt this evidence was already superfluous; everyone at Coutras and Cadillac must have been aware of Marguerite's latest affair and it would not have been long before news of it reached the ears of the King, who delighted in any scandalous tales about his sister.

By the end of April neither he nor the Queen Mother were able any longer to delay Monsieur's return to Flanders, on which he was implacably determined. They both of them blamed Marguerite for not having dissuaded him from doing so, more than unjustly, since Chanvallon, his Master of Horse, was bound to go with him. Even Aubigné claimed that she had done her utmost to deter him. And to part from her 'dearest heart' was indeed torture to her.

As soon as they had left and she was obliged to return home with her husband, Nérac, where once she had been so happy, lost all charm for her. She wore black, as if she were widowed, retired from all social life and bought several volumes of the classics, including Plutarch's *Lives*, Cicero, and a Greco-Latin-French dictionary. She had sumptuous mourning vestments and altar-cloths, all in black and silver, embroidered for a convent of nuns under her protection. Chanvallon sent her poems; she wrote him impassioned love-letters. She thanked the god of love, she told him, for having chosen her to be among his elect: '. . . like those elected by God, those holy fathers not yet in Heaven, whom He withdrew to solitude, far from human haunts, so that they might await the hour of their perfect glory in perpetual contemplation. Thus I am withdrawn in this desert, where I envy those high mountains whose heads are near to Heaven. I live with no distractions, in perpetual contemplation of my great good fortune, awaiting the hour of my beatitude. If so much perfection, my dearest heart, did not let me take it for granted that you are a divine being from whom nothing is hidden, I would tell you that the hardest rocks, in which time and time again I have chiselled your name, your beauty, and my passion, would prove to you that my soul is not one of those waxen souls transformed day by day. . . . If like those of Nature, my senses are deprived of the one being they desire, I have this advantage over her, that my Narcissus will never be deaf to my voice nor slow in responding to my passionate lamentations. I persuade myself of this, dear heart. But my God! supposing I were mistaken? But death would not deceive me; it would come to my aid. If therefore, through the envy of the gods . . . they were to place on such perfection one stain of inconstancy and your love were to change, do not think that you would have left me; I would never allow this reproach to you nor this misfortune to myself. Say: I loved her until death, and believe me that the hour when you changed would be my last, which would only depend on you. . . .'

During the next few years Marguerite wrote Chanvallon altogether twenty-one such letters. The many classical references they contain, such as the one above to the legend of Narcissus, were partly the result of her love of literature, partly a fashion of the time. But through and beneath their literary accomplishment runs a scarlet thread of naked passion; her fear of losing him, her bitter reproaches when he was unfaithful to her, are genuine cries from her suffering heart. Indeed, it is possible that this consuming passion brought Marguerite more suffering than happiness, even than the delirious ecstasy she felt when he possessed her body as well as her mind.

The rumour soon spread to Paris that the Queen of Navarre was pregnant by the Marquess of Chanvallon, to the great glee of the *mignons*, who hated her almost as much as Monsieur. It may well have been started by Aubigné, who later wrote that she had tried to bribe him into silence by consulting him with regard to her husband's joining the expeditionary force Catherine de Medici was then fitting out to reclaim the throne of Portugal—an honour he said he declined. Many years later a Capuchin friar, Father Angel, was alleged to be her illegitimate son by Chanvallon. But, considered with detachment, it seems highly unlikely that Marguerite ever bore a child at all, either to this or any other lover, and certainly, in spite of her desperate anxiety to give him an heir, never to Navarre.

Marguerite's unhappiness during her last year in Gascony was greatly increased by the climax to the Fosseuse affair, in which Navarre shamelessly used his wife to protect his mistress. As soon as they had returned to Nérac, 'Fosseuse, in order to conceal her pregnancy or to rid herself of it, put it into his head to take her to the waters of Aigues-Caude, in Béarn'—the heart of the Huguenot country.

'I begged the King my husband to forgive me for not accompanying him to Aigues-Caude; he knew that since the indignities I had had to suffer at Pau I had made a vow never to re-enter Béarn until the Catholic religion was re-established there. He insisted on my going, even angrily, but I still refused. He then told me that his little girl (which was what he called Fosseuse) needed to go there to cure the stomach trouble from which she was suffering; to which I replied that I was quite willing for her to do so. He answered that there was no question of her going without me, that it would give rise to false rumours, and became very angry with me for refusing to take her there. Finally, I managed to arrange matters so that he took her with two of her companions, Rebours, Villesavin, and their chaperon. They then went off with him, whilst I remained at Bagnères. I heard every day from Rebours (the one he had been in love with, a corrupt and double-dealing girl, who only wanted Fosseuse to be discarded so that she might take her place in my husband's affections) that Fosseuse was doing me all the harm she could, hoping that if she bore a son and could dispose of me the King my husband would marry her; that with this intention she would compel me to go to Pau and had persuaded the King, when he returned to Bagnères, to force me to go there, by fair means or foul. . . .

'At the end of five or six weeks the King my husband, returning with Fosseuse and her companions, learning from certain lords who had remained with me of the despondency and dread with which the thought of going to Pau filled me, did not press me, but only said that he would very much have liked me to do so. And as he saw that I was in tears as I told him that I would rather die first, he changed his mind, and we returned to Nérac.

'There, as everyone was talking about Fosseuse's pregnancy, not only at Court, but throughout the country, wishing to stop those rumours, I decided to speak to her. I took her into my cabinet, where I said to her: "Although for some time now you have become estranged from me, and I am told you have been trying to harm me with my husband, my friendship for you and your family still makes me want to help you in your unfortunate situation, which I beg you not to deny to me and ruin your honour, which is as dear to me as my own; and believe me, I will be like a mother to you. As there is at present an epidemic of plague here, I have a good excuse for leaving for Mas d'Agenois, an isolated country seat of my husband's. I will only take with me the suite that you might wish me to. My husband will meanwhile go hunting, in the opposite direction, and will not return until after your delivery. In this way we will put an end to the scandal, which concerns me as much as yourself."

'But instead of being grateful to me she said with the utmost arrogance that she would give the lie to those who had been talking about her; she knew very well that for some time past I no longer liked her and was seeking an excuse to ruin her. And, speaking as loudly as I had been speaking softly, she went out of my cabinet in a temper, straight to the King my husband, who was furious with me for what I had said to his little girl, and remained on very bad terms with me for several months, right up to the end of her pregnancy.

'Her pains began at daybreak. As she was sleeping in the maids-of-honours' room she sent for my doctor, and asked him to inform the King my husband, which he did. As usual we were sleeping in the same room, although in separate beds. When the doctor brought him the news he was very upset, fearing on the one hand that she might be found out, and on the other that she would not be properly looked after, for he loved her dearly. Finally, he decided to admit everything to me, and begged me to go and help her, knowing that I was always ready to serve him in every way. So he opened my bed-curtains and said to me:

'"My dear, I must confess something to you. Please forgive me, and forget everything else I told you, but get up and go to Fosseuse, who is very ill. I am sure that seeing her in such a state you will forgive the past. You know how much I love her. Please help me now!"

'I told him that I honoured him too much to be offended by anything he had done; that I would look after her as if she were my own daughter, but that he should go hunting, taking everyone with him in order to put a stop to any more gossiping.

'I immediately had her removed from the maids' room and put into an isolated one, with nurses and the doctor to look after her. God willed that she only gave birth to a stillborn female child.'

Marguerite made no allusion to the profound relief she must have felt at this. Had Fosseuse's baby been born alive and a male, her own situation might have been greatly affected. However, 'after her delivery she was carried back to the maids' room, whence, in spite of all precautions, it was impossible to prevent the story from leaking out to the whole castle.

'On returning from the hunt, the King my husband went to visit her as usual. She begged him to ask me to go and see her (as

GRAND PASSION . 175

I always did visit my maids when one of them was ill) in order to stop the gossiping. . . . He found me in bed, tired out through having risen so early and the trouble I had taken to have her properly nursed. He asked me to get up and go to her, but I told him that I had done so when she needed my help. Now she no longer did so and if I went, everyone would point their finger at me. He became extremely angry with me, which greatly annoyed me, as what I had already done for her that morning did not seem to me to warrant such a reward. She often put him in such tempers with me.'

After becoming King Henry IV of France, for centuries Navarre remained the embodiment of courage and chivalry to the French people. The first of these qualities was undoubtedly his. But Marguerite's account of this Fosseuse episode—written in such obvious sincerity and with such indignation—puts her husband in a very different light. In her anxiety to remain on good terms with him, she had abetted his passion for his 'little girl', precisely as her mother, Catherine de Medici, had abetted Henri II's liaison with Diane de Poitiers, for years apparently her best woman friend. But Fosseuse had lost her head and become impossibly ambitious. Marguerite's pride had been so badly wounded by the ingratitude of the King and his young mistress that this must be borne in mind when considering the sad sequel to it.

Henri III, said Marguerite, immediately took advantage of the situation to bring about a separation between his sister and Navarre. In describing how he set about it, once again she only told half-truths. It was the Fosseuse affair and not the King's machinations that caused their ensuing estrangement. And ever since Chanvallon had gone she was longing to leave Gascony and return to France on almost any pretext.

Yet the King and the Queen Mother did wish her to return to Court. Their motive was not to separate husband and wife, but another attempt to detach Navarre from his Huguenot allies. In spite of the Treaty of Fleix, the south was still far from pacified. So her mother wrote Marguerite several affectionate letters, assuring her of her welcome, especially if she succeeded in bringing her husband with her. The bait to lure him north was to be Fosseuse, still in Marguerite's service and therefore due to travel with her. It was assumed that Navarre would soon follow them.

Marguerite was then desperately short of money, so much so that Pibrac had sold on her behalf a house she owned in Paris.

'The King and the Queen my mother . . . sent me 15,000 *écus* so that my departure should not be delayed by financial embarrassment, and the Queen my mother informed me that she would meet me at Xaintonge; that if the King my husband accompanied me there she would confer with him regarding the King's wishes. For he was very anxious to draw him away from Gascony and place him in the same predicament at Court that he and my brother had suffered in the past.

'Neither the time I had spent in Gascony nor all these fine promises and apparent benevolence deceived me regarding what one might expect from the Court, but I decided to take advantage of his offers and stay there for only a few months to settle my affairs and those of the King my husband, believing that this would also lessen his passion for Fosseuse, whom I was taking with me, and that the King my husband, when he no longer saw her, would fall in love with someone else who was not so inimical towards me.' This he did, but unfortunately for Marguerite the remedy she hoped for turned out in due course to be worse than the disease.

'I had quite a lot of trouble in persuading my husband to allow me to make this journey, because he was angry at the thought of my taking Fosseuse with me. Being most anxious to deter me from making this trip to France, he treated me somewhat more kindly. But, having already promised the King and the Queen my mother that I would come, and even having received from them the funds for the journey, the misfortune that decided me to undertake it overcame the slight desire I then had to do so, in view of the fact that the King my husband was beginning to show me a little more affection.'

And there the Memoirs of Queen Marguerite of Navarre abruptly cease. The story of the remainder of her life sufficiently explains why she never continued nor completed them.

The years 1580-82 were a watershed. She was nearly thirty. She had reached the height of her glamour and success. She was as beautiful as ever. But her wild passion for Chanvallon and hatred for the King—never in her Memoirs referred to as her brother—had entered her blood and inflamed her judgment. In spite also of her sisterly affection for Navarre, the Fosseuse episode had destroyed her attachment to him, which until then had been quite sincere; he had subjected her to more indignities than her Valois pride could endure. From every point of view, Nérac had lost its charm for her, whilst the menace of Pau and its bigoted Puritanism, its black-clothed citizens whose black looks expressed their hatred for her as she hated them, inevitably lurked in the background.

Chanvallon was still in Flanders with Monsieur, but that war would not last for ever and in Paris they would be reunited.

When Marguerite left Gascony she may have been momentarily depressed by a sense of her failure there. But secretly her heart beat with hopeful passion and longing for reunion with her adored lover.

Part Two

13 Disgrace

Early in February 1582 the King and Queen of Navarre left Nérac with a large retinue to meet Catherine de Medici. Eighteen or twenty carts carrying Marguerite's baggage had already preceded them.

The meeting between the old Queen Mother and her son-in-law went off smoothly enough. Nevertheless, all her assurances of the King's affection did not deceive the wily Bourbon. At one moment during the Lovers' War Henri III had threateningly declared that if his sister did not prevent her husband from waging it he 'would make them both very unhappy'. If Marguerite was still willing to risk returning to Paris, Henry was not. In bland and polite terms, expressing his undying fealty, he bade his mother-in-law farewell, wrote to his brother-in-law in the same terms, and, after accompanying the two Queens as far as Vienne, left them and went back to Béarn and his Huguenot subjects.

Henry apparently showed no anxiety regarding the future of Fosseuse, proceeding northward with her mistress, who, with the Queen Mother, joined the King at Fontainebleau on 27 April. And as soon as they arrived in Paris the unfortunate girl was ignominiously driven from Court. On hearing of it, Henry sent

M. de Frontenac to inform his wife of his displeasure. Marguerite then wrote him the following letter:

'You say that it will never do me any harm to please you. This I also think, believing you to be so reasonable that you would never command me to do anything unworthy of a person of my standing, nor which affected my honour, in which you are so closely involved. And if you asked me to keep with me a girl who, as everyone knows, had a child by you, you would have to agree that this would place me in a shameful position. You wrote that to stop the King, the Queens, and others who might speak to me about it, I should tell them that you love her, and I do so for your sake. That would be all very well if it were a question of one of your men or women servants—but not your mistress! If I were of a rank that made me unworthy of the honour of being your wife, such a reply would do me no great harm, but being who I am it would be highly unsuitable, and I shall certainly not make it. I have suffered what no ordinary gentlewoman, let alone a princess, should have to suffer, having helped her, concealed her sin, and ever since kept her with me. If you do not think that by doing so I was not trying to please you, I do not know how you would have wished me to do so.'

The Queen Mother was even more implacable. When she realized that Henry had no intention of coming to Paris, it was she who insisted that Marguerite should take such a harsh line with Fosseuse. Moreover, she herself wrote to her son-in-law:

'You are not the first young and foolish husband in such matters, but certainly the first and only one who after such an occurrence addressed his wife like that. I had the honour of being married to the King, my lord and your sovereign, and when Mme de Flemming became pregnant he thought it very right and proper that she should be dismissed: in the case of Mme de Valentinois [Diane de Poitiers] and Mme d'Etampes, everything was perfectly honourable. It is not the way to treat well-born women, and of such a House, and to insult them at the whim of a public prostitute, for the whole world knows that she bore you a child. You are too well-born not to know how you should behave towards the daughter of your King and sister of the one who governs this whole realm and yourself, who, apart from that, honours and loves you as a good woman should. I have sent away this *beautiful animal* [*cette belle bête*, which Catherine italicized]; for as long as I live I shall not tolerate anything which might prevent or diminish the mutual affection those as close to me as she is [her daughter] should bear one another, and beg you that after the worst your fine messenger, de Frontenac, may tell you in order to alienate you from your wife, you will consider the harm you have done yourself and return to the right road.'

And she ended by again enjoining him to come to Paris and not allow 'a youthful folly to disturb the peace and well-being of this realm'.

Fosseuse was ruined. But her greatest fault was not to have had Navarre's baby; Marguerite had offered to take her away so that she might bear it in secret, or even have an abortion. The poor, spoilt little animal, however, had lost her head as well as her virginity; it was her ambition and the publicity she deliberately provoked that she had to pay for so miserably.

Although Catherine knew that Marguerite's own behaviour was far from impeccable, her own morality was based on the simple principle that a woman might please herself so long as she was not found out and no scandal ensued. If only her daughter had had her mother's discretion and good sense, she too might have been spared a great deal of suffering.

Henri III, meanwhile, received his sister with unusual cordiality, even conferring some new estates and titles on her. He had still not given up hope of luring her husband to Court. But Navarre —who may well have tired of Fosseuse's tantrums before Marguerite took her away—wrote most deferentially to his overlord that he would hasten to Paris as soon as the south was pacified, which, unfortunately, was not yet the case. He reverted instead to his previous method of obtaining the latest news and information of events at Court from his wife. For about a year Marguerite kept up a constant and affectionate correspondence with her husband, telling him of the considerable changes that had taken place during her absence in Gascony. The most important of these was the emergence of two favourites of the King whom she referred to as 'the dukes'.

These two bedfellows of Henri III were of a different breed from such effeminate *mignons* as Quélus and his other former playmates. They were both extremely tough and utterly ruthless. Henri III doted on them, calling them his sons. They plundered him without scruple or mercy.

The first of these two queans was Arques, whom the King—appropriately enough—created Duke of Joyeuse and married off to the Queen Consort's [Louise's] sister, spending a fortune on the wedding, part of the six million *livres* his *mignons* extracted from him.

The second, even more sinister favourite was La Valette, created Duke of Epernon. Joyeuse was made Governor of Normandy; Epernon received the Three Archbishoprics of the realm. Still they were not satisfied. Joyeuse obtained the Archbishopric of Narbonne for his brother; Epernon became Governor of Guyenne, a matter of the greatest seriousness for Navarre. Epernon was so powerful that even the Queen Mother feared to offend him.

Marguerite returned to Court to find these two *mignons* in an impregnable position there. Immediately they became her bitterest and most implacable enemies. But she was not the kind of woman to tolerate such a situation; the enmity was mutual. Unfortunately, she forgot that her former allies were no longer at her side. Bussy was dead. Her brother François was in considerable difficulties in Flanders. To have taken on this battle with Henri III, Joyeuse, and Epernon single-handed was in itself foolhardy, but to do so whilst her affair with Chanvallon was the talk of the Court and all Paris was sheer madness.

Chanvallon, in Flanders with Monsieur, was possibly still in love with her. But her heart was nearly broken when in July 1582 she learned of his proposed marriage to a rich and highly born widow, Catherine de la Mark, sister of the Duke of Bouillon.

Chanvallon's only assets were his physical beauty, charm and cleverness. He was relatively poor and badly needed financial security. In her very first passionate letter to him, Marguerite discussed at great length a marriage of convenience for him— 'to your advantage and that of our love.' Such marriages were a commonplace, put no obligation of faithfulness on the husband and provided an alibi against scandalmongering. Many years previously Guise had married in order to stop the gossip about Marguerite and himself.

She was terrified that during the Flanders campaign her 'dearest heart' might be killed or wounded:

'A criminal does not await his sentence with such furious impatience and mortal suffering as I am waiting for news of this battle, on which depends my own happiness or misery, according to whether you live or die. . . .'

Chanvallon had no intention of being killed; he had a good war. At the time of his engagement—matrimonial, not military—he nevertheless fell from Monsieur's favour. There had been an unsuccessful attempt on François' life by a Spanish agent, Salcedo. After the would-be assassin's arrest, Monsieur planned to implicate Chanvallon—who had nothing to do with it—in the plot, since under torture Salcedo would name anyone his executioners wished to accuse. At Dunkerque, where he was then meeting his fiancée, Chanvallon received a letter, unsigned, but nominally from another of Monsieur's officers, ordering him immediately to rejoin his master in Bruges. But he suspected a trap and arrived accompanied by a large troop of horsemen, who had been guarding him in case of a wayside attack. When he endeavoured to clear the situation up with François, Monsieur laughed off the whole incident as a practical joke.

On arrival in Paris, Marguerite had bought a house in the rue Culture Sainte Catherine, near the fashionable Marais Quarter, from the Chancellor, Biragues, for 28,000 *écus*. Whilst it was being prepared for her, she returned temporarily to the Louvre. She was then still on fairly good terms with the King, who was hoping that Navarre would join her. But when it became clear that he had no intention of doing so, Henri, spurred on by Joyeuse and Epernon, reverted to his old enmity towards her.

Chanvallon returned to Paris in October. In spite of his marriage in the previous August, he had no difficulty in persuading Marguerite that he still loved her. On seeing him again, her passion for him redoubled.

'My only sun, my heart, my beautiful angel': her letters to him are studded with such adoring epithets. Whether truthfully or not, Chanvallon had told her that his marriage was making him very unhappy.

'The horror of your misery', she wrote to him, 'deprives me of the power of consoling you, for it is difficult for one who needs help to give it to another. But this is nothing new for me, since marriage was the cause of all my sufferings and the blight of my life; but this time he has redoubled his cruelty to such an extent that I have been more distressed by it than by any previous malice on his part. . . . My God, my dear life, how I hate him! Oh no, let no one ever say that marriages are made in Heaven; the gods would not commit so great an injustice!'

Since Marguerite's letters to Chanvallon are undated, one can only guess at the reason for this outburst against Navarre. Both of them all their lives resented the fact of their marriage, arranged by Catherine de Medici and Jeanne of Albret for dynastic and political advantages. Yet until the Fosseuse affair they had remained on fairly good and occasionally even affectionate terms with one another. This recent slight could still have been rankling in Marguerite's mind. It is also quite usual for a married woman, as madly in love with another man as she was with Chanvallon, to feel bitter against the husband to whom she is legally bound and to denigrate him, whether fairly or unfairly, in order to arouse her lover's compassion. At that point Marguerite was no longer writing to Navarre, nor he to her, and all Paris knew of her liaison with Chanvallon.

A libellous work entitled *Le Divorce satyrique*, attributed to Marguerite's old enemy, Aubigné, claimed that whilst she was in residence in the Louvre she had Chanvallon secretly brought to her apartment in a trunk, as once she had smuggled in the rope down which her brother François climbed in escaping. 'She awaited him in a bed illuminated by many torches, between two

sheets of black taffeta, with various other little voluptuous trimmings. . . .'

Marguerite moved into her own home, the Hôtel de Navarre,
early in 1583. Chanvallon had taken lodgings in Paris. When it
was impossible for them to meet she wrote to him, sending her
letters by hand, by her 'Mercury', as she called the messenger.
Sometimes she would invent a pretext for not seeing him—ill-
health or religious duties, but in fact in order to retain his interest. The two surviving letters from Chanvallon to her show
that she succeeded in doing so:

'I would not have dared to disturb you whilst you were im-
mersed in your devotions, [possibly during Lent] but today, my
Queen, I imagine that you might begin, as they say, to send God
to Galilee. . . . It had pleased you to assure and promise me that
I would have the honour of seeing you yesterday; I very humbly
beg that you will at least do so this evening. . . . Allow me, dear
heart, to have the happiness of seeing you this evening, and do
not excuse yourself on account of ill-health, which I am sure will
not prevent you from doing as you wish, and besides, this fuss will
mean that everyone will go to bed earlier and will be more sleepy.
Adieu, my lovely mistress, I kiss your beautiful hands very
humbly.'

No doubt Marguerite covered this adoring note with kisses.
But she was violently jealous; apparently Charlotte de Sauves,
her old enemy, had dared to aspire even to Chanvallon, and there
were rumours of his other conquests:

'Do not again accuse me of cruelty; my death and my ruin are
the only links I shall have with you in future . . . and if I have
caused you some annoyance be satisfied and avenged to have reduced me to the two worst states of misery that you might have
wished on your greatest enemy. . . . Where there is such enmity
there may well be unfaithfulness. If the ardour of my sincere and
too faithful passion did not deserve a reciprocal love, at least it
should not be rewarded by such cruel hatred. Adieu, source of my
eternal sufferings! If I could only say the same to my life, which,
after you, is what I most hate. M.'

The second letter, immediately following on that one, was

much longer and even more violently reproachful, ending with the paragraph:

'I beg you, when receiving this, my last one, to return it to me immediately with the one I wrote you yesterday, for at this charming interview you are having this evening I do not wish them to be discussed at my expense by the father and daughter'—presumably her alleged rival. Chanvallon replied:

'You accused me, my Queen, of infidelity, although you cannot doubt what I am to you, nor can you be oblivious of the suffering your extreme cruelty causes me, since despising myself, I cannot but despise everything that might prevent me from expressing my infinite love for you. If therefore you have until now used such pretexts to distress and martyrize me, and to extract from me the quintessence of my heart and soul, now that with so many right and obvious reasons you admit that I am all yours, please, Madam, at least ... instead of rewarding me, do cease afflicting me with these intolerable sufferings I have endured since your perfections made me your slave. Remember, my Queen, the holy vows I renewed in your lovely hands yesterday, and admit that you read in me the sincerity of my intentions, although all I said to you was unable to express the least part of my devotion. I know you will think it strange of me very humbly to beg you for the honour of allowing me to see you tomorrow for a quarter of an hour; but today I heard something about which I cannot write, but which you should know. One of my women friends told me that you were displeased with me; you, Madam, know whether you have reason to be so, since you have only known the effects of my violent passion. So, dearest heart, take pity on me and suffer this slight annoyance for the sake of a creature who loves you so much. I kiss your lovely hands very humbly.'

But in refusing to see Chanvallon as often as he and she even more could wish, Marguerite was not always playing a comedy with him.

It must have been in the summer of 1583 that she wrote to him: 'If by flattery one could eliminate or reduce one's misfortune I would agree with you, my lovely heart, in ignoring all indications of it and rejecting all warnings. But there are so many examples of the harm done by such contempt that I could not agree to increase them by the ruin of what I hold most dear, even although after the loss of our love or your life I would have nothing more to fear, since my life, peace, and happiness depend on them. As therefore I only wish to love and preserve them, do not think it strange that my greatest fear is to lose them ... and for that reason I cannot rid myself of the fear that makes me hate and curse my life a thousand times over, knowing that it is so miserable that instead of helping and serving the one to whom it is utterly devoted, it is causing him inconvenience and unhappiness. Please God that this tempest may discharge itself on me alone, for you can imagine how much more easily I could bear it if you were not involved in it; if it were merely a matter of my own safety, I would never have passed this cruel sentence, since in so divine a cause death has always seemed to me of little importance, but to put you in danger. Oh no, my love! there is nothing so cruel that I would not suffer first. And the proof of it is that I forbid myself the pleasure of seeing you, which is as necessary to me as the sun is to the flowers of spring, which do not fade more rapidly owing to its absence than by the loss of your beautiful eyes my life and beauty lose their lustre and their strength. From this, my all, you may judge how greatly I fear that any harm may come to you. But since it is not my fault and it is only for your sake that such happiness is forbidden to us, I am bearing it, without ceasing to kiss your hands with the same affection, which will be the last to die in me.

'Please forgive this muddled letter; I am so beset by worry and anxiety that I am unable to rewrite it. M.'

And Marguerite did indeed have cause for the gravest anxiety.

When she first moved into her splendid residence she reproduced the ambience of Nérac—a round of parties and entertainments, music, dancing, and feasting. She kept open house; anyone who was cultured or talented—poets, painters, musicians, philosophers—was welcome there. This would have been harmless enough. But, throwing all self-discipline and caution to the winds, Marguerite made two cardinal errors. She was unable to conceal her passion for Chanvallon—in fact, advertised it. She had begun to put on weight and when she was indisposed the rumour was spread that she was pregnant by him. Her enemies were headed by Joyeuse and Epernon, who never ceased to poison the King's mind against her. Instead of attempting to conciliate them, or at the very least refrain from stoking their antagonism, Marguerite actually defied them, daring to lure from Court the less homosexual members of the royal circle. They came, partly from malicious curiosity, partly in search of amusement, which was not lacking. Every time one of these gallants found a willing female partner with whom to have an affair, this was gaily celebrated as a triumph over the enemy in the Louvre.

In a very short time Marguerite's breach with the King was an open one, so much so that everyone knew that to ask her good offices with him for one favour or another would do the petitioner more harm than good.

But the last straw as far as the King and especially the Queen Mother were concerned was their suspicion that Marguerite was inciting Monsieur to continue his disastrous campaign in Flanders.

Very much against the will of both Henri III and Catherine, François had insisted on returning there. Encouraged by his success in holding Cambrai, and grandly appointed Duke of Brabant by his Catholic Flemish allies, on 16 January he launched a surprise attack on the northern towns and seaports. This culminated in his attempt to take the city of Antwerp, the great port whose inhabitants had a well-deserved reputation for ferocity. The Duke's French troops were mercilessly trapped in the narrow streets, their throats cut by butchers' knives, mutilated, strangled and completely routed. The carnage resembled a second St Bartholomew.

The Duke and his defeated soldiery were mercilessly ridiculed by the victorious Flemings. The event became known as the Folly of Antwerp. As usual, Catherine de Medici was obliged to step in to patch matters up with the Protestant William of Orange and his Catholic allies against the Spaniards. By an agreement at Termonde on 18 March, the Duke was allowed to keep Dunkerque and the French prisoners were freed. But by 18 June the Spaniards had regained Dunkerque; François left Flanders and returned home.

He was seriously ill with the tuberculosis that was soon to kill him. On 11 July his mother visited him at Chaulnes, reasoned with him, and implored him to renounce his fantastic ambitions and make his peace with the King. He only pretended to give in to her. After her return to Paris, with his invincible obstinacy he went back to Cambrai for the month of September, then, desperately sick, on 9 November he left for Château-Thierry, where Catherine again visited him, but was still unable to influence him to renounce his Flanders aspirations.

Both she and the King were more and more anxious with regard to Philip of Spain's intrigues against France. The Catholic King was making overtures to the Huguenot Henry of Navarre, offering him funds to raise the southern French Protestants against the throne of the Valois. But it was already obvious that Monsieur was unlikely to live long enough to succeed to it. Henry of Bourbon was clearly in due course going to become King Henri IV of France. Henri III therefore wished to remain on good terms with his cousin. He offered him a present of 100,000 *écus* for refusing the Spanish bribe; Navarre declined it, replying that he had only wished to prove that 'one could be at the same time a good Huguenot and a good Frenchman'. Their understanding was apparently only impeded by one obstacle, the obstinate devotion of Henri III's sister and Navarre's wife, Marguerite, to her younger brother and his mad schemes.

Until then the Queen Mother had always tried to protect Marguerite from the King's spite. In June she made yet another vain attempt to bring her daughter to reason.

Some years previously Henri had forced his sister to dismiss her favourite lady-in-waiting, Gilonne de Thorigny. He now reverted to the same tactic.

At the Hôtel de Navarre Marguerite's two favourite ladies were Mmes de Duras and Béthune. Mme de Duras was highly born and cultured, an intimate friend of Montaigne, who dedicated

to her Chapter XVIII of his *Essays*. Yet there was no doubt
that both ladies knew of and abetted Marguerite's affair with
Chanvallon. Moreover, the King held them jointly responsible
with their mistress for luring away from Court certain of his
favourites, to his no uncertain displeasure. He accused them not
only of immoral behaviour; he denounced them as procuresses
and abortionists, instructing the Queen Mother to order his sister
to dismiss them forthwith.

With foolhardy audacity Marguerite refused to do so, and even
dared to remind Catherine that Charlotte de Sauves and other
members of her Flying Squadron were still in her service. Why,
then, should she dismiss her own ladies?

The Queen Mother might conceivably have overlooked this
disrespectful, even impudent rejoinder. But when it came to
affairs of State, the security of the realm, it was a far more serious
matter. On 31 July Catherine wrote to her Chancellor, Bellièvre,
that Marguerite had 'sent a special messenger to my son [Fran-
çois] to win him over and deter him, if possible, from his good intentions to conform to the plans of the King, my son, and to
induce him to adopt some bad resolution . . . which could only
bring disaster both to himself and to this realm.'

And, finally, Henri III suspected his sister of ordering the
murder of a messenger whom he had sent to Joyeuse in Italy,
with a letter telling him of her affair with Chanvallon.

Small wonder that Marguerite, having so gravely and need-
lessly antagonized her mother and so recklessly defied the King
her brother, feared the storm about to break over her head, and
took all the steps she could to protect her beloved from perishing
in it.

Scandal stories about her feud with the King flew around
Paris like leaves in an an autumn gale. One of these found its
way into history, although it was totally untrue. It was said that
on the pretext that Queen Louise was indisposed, the King had invited his sister to preside at a banquet and ball in the Louvre.
There, in full Court, he suddenly turned on Marguerite as
viciously as a snake, denouncing her publicly for her adulteries, as
a whore and common prostitute, and then drove her out. His

alleged vituperations were so violent that at least one commentator preferred to disguise them in Latin, veiling, as Gibbon said, 'all licentious passages' in *The Decline and Fall of the Roman Empire* 'in the obscurity of a learned language'.

It is not at all unlikely that in private Henri III might well have given vent to his *mignons* of such an opinion of Marguerite. But, as serious historians have pointed out, such a public scene could not have occurred. At the period in question the King was having one of his recurrent bouts of religious mania. Dressed as a penitent, he was taking part in street processions, floggings, and other masochistic practices, to the general contempt of his people. In March 1583 he founded a new brotherhood of penitents; in April he went barefooted, dressed as a flagellant, with a string of little ivory skulls dangling from his waist, on a pilgrimage to Chartres, to pray to the famous Virgin there for an heir. He dismissed all his musicians and would have no more balls or concerts at Court. On 27 May he left Paris with Queen Louise and the Queen Mother for Mézières. On 21 July he was at Monceau, having left Catherine as regent in Paris.

When she transmitted to Marguerite the King's orders to dismiss Mmes de Duras and Béthune, the Queen of Navarre threatened to leave Paris herself, and to return to Gascony. Catherine, only too pleased that she should do so, on 25 June ordered Bellièvre to pay her daughter for this purpose 50,000 *livres* that were owing to her. But as Marguerite was then living only for Chanvallon, it is extremely unlikely that she ever intended to carry out her threat.

The King returned to Paris on 3 August, staying at the Castle of Madrid in the Bois de Boulogne, where he was in close touch with his mother. On learning that Marguerite had not obeyed him, he was naturally furious. He immediately wrote a personal letter in his own hand to Henry of Navarre, informing him of the two women's scandalous behaviour, and his royal intention to dismiss them forthwith himself as 'very pernicious vermin and not to be tolerated in the company of a princess of such descent'.

Whilst this letter was being taken by special messenger to the

King of Navarre, Henri III again ordered his sister to dismiss the two women. When with the greatest imprudence Marguerite still defied him, he decided on a final and drastic end to the whole business.

On 7 August 1583 the King, whose word was law, ordered Marguerite herself to leave Paris on the instant. And, finally, he sent two sergeants of the Watch that very night to Chanvallon's lodging, presumably to arrest him. Whether Marguerite managed to warn her lover in time or whether he himself had thought discretion the better part of valour, he had disappeared.

It was not until 12 August that Henry received the King's letter, to which he immediately replied in one of his best ironical styles. Very deferentially and humbly, he thanked His Majesty for the interest he took in his matrimonial affairs. 'For a long time', he continued, 'rumours of the evil and scandalous behaviour of Mmes de Duras and Béthune have been reaching me . . . but I considered that as my wife had the honour of being what she is to you, and to be living so near to Your Majesties, I would be misjudging your good intentions if I were to show myself more zealous to deal with the situation at a distance than Your Majesties were on the spot.'

Henri III did not in fact see Marguerite at all. The very day after his curt and brutal order to her to leave Paris immediately, he himself left for Bourbon-Lancy.

Marguerite had no option but to obey her brother and King. Her departure from Paris was almost a flight. She stopped for dinner at Bourg-la-Reine, where she knew the King would be passing on his own journey. Hoping against hope for an opportunity to speak to him, she had the windows of her carriage let down and watched out for his arrival. In due course he came— but swept past her without so much as a glance in her direction. Worse was to follow.

On the King's instructions, the next evening Marguerite's litter and all her escort were held up by a captain of the Royal Guard. When travelling in public, ladies of high degree wore a mask to conceal their features from vulgar eyes. Marguerite was ordered to unmask, an intolerable affront. Her gentlemen-in-waiting, secretary, doctor, and others, numbering ten, were then arrested and taken away by the Guard. They were joined later on by Mmes de Duras and Béthune, and even one of Marguerite's chambermaids, Barbara, who on the King's orders were travelling south by another route. All of them were put into solitary confinement, unable to communicate with one another, at the Abbey of Ferrières, near Montargis. There, according to L'Estoile, the King 'in person questioned them separately and demanded from each of them written and signed depositions; after which he sent certain of them to the Bastille. . . . He personally interrogated them regarding the relationships, morals, life and honour of the Queen his sister and even questioned them regarding the child that rumour said she had borne since her arrival at Court, whom it was suspected she had had by young Chanvallon, who in fact had already gone away. . . .' However, 'the King was unable to discover anything from the said prisoners'.

Whilst her ladies and servants were being so roughly handled by the King and his Guards, Marguerite waited all day at Palaisau for news of them. She waited in vain, and was finally obliged to continue her journey southwards. But before doing so she made a desperate appeal to her mother:

'MADAM,

'Were it not that in the misfortune in which I find myself I remembered that I have the honour of being your daughter, and hoping for your kindness, I would already by my own hand have ended my cruel fate; but remembering, Madam, the honour you have always shown me, I throw myself at your feet and very humbly beg you to take pity on my unendurable misery, and taking your creature under your protection to arrange that the King will be satisfied by my suffering and in future will accept me as his very humble servant, which I would always have wished to be, had I thought it agreeable to him; and, having received this kindness from you, Madam, I pray that you may give me a second life which I only wish to devote to your obedience and at all times sacrifice to your will, Madam, my soul being so troubled that I know not what I am writing. I end by very humbly kissing your hands and pray to God, Madam, to give you health and a long and contented life.'

But there was no reply.

The King had indeed kept his promise to make his errant sister very unhappy.

14 *Poison in the Air*

Marguerite slowly continued her miserable journey southwards. Whether or not it was a consolation to her that the King's sergeants had not found Chanvallon, she realized that they would never meet again. He was said to have fled to Germany. Unlike La Molle and Bussy, he enjoyed a long life, dying in 1630, when he was more than eighty. But all that remained of him to Marguerite were a few letters, poems, and the scandal for which she was now paying so bitterly.

Although she did not then know it, she was never again to see her mother, either.

Catherine, however, soon got in touch with her unhappy daughter. The Queen Mother disapproved as strongly as the King of Mme de Duras; nevertheless, she could not give her approval to the appalling indignities inflicted on the Queen of Navarre by the Royal Guard; the holding-up of her travelling coach, her compulsory unmasking, and the arrest of her servants. One simply did not, in any circumstances, inflict such insolence on a princess of the Blood Royal.

Yet Catherine was obliged to proceed with the greatest caution. She was old and ailing, the *mignons* Joyeuse and especially Epernon so possessed their self-styled 'father', the King, that her influence over him was by then almost negligible. In order to justify his treatment of Marguerite to the Queen Mother, Henri actually sent Epernon to explain matters to her, and when she dared to write to him regarding Mme de Duras—whose mother, the Duchess de Gramont, was moving heaven and earth to obtain her daughter's freedom—he was 'displeased' by her letter, although he did in due course release the two ladies-in-waiting, as he was bound to do.

With regard to Marguerite, however, Henri III showed unusual stubbornness, undoubtedly under Epernon's influence, Catherine advised her daughter to write to the King. Marguerite replied:

'MADAM,

'Following your commands in several letters and the advice of M. de Bellièvre, I am writing to the King. You know, Madam, how often I have sought his favour. God grant, Madam, that I shall be more successful this time. Since he cannot love me for my services to him and my very humble affection, I hope, Madam, that now that I am burdened with so many ills and annoyances, he will love me for pity's sake; and since, as it is said, kings resemble the gods, who love afflicted hearts, mine should be very pleasing to him. I do not doubt that he can do me much good, as he has done me harm, when it pleases him to help me to the one, as he has made me suffer the other. Apart from thus showing his good nature, he will oblige one who has the honour of being his sister, who was naturally most disposed to honour and love him, until he rewarded my affection with hatred, which if he pleases he can now cease to show me, by proving to the King my husband that on my side he has known only helpfulness, and will not allow the peace to be broken, the cause to which my life is devoted. I therefore very humbly beg you, Madam, to lend me a helping hand, and to believe that when I rejoin the King my husband—as I understand from Frontenac will be soon—I will render all the good services and offices in my power for the good of this kingdom, and very humbly pray you, Madam, to keep me in your good graces as your very humble and obedient servant, sister, and subject,

'MARGUERITE.'

The tone of this letter expresses far more hatred than love for the brother whom she blamed for all her unhappiness. Her letter to the King was as brief as it was proud:

'SIRE,

'If misfortunes had fallen on me alone, only I would be miserable, but since this is known not to be so, although they are of a different kind, this difference is not any more my fault than is the malice of those who, by their calumnies, would wish to condemn me as having deserved my misfortune, which is not the case.'

This was clearly a reference to the maltreatment of her two ladies and other servants involved in her disgrace. And the bold allusion to her calumniators was another open challenge to the Dukes Joyeuse and Epernon. Marguerite continued:

'Sire, putting all passion aside, let your own judgment therefore be my equitable judge. May it please you to consider dispassionately what I have had to endure to obey you; for those who have not felt such passions may blame the behaviour of those who have, without having considered them. Consider them, therefore, Sire, on the basis of the situation in which you find me. Even were I not your sister and servant and you my sole support, I would hope for your kindness as a Christian King, and that God, whom you serve so well, will preserve in you the pity you owe to all, and even more to myself as my King, and for which I beg you in bending the knee of my heart, which prays to our Lord to give Your Majesty permanent good health, as wishes the one who can only remain your very humble and obedient sister and subject.

'MARGUERITE.'

At that moment Marguerite's difficulties were increased by an almost total lack of funds. Catherine, who was still acting with the greatest caution, behind the scenes and mostly through Bellièvre, sent her 200,000 *livres*.

But Marguerite was over-optimistic in believing that she would soon rejoin her husband.

Shortly after the end of the Fosseuse affair, Navarre had found a new and very different mistress, who for several years completely dominated him and was even more inimical to Marguerite than her silly little predecessor had been. She was Diane d'Andouin, the widow of the Count of Guiche, a highly born and rich Catholic and, curiously enough, a kind of cultural imitator, almost a caricature, of Marguerite herself. Partly owing to his Queen's influence at the brilliant height of the Court of Nérac, partly perhaps because as he matured Henry of Navarre became far less uncouth, he began to take an interest in the arts and literature. Either he or Diane herself altered her name to Corisande, that of the heroine of a fashionable tale of the period, *Amadis des Gaules*, which he had read aloud to him. But this did not alter his mistress's ambitions. Like her unfortunate little predecessor, but rather more cleverly, Corisande aimed, after Henry should have discarded Marguerite, at becoming Queen Consort of the Bourbon heir to the throne of the Valois and even at ultimately placing on it her son, whose father might have been her former husband or Navarre himself.

Henry at that period had no personal interest in forgiving or taking Marguerite back. There were, however, two other matters involved. The first was to obtain from the King redress to his own honour, involved in the affront at Palaisau to his wife's. The second—Navarre having as usual a sharp eye to the main chance —was to use this scandalous incident as a bargaining counter in his attempt to regain some of the Huguenot strongholds in Gascony wrested from him by the Catholic King. The price of these was to be Marguerite's public rehabilitation by her husband. For if, as her brother the King had so clearly intimated, she was an adulteress and a whore, Navarre was under no compulsion to take her back. Henry's first move was to consult his Council; then, on 17 August he sent Duplessis-Mornay to the King, who was at Lyons, to ask him to clarify his charges against Marguerite:

'The Queen your sister', Duplessis tactfully but firmly pointed out to His Majesty, 'is on the way to rejoin the King her husband. What, Sire, will Christians say if the King of Navarre receives her and embraces her without hesitation, after she has been sent back to him so besmirched?'

'What can they say?' was Henri's cynical rejoinder, 'except that he is receiving his King's sister? What less could he do?'

Navarre did not consider this good enough, yet Henri obstinately refused to retract his accusations against Marguerite, only offering to send Bellièvre to discuss the matter after his own return to Paris two months later.

Bellièvre's first visit to Gascony was abortive. The King, unrelenting, was determined that Henry should take back his wife unconditionally. Bellièvre's instructions were to place all the blame on Mmes de Duras and Béthune, and to deny altogether the 'rumours' that any affront had been intended or done to the Queen of Navarre.

According to L'Estoile, in one of his letters to Bellièvre Henri III stated that Navarre 'knew how kings were liable to be deceived by false reports, and that the most virtuous princesses were not exempt from calumny, even in the case of his late mother [Jeanne of Albret], of whom he knew what had been said and how badly she had always been spoken of.

'The King of Navarre, having seen those letters, began to laugh, and in the presence of all the nobility there said to M. de Bellièvre: "The King does me much honour in his letters; in the earlier ones he called me a cuckold, and in the later ones the son of a whore. My thanks to him for it."'

When Navarre demanded the return of his strongholds, Bellièvre having no instructions to deal with that matter, negotiations were broken off. Navarre lost patience and on 21 November recaptured Mont-de-Marsan by assault. He further categorically informed Bellièvre that he would not receive Marguerite until all the royal garrisons in the towns adjacent to Nérac were withdrawn.

Marguerite meanwhile found herself between the devil, her brother the King, and the deep blue sea, the King her husband. On 23 September, when she was at Jarnac, Navarre wrote to her forbidding her to come any further until his demands were satisfied. Pitifully she replied to him that the King had ordered her to proced to Coutras, and that she dared not disobey him. There she remained from the end of October until the end of November.

Early in December she arrived at Agen, where she wrote desperately to Bellièvre for news of his negotiations with Navarre:

'. . . Having since [last writing to him] heard that you were with the King my husband, to whom I am sending this messenger to receive his instructions regarding the decisions he took with you; living in such anxiety that I can find no rest until I am out of this purgatory, as I may well call it, not knowing whether it will lead me to paradise or hell; but whichever it is it can hardly be worse than what I have been made to suffer during the past six months.'

Perhaps in order to mitigate the blatancy of his bargaining over her with the King, Henry wrote to his wife on 17 December, explaining to her in friendly terms that:

'It is necessary that when we meet it should be of our own free will; in my opinion, you would do well to tell the Queen your mother so, and I will then make it plain that I cannot be forced to do anything under compulsion. And also I do not believe any of the calumnies. That is all, my dear, I can tell you at present. Without all these complications, we might have had the pleasure of being together by now.'

Marguerite was not taken in, yet she had no option but still to wait for the outcome of the sordid haggling between the two kings in which she was involved. Henry meanwhile dug in his heels:

'As soon as I hear that the garrisons have been removed according to the King's instructions', he wrote on 8 February, 'I shall leave for Nérac to receive my wife there.' And later in the same month: 'Withdraw from Condom and Agen the two companies that have been placed there, in order that I may with pleasure receive my wife at Nérac.'

In January Henri III had ordered the garrisons to be partially withdrawn. But he himself had not withdrawn one word of his accusations against Marguerite, leaving it to Catherine and Bellièvre to explain them away to Navarre.

The basic reason why the two kings found it necessary to come to an understanding was the obvious fact that Monsieur was dying. After more strenuous efforts by the Queen Mother to persuade him to give up his Flanders adventure, François finally capitulated, and on 11 February arrived in Paris, where once again he was reconciled with the King.

Henri III and Navarre reached a compromise satisfactory to both. The garrisons of Agen and Condom were withdrawn and only fifty, a token number, of royal troops continued to occupy Bazan, whilst Navarre retained Mont-de-Marsan.

Bellièvre was instructed by the Queen Mother privately to give her daughter some maternal advice. In spite of the official versions of Marguerite's 'purity and the honourable behaviour she had always shown as the result of her birth and education', Catherine had no illusions in the matter.

'Please tell her before your departure', she wrote to her envoy, 'reminding her of all the things ... that should be remembered and done by a person of her quality, that she should be accompanied by honourable people, men and women; for others beside ourselves may do us honour or dishonour. The company we keep has a great deal to do with it, and especially in the case of princesses who are young and think themselves beautiful. ...' Catherine herself had once thought her daughter the most glamorous princess in Europe and had encouraged her in this view of herself. That small slap in her face might not have been due to her changed opinion of Marguerite's attractiveness, but simply a mark of disapproval of her use of it. And, very bluntly alluding to the Fosseuse incident which had so seriously annoyed her, the Queen Mother added: 'Especially let her not make a fuss over those girls to whom her husband may make love, for he will think that she is very pleased for him to make love to someone else, so that she may do the same; let her no longer allow him to make love in her house to her women and girls, for a woman who loves her husband will never love his whore.' Had Catherine but known it, there was no longer any danger of that.

At long last, almost exactly eight months after Marguerite's expulsion from Paris, the King and Queen of Navarre met at Port-Sainte-Marie, leaving the same afternoon for Nérac.

The final delay before their reunion occurred for two very

different reasons. During her previous residence in Gascony, Marguerite had always spent Lent—with her husband's consent—in one of the Catholic towns, notably Agen, and this she again did.

Henry was at Pau, the Huguenot centre she most detested. His counsellors were not at all delighted that he should welcome back his adulterous Catholic Queen. Christian charity and compassion were not the basis of the pastors' creed; there were even murmurings that she deserved to suffer the fate of the Biblical woman taken in adultery. Nor were they gratified that their Huguenot ruler had installed in the castle of Hagetmau, close to Pau, his reigning mistress, the Catholic Countess of Guiche. By then Corisande had acquired an influence over Henry that seemed to make his affair with Fosseuse a mere passing fancy. Gossip even said that she had cast a spell on him; certainly he was almost completely under her thumb. Even more vigorously than the pastors, Corisande objected to her lover taking back his morally bedraggled Queen. Yet there was hardly any need for her to order him as she apparently did, to do so only for appearances' sake.

No husband, however profligate himself, however willing that his wife should also amuse herself sexually so long as she did so 'in her privacy', could help feeling resentment towards a wife like Margot, whose love-life had become a public scandal. As he had never been attracted by her when they were still on the best of terms, it was unlikely that he would then be so.

The King and Queen of Navarre appeared together for the first time in the Long Gallery of the Castle of Nérac, where, said an eye-witness, La Huguerye, 'I saw this Princess constantly dissolving into tears, so much so that when they were both at table, where I wished to see them (it was very late, by candle-light in those days), I never saw a more tear-stained face, nor eyes redder with weeping. And I felt great pity for this Princess, seeing her seated next to the King, her husband, who was being entertained by I know not what frivolous conversation by his courtiers, whilst neither he nor anyone else spoke to this Princess, which made me agree with what Du Pin'—Henry's secretary and Marguerite's old enemy from Pau days—'told me, that the King had been forced to take her back.'

Commenting on this pathetic picture, Mariéjol, Marguerite's most distinguished biographer, suggested that she might have been weeping tears of joy! In her public isolation and ostracism, this seems somewhat unlikely. Yet a few days later Marguerite was indeed writing both to her mother and her brother the King, telling them how delighted she was to be back at Nérac. It seems more probable that, knowing herself to have absolutely no choice in the matter, she had decided on a face-saving policy. After having so unfortunately publicly broken down on the night of her return, as soon as she recovered her self-control she was not going to give her enemies the satisfaction of gloating over her misery. And she was surrounded by enemies, with not a single influential friend to support her against them.

In this situation the death of her beloved brother François was a tragedy for Marguerite. He died on 10 June 1584 at the age of thirty, 'of an hæmorrhage accompanied by a slow fever, which had so shrunken him little by little', wrote L'Estoile, 'that he was all dried up and emaciated'. He was only sincerely mourned and regretted by his old mother and his adored and devoted sister.

With the death of Monsieur the political scene in France underwent a new series of upheavals and convulsions, leading to the last Wars of Religion, in which Marguerite became personally and disastrously involved.

The immediate result of this new situation was a mutual attempt by Henri III and Navarre, his acknowledged heir, to draw closer together. Had Henry then reverted to Catholicism, as in due course he was obliged to do, much bloodshed and suffering might have been spared the French people. Henri III and the Queen Mother both foresaw that this would be the case, but in spite of his obstinate Huguenoterie they were forced to come to friendly terms with Navarre owing to the growing threat to the Valois crown.

Henri of Guise, Scarface and Marguerite's former admirer, had become an agent of Philip of Spain, from whom he was drawing heavy subsidies in order to oust the Valois and, as he dared to hope, ascend the throne of France himself. He was immensely popular with the predominantly Catholic nation. The French people, always clearsighted and cynical regarding their rulers, were perfectly aware of and disgusted by their King's homosexuality, the power over him of the Dukes, and the vast sums they were extorting from him and the nation. Playing on this potential disloyalty of the Catholic aristocracy and citizenry to the throne, Guise, with his Spanish subsidies, had forged the League into a powerful instrument of revolt and was beginning military operations. He was joined by thousands of Catholics who might otherwise have remained loyal to the Valois had they not feared the accession in due course of the Bourbon Huguenot, Navarre, who might well then turn the tables on them to avenge the Massacre of St Bartholomew.

In order to cement his alliance with his heir and brother-in-law and hoping to achieve his conversion, Henri III, with the Queen Mother's full approval, decided to send to him his most trusted envoy, his 'son' Epernon. Since François' death, only Henri, whom she had always adored, and Marguerite, who had given her so much trouble recently, remained to Catherine. Both she and the King were well aware of Marguerite's implacable hatred for Epernon and his for her. But in their view it was necessary that both the King and Queen of Navarre should receive the super-*mignon* with the fullest honours. Henri used his old mother as his instrument in transmitting his instructions to this effect to his sister. Navarre, anxious to conciliate his liege lord and ally, whom he would need in his own defence against Guise, expected the same conciliatory behaviour from his wife.

So soon after François' death, this situation placed another almost intolerable strain on Marguerite. She realized very clearly that her arch-enemy would gloat on seeing her, helpless and defenceless, at Nérac. Catherine decided that it was necessary to make her duty in the matter clear to her. So she wrote to Bellièvre, who was still there, that so soon after the death of their brother it would be a bad time for her to do anything that would offend the King, 'as I know that it will do if she does not see M. d'Epernon, I mean, as coming from her King and elder brother, bringing her letters from him. I am sure that if she does see him she will be on as good terms with him [Henri] as she ever was, but if she does not, she will cause me a great deal of trouble.'

And she wrote to her daughter to the same effect.

On 7 July Marguerite herself wrote to the Marshal de Matignon, telling him how she felt about this appalling dilemma. Her mother had ordered her to receive M. de'Epernon '. . . with such comminations and threats that, as I love her and wish to set her mind at rest, I am forced to obey her; nevertheless, I have postponed doing so until I receive the commands of the King my husband, to whom I owe this mark of respect. I expect a reply in six or seven days. She is so distressed by our loss that my fear of adding to it compels me to put such a strain on myself as I would have thought to be beyond my endurance.'

Navarre had already met Epernon at Pamiers, where they had apparently reached a good understanding. For appearances' sake, Henry pretended to consult Marguerite before inviting him to Nérac, but, as they both knew, she had absolutely no choice in the matter.

'I realize', she wrote to Bellièvre, 'that I can neither escape from nor avoid the misfortune of this meeting. It is not the first nor the last that I believe will come to me from that quarter. But since my life has become like that of a slave, I shall have to bow to the force and power I am unable to resist.'

That was in fact what she had become. But was her slavery due solely to the extreme malice and hatred of Henri III and Epernon? Her critics did with some justice claim that she had at least partly brought it on herself by her unconcealed passion for Chanvallon, and the licence she had allowed to pervade her establishment in Paris. That was undoubtedly the Queen Mother's view.

When they met on 4 August at Nérac, where Epernon remained for the following two days, both she and he outwardly observed the conventions and there were no disagreeable incidents. Marguerite's first lady, Mme de Noailles, who at the Queen Mother's suggestion had succeeded Mme de Duras, hastened to assure Catherine that they had been on the best of terms. According, however, to Brantôme, 'the King and M. d'Epernon were satisfied, but those who were more clearsighted and who knew the Queen's character, understood very well that she was on her guard, and she herself said that she had been playing a part in this comedy very much against her will.'

But if Navarre was satisfied with his Queen's submission, this did not in any way change his attitude towards her. No sooner had Epernon left to rejoin Henri III at Lyons than on 7 August Henry promptly departed also, once again for Hagetmau and Corisande.

Marguerite knew that her only chance of recapturing him was to give him the much-needed heir who might restore his affection for her. With this in view, whilst Henry was spending all his time in Corisande's company, Marguerite set off on a pilgrimage to Notre-Dame-de-Bonne-Encontre, near Agen, to pray for the son she so urgently longed for. And from 20 September until 10 October she was taking a cure at Encausse, possibly to aid this miracle to occur.

But it takes two to make a baby. However ambitious and domineering Corisande may have been, Henry had no desire nor intention in any case to resume sexual relations with his wife. Although he had written that he did not believe the calumnies against her, there was a risk that if he did sleep with Marguerite and she did not become pregnant she might still conceive a bastard by some other man and pass it off as his heir.

L'Estoile wrote that 'the Queen appeared greatly displeased with her husband, who neglected her, having slept with her only on one night since the affront to which the King her brother had subjected her in August 1583 . . . cajoling her with fine words and an outwardly friendly manner, but nothing more'.

Marguerite may already have been seeking some form of escape from her sterile life of slavery. Her tribulations were increased by the return to Nérac at that time of her former transient lover, Turenne. He had left Gascony to fight in Flanders, where he was captured by the Spaniards and released only a few days before the death of François.

Turenne was a firm Protestant and his captivity had not made him hate the Catholics any less. It was also said that at the time —three years previously—when he had been Marguerite's lover, she had taunted him with his apparent sexual inadequacy. Whether or not this was the case, he now intrigued against her and it was on his instigation that Navarre took a foolish step. He arrested one of Marguerite's secretaries, Ferrand, who acted as her travelling messenger between France and Gascony. The charge against this victim was that he was carrying compromising messages from the Queen of Navarre to her former aspirant, Henri of Guise, the head of the League, at enmity both with the King of France and the King of Navarre.

As subsequent events were to prove, this was not an unfounded accusation. But at that stage, in spite of being taken to Pau and put to the 'question', Ferrand provided no evidence against Marguerite. Navarre had no authority to arrest him in France and in order to justify himself claimed that as his wife's servant, Ferrand was also his own. He also trumped up the charge that Marguerite had ordered Ferrand to poison him.

Fortunately Henri III and the Queen Mother supported Marguerite in this crisis, not so much for love of her as in indignation that her husband should have infringed the royal prerogative. The King sent a personal envoy, Brûlart, President of the Paris Parliament, to Navarre, who, seeing that he had gone too far, apologized both to him and to his wife for having thus maltreated her secretary. Marguerite replied dryly to her husband that had she thought him so interested in her affairs she would first have shown him the messages she was sending.

But not only accusations of poisoning were in the air; their personal relationship was by then equally poisoned. Marguerite began to fear for her own life if she remained at Nérac; she well knew how impatiently Corisande was waiting to step into her shoes. And by then she had completely given up hope of any reconciliation with her husband, or of having a child by him.

On 19 March, which was the beginning of Lent in the year 1585, Marguerite left for Agen, where with her husband's usual consent she apparently intended to do no more than perform her Easter duties. Had Henry suspected that Marguerite was never to return to Nérac he might not so easily have let her go.

15   Disaster at Agen

At one time Agen had belonged to England. Richard I's sister, Joan, was given it as part of her dowry on her marriage to Raymond, Count of Toulouse. The city did not finally revert to the French Crown until 1453.

The centre of the district known as the Agenois, the town was always an important military site. Situated on the Garonne, it was encircled by walls with twenty-one towers, well equipped for defence.

The citizens were fervent Catholics and possessed considerable civic pride. Navarre had occupied Agen in 1577, and ever since then their principal anxiety was that he might do so again.

Under the Valois monarchy Agen formed part of Marguerite's own appanage or royal endowment: Countess of Agen was one of her subsidiary titles. She had always been popular with the inhabitants, partly because it pleased them to have a Daughter of France as their mistress, partly on account of her piety, and partly because of its practical value to them. In addition to a fine Cathedral dating from the twelfth century, there were many churches and religious foundations, to the upkeep of which Marguerite had generously contributed during her four months' previous residence there before her second sojourn at Nérac.

When she returned to Agen on 19 March in the following year, ostensibly to perform her Easter duties, she was accompanied by only a few ladies and gentlemen-in-waiting. To have brought all her Court with her would have immediately aroused Henry's suspicions.

The Countess took up her quarters in a fine house—Agen contained many admirable examples of domestic architecture—belonging to Mme de Cambefort, widow of a prosperous citizen. When the rest of her retinue joined her, and the local Catholic nobility flocked into the town from all over the Agenois to do her homage, she soon re-formed her Court, and these social activities added to the revenues of the local tradesmen and purveyors. All appeared at first to be perfectly normal and tranquil.

But Marguerite had reached a point of no return. Although she had never loved Henry, she had until then sincerely liked him, in spite of his many infidelities. Fosseuse was the beginning of the end, however. Almost certainly she did not in her heart of hearts believe that Navarre intended to poison her, yet owing to Corisande's influence, his ingratitude and callousness towards her, and the bitter tears she had shed on the night of her return to Nérac, her mind had become riddled with hatred for him.

A return to Paris was out of the question. The King himself had barred that way of escape to her, and their mutual hatred was even deeper than her resentment towards her husband.

Nor could Margot rely on her mother's sympathy. Whenever it came to a clash between her adored son and wayward daughter, Catherine invariably supported the King, although she did endeavour to help Marguerite, perennially penniless, financially —latterly through Bellièvre mostly, or other intermediaries. The Queen Mother had been shocked and grieved by the scandal of the Hôtel de Navarre, for which, however, she had placed all the blame on Mme de Duras, insisting that she, too, left Paris. To replace her she had provided her daughter with a blameless first lady, Mme de Noailles. It was therefore the height of defiant imprudence for Marguerite, as soon as she was settled at Agen, to take back into her service both Mme de Duras and her husband.

At this crisis in her life Marguerite lost all the good sense, brilliance of intellect and philosophical understanding that were her Medici heritage through her birth and education. She reverted wholly to the Valois tradition of unwise gratitude and devotion to such unworthy retainers as the Duras couple, and of wildcat schemes and ambitions. It was as if the spirit of her departed brother François had entered into her. Its final manifestation was that she, as he had so often done in the past, decided to play at soldiers.

Her rationalization of her hatred for Navarre took the form of persuading herself that she had a mission to save Guyenne from his Huguenoterie and Protestant desecration. Her hatred for the King was sublimated by her contempt for his homosexuality and passion for Epernon into the cause of rescuing the throne and France from those upstarts, the Dukes. Only one man appeared to her worthy of her support and able to give her the protection she needed, the powerful Duke of Guise, head of the Catholic League.

At a meeting on 4 April, the assembled Council of Agen resolved to bar the approaches to their town to Henry of Navarre. This was the moment for which Marguerite was waiting. She had already proved herself an able public speaker and her natural eloquence did not then fail her. Whilst warning the Council to be on their guard against any Huguenot offensive led by her husband, she informed them at the same time that she was proposing to raise two companies of infantry for her own greater protection. To this proposal they gave their consent.

At first neither Marshal de Matignon, the King's commander in Guyenne and one of Marguerite's loyal admirers, nor Bellièvre suspected her of anything more than justified self-defence. Matignon wrote reassuringly to Henri III that 'as regards the said lady she does not wish to do anything to displease the King, but has taken refuge there as she no longer felt safe at Nérac, knowing the ill-will towards her of the Countess of Guiche and her power over the King of Navarre', and he reported that he himself had provided her with a company of men-at-arms and another of infantry. Bellièvre took a similar view, even informing the Queen Mother that he had 'not failed to point out to M. de Clervault [one of Navarre's courtiers] the harm the King of Navarre is doing himself by preferring the friendship of the Countess to his wife's. . . .'

Both Marguerite and Mme de Noailles wrote to Catherine for financial assistance. Knowing nothing at that point of the final break-up of the Navarre marriage, the Queen Mother asked Bellièvre and Villeroy to request some help for his sister from the King, since her necessity was so great that 'she did not even have enough meat to eat'.

The King might possibly have granted Marguerite some relief, not for her own sake, but because Agen was one of his important citadels, to be held for the Crown against both Navarre and the League. But Marguerite's intention to link herself with Guise was betrayed to Henri III on 1 April. And she had indeed already sent Choisnin, her former secretary, whom she had previously dismissed, but, unfortunately for herself, reinstated, to negotiate with Guise and ask him for funds. Choisnin proved himself a scoundrel, handed Guise his mistress's letter, but suppressed her instructions, which he later published.

By the time Matignon received the King's command to withhold all military support from the Queen of Navarre it was too late.

The situation came to a climax on 15 May.

Having placed her troops on guard at strategic points, the Daughter of France, Queen of Navarre and Countess of Agen, summoned all the leading local officials to a meeting at the Bishop's seat. Here she made a crucial speech to them. After repeating her accusations against Navarre, she informed them that the King's Marshal, Matignon, was also conspiring against her. As their Countess and ruler, she warned them that civil war was about to break out, and on the pretext that she wished still further to strengthen the town's defences she peremptorily demanded that they hand over to her the keys of the city. There were a few murmurs of dissent and objections, but, only too conscious of the presence outside of the two military companies, the citizens finally, with as much good grace as they could muster, did hand over the keys to their liege lady.

This public act of taking over the town of Agen on behalf of the League was Marguerite's final severance of her own loyalty to her brother the King and the Crown of France, to which, had she been a male, she would have been the heir. The Salic Law, however, disinherited her as a woman from the succession, which would therefore pass to that renegade Bourbon, her husband. Quite possibly her inner resentment at this fact inspired her ruthless militancy at that point.

When news of this *coup* by her uncontrollable daughter reached the Queen Mother, Catherine was naturally furious. At that moment she herself was once again endeavouring to act as the King's mediator in coming to terms with Guise and the League. From Epernay she wrote to Bellièvre on 28 May that Marguerite was 'now fortifying Agen and filling the town with soldiers' and that, to add insult to injury, Duras and his wife were with her. She declared that her daughter was giving her so much trouble that it was enough to kill her, and she added bitterly that 'God has left me this creature as a punishment for my sins and a scourge'.

Marguerite's forces in Agen were, however, growing, as local Catholic recruits joined them. The two companies which formed their nucleus were commanded respectively by two young officers, Ligarde and Aubiac.

Aubiac was the brother of one of the Queen's maids-of-honour. But he was a soldier, not a courtier. He was young, sturdy, red-haired and red-nosed, and freckled. When he was first received by Marguerite he was instantly swept off his feet by her glamour and beauty.

'Let me be hanged,' he exclaimed, 'if I might only once sleep with that woman!' A wish that the poor young man's bad fairy was in due course to grant him.

On 14 September Guise wrote personally to Philip of Spain, requesting him urgently to provide Marguerite with 'a good round sum' of money in order that she, his ally at Agen, should not be abandoned by her people, 'now that we are most in need of her assistance'. He himself, meanwhile, sent her reinforcements under François de Lignerac, the League's delegate in High Auvergne.

Lignerac took over the defence of Agen. He was an extremely tough and wily soldier, a dour Auvergnac. If, like the young captain, Aubiac, he then fell in love with the beautiful adherent of the League whom he was sent to protect, he was also realistically aware that as Daughter of France and Queen of Navarre she might prove to be his trump card if he played his hand correctly.

After she lost Chanvallon, Marguerite never fell in love again. During her brief and unhappy second stay at Nérac she had no known liaison; Henry's fear that if he slept with her she might foist a bastard on him was based on no actual evidence that this would have been the case.

In the second half of the twentieth century an increasing number of young women would not refrain from sexual pleasure because they were not in love with their partners. At the age of thirty-two Margot's instincts were strong and normal. In neither suppressing nor sublimating her sexual desires she was 400 years ahead of her time and, understandably enough, was regarded as a nymphomaniac by her shocked contemporaries and by her biographers in her own country right down to the present day.

But until then she had been fastidious in her choice of lovers; they were handsome, well-born men, poets as well as swordsmen, courtiers experienced in the refined and almost ritualistic approaches to a princess's favours. At Agen, however, Margot was surrounded almost solely by military men with no courtly airs and graces whatever. Possibly their very uncouthness might then have attracted her, since she was seeing herself as a semi-Amazonian figure. Aubiac undoubtedly did become her lover; at that stage in their relationship Lignerac did not. She never liked him, but it is uncertain whether she had already begun to fear him.

Yet even if it was Lignerac and not Marguerite herself who was chiefly responsible for the tragedy that was shortly to fall on the helpless citizens of Agen, their Countess at that stage showed none of the finer feminine feelings—compassion, concern for the welfare of the common people, and great generosity towards them—that until then had made her so popular with them.

After taking over the keys of the city the Countess of Agen immediately began considerable works of fortification, which were highly unpopular with the townsfolk. Her military advisers decided to build an impregnable citadel, which would take in roughly one-third to one-quarter of the entire city. The focal point of this fortress was to be the Jacobin Convent, which would be linked to Marguerite's residence in order that if need be she might take refuge there at short notice. The fortifications were also to include three sets of ditches and ramparts on the outskirts.

An entire quarter, the best in the town, was ruthlessly pulled down to make way for these extensive operations.

'The Queen had bought a few of the houses', wrote Merki, 'but lacked the money with which to pay for them . . . and the owners themselves were forced to pull down their own homes, even the stones of which were used on the new works. In this way fifty houses were destroyed in a few days and another fifty were in course of destruction.' The peasants and agricultural workers of the surrounding countryside were conscripted into digging the trenches and waterworks; there was no money to pay them either, although they were provided with bread and wine.

M. de Duras, meanwhile, was leading a small offensive against the King of Navarre, which was inevitably to prove abortive. Henry refrained from taking the initiative against his wife, preferring at that point to remain on as good terms as possible with the King and Matignon. In a letter dated 28 June he wrote:

'. . . Those of Agen are getting busy'—the Duras couple were triumphant—'you would not believe the insolent things they are saying. We are being as patient as possible; please God that we may continue to be so.' And, writing to Turenne in August, he informed him that 'Duras is going to see the King of Spain and in spite of whooping-cough and the plague, which are sparing few [of the unfortunate inhabitants of Agen], he is asking our enemies to provide the Queen with funds to defeat the heretics who are allied with her husband.'

The Catholic King, however, did not respond, either to Guise's or to Duras's requests. Marguerite's finances continued to worsen.

According to her household accounts for 1585, she was maintaining a Court of 235 people, not including the pages. There was no money to pay the troops, and although the homes of the few unhappy local Huguenots were sacked, this yielded next to nothing.

There followed a compulsory levy on the citizenry, the richer of whom were taxed up to ten *écus* daily, and if they were unable or unwilling to pay they were pillaged by the soldiery or imprisoned. The usual atrocities by uncouth mercenaries were committed; one housewife was raped by three men in the presence of her husband, whom they then garrotted. Although they were beheaded for this crime and their heads were exposed as a warning to their fellows on the Gate of the Pine, indiscipline continued, and the Bishop and other notables went in deputation to their Countess to beg her to order the persecution of the Huguenots to cease.

When Catherine succeeded in concluding the Peace of Nemours with the League, Marguerite's name was deliberately omitted from the list of its leaders. Nevertheless, on 17 August she had a great bonfire lit in the middle of Agen and a *Te Deum* sung in the Cathedral in celebration of this event.

The aggressors from Agen under Duras were driven back by Navarre, and therefore the necessity to complete the fortifications against possible Huguenot attack seemed still more urgent. But matters did not turn out that way.

The plague. . . .

This terrible scourge, mentioned in Navarre's letter, broke out in Agen during that summer—not surprisingly, considering the upheavals the building of the new fortress and fortifications were causing, with the release into the open of thousands of infected rats. Between 1,500 and 1,800 inhabitants died of it in a few months. Almost incredibly, and showing to what extent she had by then lost all practical common sense, Marguerite refused to believe in its presence, complaining that it was a mere rumour spread by the Huguenots to compel her to evacuate her city. And when some of the more sensible citizens attempted to fly from it, all departures were forbidden: neither men, women, nor children and no household goods were allowed to pass through the heavily guarded gates.

This was the last straw.

The defenceless people of Agen, their houses destroyed over their heads, their wives and children half-starved and dying of a horrible disease, the undisciplined soldiery quartered on them having to be fed first from their few remaining victuals, crushed by taxation, yet unable to move out, decided to rebel. Yet it never occurred to these good Catholics, who were also loyal Frenchmen, to hand over their city to the hated Calvinists. All they wished for was to re-establish their former situation, when they had lived under the King in quiet and comfortable prosperity. Marshal de Matignon was His Majesty's representative in the Agenois, and to him they sent a delegation, begging him to deliver them from their Countess, her brutal soldiery and their excesses.

Matignon could no longer believe that Marguerite was innocent of treason to her brother and King. But she was Henri's sister, the Daughter of France, and he could not completely rule out the possibility of a future reconciliation between them. He therefore took care to protect his own interests in such an event, remote though it might be. From Tonneins, on 20 September, he sent a reply to the citizens of Agen, giving them precise instructions:

'Following His Majesty's orders', it ran, 'we empower you to return the town to its former liberty and obedience to the said Lord; to seize and hold its forts, and to expel by force of arms if necessary the captains, soldiers, and other men of war there, and to admit us to hold it in His Majesty's service.' But in unmistakable terms Matignon added that they should do this 'with all honour, respect, and very humble obedience due to the Queen of Navarre, her ladies and maids'.

After receiving this authorization, at dawn on 25 September a group of armed citizens, most of them leading officials and certainly no disorderly rabble, numbering around thirty, marched to the Gate of the Pine, where they surrounded and surprised the guard. But very soon the captains and soldiery counter-attacked them so ferociously that all but eighteen of them fled. These brave men, however, managed to barricade themselves inside the Gate whilst awaiting reinforcements.

Although the work on the citadel was not yet completed, a few days previously Marguerite had taken up residence in the Jacobin Convent, where a large quantity of food, arms and gunpowder had already been stored.

The revolt spread from below and a howling mob advanced on the Convent. According to one of the fathers, an eye-witness, 'a soldier of the King of Navarre, who had managed to gain entry, set fire to the ammunition, which immediately exploded, bringing down the novices' quarters and burying the novices as well as two of the fathers in the ruins.'

When this disaster occurred and the entire city was in an up-roar of civil war, Marguerite was about to sit down to her mid-day meal. She was apparently totally unaware of her betrayal by the outraged citizens to Matignon, to whose advancing troops they were already opening the gates. Had she remained, she would inevitably have been handed over by them to the Marshal and possibly by him to Navarre. In her terror and despair, she completely lost her head. It was Lignerac who, with a soldier's presence of mind, whisked her away through the New Gate, the one remaining gate to safety.

'The poor Queen', Brantôme, staunchly loyal as usual, wrote, 'all she could do was to mount pillion on the horse of one gentle-man whilst Mme de Duras did the same with another, and so saved themselves with all possible haste', leaving the entire Court to survive the rabble as best they might, escaping with their lives, but nothing else whatever.

'On that day, 2 October 1585', L'Estoile wrote with uncon-cealed sympathy, 'the burghers of the town of Agen, unable to bear any longer the tyrannies and indignities inflicted on them by the League, under the command and orders of the Queen of Navarre, rose against her, beat, drove off and killed her soldiers, and forced her to leave their city, and had it not been for Marshal de Matignon they would have thrown her over the walls in spite of her rank and quality, having furiously mutinied against her owing to the bad treatment they had suffered from her.'

Understandably enough.

It was said of the later Bourbons that they learned nothing and forgot nothing. Of the Valois it might have been said that they learned nothing and forgot everything.

In that unfortunate six months for herself and the people of Agen, Marguerite of Valois showed that she was indeed a Daughter of the Blood Royal.

16   Aubiac's Bad Fortune

It is uncertain which of her cavalry officers bore Marguerite away from Agen, but very probably it was Aubiac, since Lignerac had to remain to cover her retreat.

There is no doubt, however, that her flight was as painful and exhausting as it was precipitate. She had no time to take anything with her, not even her jewels. There was not an instant to be lost, and when she was hoisted into the saddle she was not even provided with the small cushion used on such occasions by ladies to mitigate the jolting and bumping on unsurfaced roads and stony tracks. She was, of course, riding side-saddle, and soon her leg became intolerably painful and abrased from contact with the hard leather.

But Marguerite bore the soreness and discomforts she was suffering with fortitude, since all that then mattered to her was to reach her refuge as quickly as might be. She was followed by a troop of eighty cavaliers and lancers to guard her on the journey from the brigands and marauding soldiery infesting the country-side, as well as the more orderly men of war—those of the King under Matignon, and Navarre's Huguenots—into whose clutches she so dreaded falling.

Her destination was the stronghold of Carlat, a fortress in High Auvergne under the command of Lignerac's brother, de Marzé. Carlat was another of the Queen of Navarre's appanages, which had come down to Marguerite through her mother, Catherine de Medici. It was perched on a precipice amongst wild and rocky mountainsides and gorges. There, she felt, she would find safety from her enemies.

It was on a Wednesday that her painful journey began, and on that day she rode in that manner for over 30 kilometres, spending a brief night's rest at the Castle of Brassac in the Tarn and Garonne. On the following day, off again at dawn, she rode nearly twice as far, and on the Friday still another 40 kilometres. By the Saturday she was understandably exhausted. But as she had by then reached the foothills and was approaching the mountains guarding Carlat, she felt able to relax a little. She spent the Sunday in prayer and hearing Masses at the Abbey of Montsalvy. There she also met de Marzé, who came to receive her with 500 local gentlemen, who had descended from their fastnesses to welcome the Daughter of France and accompany her to Carlat with the honours befitting a Queen.

For so Marguerite was received when she finally arrived at Carlat on Monday, 20 September, after having spent up to ten hours daily for nearly a week in her excoriating and exhausting flight.

Carlat was an ancient feudal fortress which had originally belonged to Jacques d'Armagnac, Duke of Nemours, one of the great landowners who had matched their strength against King Louis XI in the fifteenth century, and lost their heads and possessions to him. It had remained, however, an almost impregnable stronghold. Built on a mountain spur of black basalt, on all sides the ramparts dropped precipitously down to the banks of two small streams, the Embenne and Restenne, which in spring and autumn swelled into torrents. Within these double ramparts rose crenellated towers, protecting the enclosed buildings forming a miniature city—barracks, a church, a nunnery and two palaces. In medieval times, and under the Duke of Nemours, who was a man of culture and erudition as well as a rebel, Carlat had been a centre of splendour and luxury, richly furnished and decorated, with renowned sculpture and tapestry. But since it had passed to the Daughters of France as their appanage, the fortress had fallen on sad times. No princess, unless she found herself in Marguerite's desperate situation, would have wanted to bury herself alive in such a wild and lonely spot. The palaces, abandoned over the years, had been pillaged and denuded of all their treasures, even of the barest furniture and necessities. Yet even this wild retreat had not escaped the ravages of the Wars of Religion: it had changed hands several times between Huguenots and Catholics, and its former elegant buildings had been used for the quartering and stabling of rough soldiery and their mounts. Although Carlat was one of Marguerite's appanages, as a strongpoint it was—like Agen—under the King's command, and de Marzé had recently occupied it on the orders of Henri III.

Arriving at Carlat in the autumn darkness, to the sound of rushing torrents and wailing winds, Marguerite might well have been appalled when, after crossing the drawbridge and court-yards, she was led into her new palace, and by the light of flicker-ing torches and candles was conducted up the cold staircase to her bedroom. Its high walls, on which decaying tapestries were still hanging raggedly, rose to an almost invisible ceiling, blackened by age and neglect. And although the cobwebs had been hastily brushed away, the room contained hardly any furniture, not even a small bedside table.

The invaluable accounts of her household, preserved in the French National Archives, reveal these depressing details. The Queen of Navarre had to send for a carpenter to the nearby town of Aurillac, to make some hasty repairs to her residence and the chapel, including new window-frames and pews, and to provide some makeshift furniture until her own should have arrived.

Matignon entered Agen on 26 September. He rewarded the local councillors and officials for their loyalty to the King and their rebellion against Marguerite and the Leaguers. But he took care to see that none of her staff were molested or prevented from joining her at Carlat, and that all her possessions were in due course sent on to her. Her account books for the year 1585 gave a list of all those goods, for the removal of which she paid: 'trunks and boxes, linen, furniture, carriages, horses and mules'. No doubt Marguerite was most relieved by the delivery, a few days after her own arrival at Carlat, of her bed-of-state. Her coachman was paid for driving her elaborate gilded coach there, the local peasantry in the villages through which it passed flocking to gaze at it. Even bottles of toilet waters were delivered by messenger and figured in the inventory.

Marguerite's secretary, Choisnin, whom she had sent to Guise, had remained in Agen in charge of her voluminous wardrobe, jewels, and silverware. De Marzé was sent to escort him to Carlat, chiefly to protect the Queen's valuables he was bringing with him, whilst her treasurer, Antoine Charpentier, and the controller of her household, François Rousselet, remained at Agen to settle up her bills. By the end of the first week in December most of Marguerite's possessions had arrived at Carlat, and she was able to install herself in the so-called Palace of Bridoré in the comfort and near-luxury which until then she had so badly missed. But her troubles were merely beginning.

The only piece of jewellery that vanished during the removal from Agen was a valuable string of pearls, which so incensed Marguerite that she threatened to return there and burn the place down if it were not restored to her. It never was: the threat, as she herself was compelled to realize, was a hollow one.

With Matignon's approval, Alain de Vaurs, a local Councillor, visited the King to report to him on the events of 25 September. Henri III did more than approve of the loyalty of the citizens: he rewarded it by a remission of taxes for five years in compensation for the losses and damage they had suffered. And by a decree of 19 December 1585 the King revoked Marguerite's appanage of Agen and the Agenois district, which were returned to the Crown.

Marguerite's two honest servants, her treasurer and controller, arrived at Carlat a few weeks after Choisnin, when the secretary was obliged to render account of the moneys he had spent, which amounted to 14,000 or 15,000 écus. Choisnin not only held on to this sum, but claimed another 6,000 for his personal services. He made himself so obnoxious to the Queen that she refused to receive him, whereupon he boxed the ears of the footman guarding her door and was forbidden to return for a week. Choisnin spent this period in writing a vile lampoon, which, on the pretext that it was dedicated to his mistress and that she was fond of learned works, he went about reading aloud to anyone in the fortress willing to listen to it. Certain gentlemen-at-arms, disgusted by this sly and treacherous creature, gave him a beating and threw him out of Carlat. Choisnin, however, had the last word. He declared that he would take to the King the instructions Marguerite had given him when she sent him to the Duke of Guise, and he made good his threat that he would ruin her.

The King and the Queen Mother were keeping themselves well informed of events at Carlat. The King was most anxious that his sister should not remain there; he needed the fortress as a base in his war against the Huguenots. Catherine had offered Marguerite, instead, another of her castles, Ibois, in Low Auvergne. But her daughter refused this offer in a letter from Carlat that was little short of arrogant, and no way in which to write to the Queen Mother:

'I thank Your Majesty', she said, 'for the castle it has pleased you to offer me. Thanks to God I do not need it, as I am in a very good place which belongs to me, supported by many honourable gentlemen and living in high honour and complete security. And as it pleased you, Madame, to order M. de Suraine [Catherine's messenger] to tell me that it was not my business to go to war, it was, nevertheless, Madame, up to me to protect myself. Nor have I done anything else, but did so in order not to fall back into the power of those who wish to deprive me of my possessions, my life and honour. As I very humbly beg you to believe, I will spare nothing to this end, nor for the remainder of my life make myself troublesome to you.' Harsh words, which not long afterwards their writer was bitterly obliged to eat.

Marguerite had rushed to Carlat as a refuge. She had not been there more than a month or two before she realized that it was a trap, a prison, in which she was being held by Lignerac and his brother, Marzé. These two fierce Auvergnats were in fact a pair of ruthless conspirators. Although Lignerac was sexually attracted by his still beautiful captive, he did not, uncouth as he was, attempt to court her. No doubt he sensed and enjoyed her growing fear of him, and this sense of power was a flattering compensation to him for Marguerite's undisguised antipathy and antagonism. Marzé controlled the garrison on the King's behalf.

Like her mother, Marguerite had an exceptionally strong constitution. Nevertheless, from March to December 1585 she had been through experiences that might have undermined the strongest female body. The turmoil of Agen, the rigours of her flight, the bitter cold and draughts that swept through Carlat in winter, all these physical strains, coupled with the increasing mental strain she was enduring; her constant lack of funds, owing to which she even had to borrow heavily from Lignerac to pay the troops, and also to send some of her jewels to an Italian broker in Lyons, who sold them for her at a considerable loss, all these factors contributed to her breakdown in the early months of 1586.

The serious illness which then attacked her may well have been pneumonia. For weeks she lay in high fever and at times barely conscious. Since the last thing Lignerac and Marzé wished to happen was the death of their precious captive, they sent for doctors from near and far. None of them appeared to have an immediate cure, and almost certainly her infection was pulmonary, since above all she needed constant and most careful nursing.

The 'nurse' who devotedly undertook these strenuous duties was a mere lad, the local apothecary's son. For weeks he attended her day and night, hardly for a moment leaving her bedside. And when the days lengthened and the glorious spring of April and May burst on Auvergne, Marguerite took a turn for the better. As her health improved and her strength gradually came back to her, it would have been less than natural had she not shown gratitude and even in her usual impulsive way genuine affection for the boy who had so wholeheartedly nursed her and to whom she probably owed her life.

Her slanderers propagated the story that the apothecary's son had become her lover, and their libels might have been based on circumstantial evidence of a particularly grim kind.

Marzé, Lignerac's brother and the King's commander of Carlat, suddenly died that summer, apparently of poisoning. Again it was assumed that Marguerite had taken this sinister step to rid herself of one of her two jailers, though the accusation was unproven.

Catherine, still optimistically hoping to reconcile the Navarres, had offered to receive Marguerite at her magnificent Chenonceaux. At that moment even the King was preparing to grant his sister some financial assistance. But their hopes and plans were, to say the least, frustrated when Their Majesties received a sensational report of the latest scandal at Carlat.

By June Marguerite had wholly recovered and even made a few visits to the seats of the local gentry, attending a fête in her honour at one of them. But on 19 July Mendoza, the Spanish Ambassador to France, reported to Philip II:

'I hear that the Queen Mother was recently lamenting that M. de Lignerac had stabbed to death the son of an apothecary in her [Marguerite's] room; so close to her bed that she was covered in bloodstains, and the worst of it is that his motive was jealousy.'

For the second time in her life the Queen of Navarre's gown was spattered with the blood of an innocent man, and this unfortunate boy she was unable to save as, years ago, on St Bartholomew's Night, she had saved the life of M. de Léran.

What had happened was that Lignerac, who had been absent from Carlat, suddenly returned, and in a frenzy of jealousy burst into Marguerite's room, stabbing the poor lad several times, without uttering a word, then leaving the horrified Queen, still not addressing her.

This brutal incident finally convinced the Queen Mother that the Navarre marriage would never be patched up again. There was no further invitation to Chenonceaux, nor were any Royal funds made available to Marguerite.

Yet the assumption that when Lignerac murdered the young apothecary Marguerite was in bed with him seems all the more tenuous since during this whole period Aubiac, her adorer and rescuer from Agen, was living in the castle. At what time he became Marguerite's lover is not precisely known, but the fact that he did so is incontrovertible. During the autumn and winter of 1585 and the first six months of 1586 not even Marguerite's enemies openly accused her of living with him. Only after the death of Marzé and the temporary departure from Carlat of Lignerac, who from time to time descended on the castle like some hideous bird of prey, did Aubiac become Marguerite's accredited lover. She placed him in command of her bodyguard and sent his cousin out into the countryside to recruit more troops for it. With the death of Marzé and with Lignerac at a distance, she apparently felt renewed confidence that she could hold on to Carlat against all her enemies. But her confidence was injudicious and miserably misplaced.

When Lignerac returned yet again the garrison under Aubiac offered him no resistance. Marguerite was then completely in his power. He threatened to throw his successful rival over the cliffside, and would undoubtedly have done so had she not flattered his vanity by her passionate pleas for Aubiac's life and paid part of the large sum she owed him, on which he was insisting, even adding some of her rings in pledge for the remainder. And there was nothing she was not prepared to give Lignerac in return for Aubiac's life; even her own body. Lignerac finally agreed to spare him, but insisted that he leave Carlat immediately. Marguerite declared that she would never part with him; if he went, she would go with him. She remembered the castle of Ibois her mother had offered to lend her; in her pride she had refused it, but now, in her terrible dilemma, since there was no other refuge, she resolved to go there, taking Aubiac with her.

On the basis of this resolution, all Marguerite's biographers assumed that she was madly in love with Aubiac. This was not the case. Chanvallon was the last man for whom Marguerite of Valois felt that overwhelming passion that sweeps a woman off her feet. It had left her disgraced, with an aftermath of disillusionment and bitterness. Yet had she not suffered so deeply she still could not possibly have had any such romantic emotions about a red-faced, red-nosed, red-haired, freckled young soldier like Aubiac. He was madly in love with her from the moment when he had first seen her at Agen. And it is unnecessary to postulate that she felt so deeply and romantically about him that she was unwilling to remain at Carlat without him. Had she done so, she would have been utterly at the mercy of the bestial Lignerac, who, she was well aware, might then have sold her with unabashed cynicism to the highest bidder—the King, Guise, or even Navarre had he wanted her back. No, Marguerite was not passionately in love with Aubiac; she simply needed him desperately; and equally desperately she needed to leave Carlat, which, without Aubiac's support, would have been physically impossible. She did love him, however, with genuine affection and gratitude for his selfless devotion to her.

Lignerac finally agreed to let them go together; he even saw them a short way on their journey and then returned to Carlat, of which he was at last complete master on behalf of the King, on whose gratitude he would be able, he knew, to count.

In his latest campaign against the southern Huguenots, Henri III appointed as commander of his forces the Duke of Joyeuse, the *mignon* who shared the royal bed with Epernon. The mere fact that Joyeuse was in the vicinity would have been enough to decide Marguerite to leave Carlat. But Joyeuse, who was no great soldier, made an error in appointing as his own two principal aides M. de Lavardin and the Marquess of Canillac, neglecting to offer a post on his staff to M. de Randan, titular Governor of Auvergne, who thereupon became his enemy.

Marguerite's journey from Carlat to Ibois was an even more fantastic one than her flight from Agen. She left with Aubiac after the mid-morning meal on 14 October 1586. Before them lay a string of precipitous mountains, covered with trees then blazing with their magnificent autumn foliage; below them nestled valleys threaded by rivers and streams, on the banks of which the local towns and castles were situated.

Owing, however, to her defenceless state and her ever-present fear of capture, Marguerite was obliged to avoid all the easier roads in the plains and keep to the dangerous and narrow paths along the mountain-crests, until she reached the pass known as the Father's Tomb, between the two peaks of the Plomb du

Cantal. Her journey was so perilous that Catherine, when she heard of it, wrote that 'having neither horses nor weapons, I think that some spirit or genius of the air must have borne her over them. God will that it was a good one. . . .'

But no angel bore Marguerite on his wings; it was Aubiac who escorted her on this terrible enterprise. According to one account, she set out, as from Agen, riding pillion behind him, with only one waiting-woman and leaving her ladies to follow on later; another, that she was accompanied by a few officers and her maids-of-honour, including Aubiac's sister, Madeleine, and that for the worst part of the way the Queen rode in an ox-cart. Whichever was the case, the first day's ride, from Carlat to Murat, where she spent the night, took from eight to ten hours. Next day she set out for Allande, another ten kilometres distant. On 16 October her worst experience faced her, when she travelled ten kilometres uphill in the morning, and another thirty downhill in the afternoon.

Ibois was near the town of Issoire, where there was a bridge over the River Allier. But as Issoire was in the hands of Joyeuse's army, Marguerite dared not approach it. She had therefore arranged in advance with a local landowner, M. de Châteauneuf, that he would meet her at Pertus, where there was a ferry, and where he had promised to see her across the water. Many of the Auvergnat gentry who had flocked to serve Marguerite at Carlat had already abandoned her to join the King's men. When she arrived at the river's edge, in darkness and at the point of utter exhaustion, there was neither ferry nor Châteauneuf. Desperate, almost in sight of her goal, Marguerite resolved to ford the river on horseback behind Aubiac, emerging drenched and shivering on the farther bank. When at last they arrived at Ibois late at night on 16 October, they found the gates had been left open for them, but there was seemingly no other welcome.

In these appalling conditions, jolting and bumping over old Roman roads and remote tracks high up in the mountains, slithering down their steep slopes to the river's edge, Marguerite had travelled no less than fifty miles in three days. She knew that she owed her safe arrival entirely to Aubiac's unfaltering devotion:

there is no need to imagine that she was in love with him to appreciate her heartfelt gratitude and affection for him.

But no repose was to be theirs.

From the moment when she finally left Nérac Marguerite had invited the anger and inevitable retribution of the King and the Queen Mother.

Choisnin had carried out his threat and taken his former mistress's instructions and copies of her letter to Guise to Henri III. By allying herself with the head of the League at Agen, she had openly sided with the would-be usurper of the Valois throne; at Carlat, where she thought herself in safety, she had written a defiant letter to her mother, which on her flight appeared a superflous act of disrespect. By making a return to Navarre impossible, she had deprived herself forever of the chance of becoming Queen of France one day and seriously impeded the negotiations in progress between the heir-apparent and the King, in which the Queen Mother was acting as intermediary. Finally, her Royal relatives had had to suffer the scandal of Lignerac's murder of her alleged lover, the young apothecary, and the even greater loss of face caused them by her unconcealed and unashamed attachment to Aubiac, who in their opinion was barely a gentleman and no more fitting mate for a Daughter of France than a valet might have been.

The King had been determined to oust Marguerite from Carlat, and when Lignerac succeeded in doing so she was entirely at Henri's mercy—or lack of it. The moment she arrived at Ibois she delivered herself into his hands.

The Marquess of Canillac, serving on Joyeuse's staff, on being informed of her arrival, immediately set off for Ibois with a troop of around fifty horsemen. At first Marguerite actually thought of resisting his entry. In her fury at having been lured, as she was convinced she had been, into this trap, she wrote a letter to M. de Sarlan, the Queen Mother's *maître d'hôtel*, which in fact was intended for Catherine herself:

'Monsieur de Sarlan,
    'Since the cruelty of my misfortunes and of those to whom I have

never rendered anything but service is so great that not satisfied by the indignities that for so many years they have made me suffer, they now intend to persecute me to the end of my life, I desire at least before my death to have the satisfaction that the Queen my mother should know that I had courage enough not to fall alive into my enemies' hands, which I assure you I shall never do. Assure her of this, and that the first news she will have of me will be of my death. On her promises and orders I fled to her property, where instead of the good treatment I was expecting I have only found shameful ruin. Patience! She gave me life and she wishes to deprive me of it. But I know that I am in God's hands; nothing will happen to me against His will. I trust in Him and will receive all at His hands. Your most faithful and best friend,

'MARGUERITE.'

Whether or not she was really contemplating suicide when writing that letter, Marguerite thought better of it afterwards. Nor was her faith misplaced. In spite of their merciless indignation, the King and Catherine were not prepared to take her life, although had God done so they would have shed no tears. Aubiac's case, however, was a more tragic one.

Realizing that it was futile to attempt to barricade herself against Canillac, Marguerite gave orders that he was to be admitted. She did not spare him the lash of her tongue, the only apparent weapon then remaining to her. She apostrophized him contemptuously in the second person singular:

'Marquess,' she said to him, 'you think that in capturing me you have brought off a great *coup*. But it's a very small thing for you, and even less for me. Joyeuse, who is cleverer than you are, saw what little honour or merit he would derive from carrying out this order. That is why he passed it on to you.'

As she addressed him so scathingly Canillac could not refrain from a secret sensation of admiration and desire for this proud and indignant Princess, her eyes blazing and her cheeks flushed with anger. A beautiful woman is never more desirable than when she is in a rage. Nevertheless, he answered her quietly but firmly that he was acting on the King's direct instructions, to which Marguerite replied that 'Brother and sister will in due course make it up, and you will be left in the lurch.'

But in saying so she was merely bolstering up her own courage. She knew that never again would she and the King be reconciled. And secretly she was terrified, not so much for herself as for Aubiac. She tried to smuggle him out of Ibois disguised as a woman. When this trick failed, she hid him away. Canillac declared that if necessary he would tear down Ibois stone by stone until he was found. Finally, desperately lamenting both their fates, Marguerite, in tears, was forced to hand over her defenceless lover to their enemy. She knew that his death was a foregone conclusion; at least she did not know how horrible it was shortly to be.

Catherine, who was then at Tours, learned before the King of her daughter's and Aubiac's arrest. Implacable as she always was when her considerable patience was finally exhausted, she ordered Villeroy to ask the King to take the firmest measures against Marguerite: 'I beg him to lose not an hour in giving the necessary orders; otherwise she will inflict yet another disgrace on us.' Henri III soon granted his mother's request.

Whilst Canillac waited for his instructions, Aubiac was imprisoned at Saint-Cirgues. Marguerite and her ladies were taken under heavy escort to the castle of Saint-Amand-Tallende, on the left bank of the Allier, and shortly afterwards to nearby Saint-Saturnin. At the former, Marguerite, thoughtful as ever of those who served her, sent Aubiac's sister, Madeleine de Birac, back to her home in Gascony, paying all her expenses; the remainder of her suite were also paid off and dismissed.

At the beginning of November Canillac received the King's personal orders through Villeroy. Henri III had already impounded all Marguerite's available property to pay the wages of the fifty to one hundred Swiss whom the Queen Mother thought the necessary number to guard her imprisoned daughter; they were to be chosen by Matignon from men personally known to him and completely loyal. Her debts were to be examined and those considered justified to be paid off, but the King himself expressly forbade anything at all to be paid to the detested Mme de Duras.

Canillac was further instructed to draw up an inventory of all the Queen of Navarre's rings, which were to be brought to the King personally as soon as possible. And Canillac's own expenses were to come out of the moneys raised on Marguerite's confiscated possessions and other forms of revenue.

'As for her men and women', Henri III wrote to Villeroy, 'he is to sack them immediately and to replace them temporarily by some honest lady-in-waiting and chambermaid.' In his petty spite as well as hatred, he ordered that in the letters-patent Villeroy was to draw up in the King's name in all these matters, Marguerite was to be referred to 'only as "sister", with neither "dear" nor "well-loved"'—the customary terms. And he finally added that the Queen Mother had begged him to have Aubiac 'hung in the presence of this miserable woman, in the courtyard of the Castle of Usson, so that plenty of people may see him.'

This was undoubtedly Henri's desire and would certainly have been done but for considerations of policy. For such a public execution of Marguerite's lover, which she would have been forced to watch being carried out, would have been an equally public acknowledgement of her adultery—all Henry of Navarre needed in order to have their marriage annulled, as he had for so long wished. And at that moment the Queen Mother was again negotiating with her son-in-law and endeavouring to bring him back into the Catholic fold, in spite of his excommunication by the Pope a short time previously. It was therefore decided as more politic that Aubiac should be executed for the alleged poisoning of de Marzé, the King's commander at Carlat.

Aubiac was taken to Aigueperse, the capital of the Dauphiné of Auvergne. On the outskirts of the town his tormentors executed him, not by cutting off his head, the usual form of death inflicted on an officer and a gentleman, but by hanging. They gave themselves the added amusement of hanging the poor young victim upside down—as Mussolini was hanged by his compatriots four centuries later (in case any reader should think that such horrible forms of death-dealing were peculiar to the sixteenth century)—and before he had even stopped breathing they threw him into his grave and piled the dirt on him. He was said to have still been clutching a little muff of Marguerite's that she had given him. His bad fairy thus granted him the wish he had so rashly uttered when first he had seen and fallen in love with the Queen of his heart.

17   Ark of Refuge

In a second letter to Villeroy, the King wrote that the more he thought about it the more he felt the shame 'that miserable woman has brought on us. The best thing God could do for her sake and for ours, would be to take her,' and, no doubt, had Marguerite then been available, His Majesty might well have assisted such a divine plan. Meanwhile, he continued, he had written personally 'to the Marquess of Canillac regarding her women.' He was to allow her only two of her chambermaids and one lady-in-waiting who he considered 'would be better suited to sharing her imprisonment than those who did not deserve it.'

Having given Canillac these detailed instructions Henri III postponed further action against his hated sister until the following January. Owing to the ever-increasing menace of the League, the King and especially the Queen Mother were again making strenuous efforts to come to terms with Henry of Navarre. Marguerite was more than a pawn in that game. They unashamedly held out the possibility of her imminent death as bait to attract her husband to their side—away from his Huguenot supporters and back to the Catholic Church. At the end of October Catherine left Chenonceaux to meet Navarre at St Brice, near Cognac. As, some years previously, she had taken Marguerite south with her in order to patch up their marriage, now that it was irrevocably broken she was accompanied by her granddaughter, Christine of Lorraine, a possible future bride for Henry when Marguerite should have died or, failing that desirable solution, be confined for life to a nunnery after the dissolution of her marriage by the Pope. To Henry's honour, however, he firmly repudiated any such detestable action or bargain. By doing so, he possibly saved Marguerite's life. For, seeing that her husband was still not prepared to renounce his Huguenoterie, her brother had no wish to set him free to marry a Protestant princess provided for him either by his German allies or Elizabeth I of England.

Still another castle that was an appanage of Marguerite's was Usson, four leagues from Brioude, bestowed on her by the decree of 1582. Knowing it to be one of the most sinister and depressing as well as impregnable fortresses in his realm, Henri deliberately ordered his helpless sister to be imprisoned there. Brantôme described Usson as 'a stronghold which that wily old fox Louis XI had made so, in order to hold his prisoners in a hundredfold greater security than either Loches, Bois de Vincennes, or Lusignan'. Usson stood on a commanding cliff, on top of which, wrote Scaliger, who visited Marguerite there later on, 'were three towns superimposed one above the other, rather like a papal mitre'. On the summit was the castle, with a few dwellings nestling below it. Another commentator devoted to Marguerite, Father Hilarion de Coste, said that 'even the sun could only enter there by force'.

So it was to Usson that on 13 November 1586 Marguerite was taken by Canillac. The Swiss Guard and other Royal troops made any possibility of escape unthinkable.

Marguerite had no illusions regarding the danger in which she stood. At Court her death was expected within a matter of weeks. Yet in spite of her genuine piety she was not the woman to neglect the maxim that God helps those who help themselves. She had no protector, no weapon left with which to defend herself except her wits. But only when she was in love did her otherwise shrewd intelligence fail her. In her account of her Flemish voyage she showed herself an astute judge of character. Now she had ample leisure to study the personalities of her jailor and his wife, the Marchioness of Canillac, who was residing in the Castle with her husband.

One small but important point in Marguerite's favour was that, through his wife, Canillac was related to Mme Charlotte de Curton, Margot's former governess, who had brought her up with so much affection. The Marquess was not by career a soldier but a diplomat. At the King's command, he had given up an ambassadorship to support Joyeuse's campaign, and then to arrest and take charge of the Queen of Navarre. Henri III had made him generous promises of returning in due course to his diplomatic career, and of considerable financial and other benefits for his guardianship of his prisoner. As usual, however, when it came to paying up, the King vacillated and procrastinated, so that with the passing months Canillac's loyalty and patience began to wear thin and his sense of grievance to grow.

During her Flemish excursion, when Marguerite was planning to win over the powerful Count of Lalain for her brother François, she had begun her campaign by first concentrating her attention and flattery on his young Countess. In Flanders the Queen of Navarre had been at the height of her youthful beauty and success. At Usson her career had to all appearances reached its nadir: she was alone, helpless, and disgraced. Nevertheless, her glamour was still intact, and although she had already begun to put on too much weight she was beautiful, even desirable. She was also and would always remain a Daughter of France, the greatest lady in the land after the ageing Queen Mother and Queen Louise, the Queen Consort, who was a mere shadow. And when Marguerite chose to be charming and beguiling, neither woman nor man could resist her.

She now began her campaign by showering compliments on the Marchioness, telling her that she was made for the Court, where she could not fail to become a huge success. In preparation for this brilliant future, Marguerite gave several of her own jewels and dresses to the bedazzled Mme de Canillac, teaching her how to wear them and giving her lessons in the correct deportment of a great Court lady. Since even in her worst moments Marguerite's sense of humour was always latent, this charade may have given her a good deal of quiet entertainment whilst she pursued her further and daring plan.

For this was not merely the trivial matter of winning over the Marchioness. Canillac himself was the bird for whom she was spreading her nets. Incredible as it might seem, the truth is nevertheless sufficiently authenticated that Marguerite completely captivated this middle-aged man, as she had captivated Pibrac and even won the admiration of that detached philosopher, Montaigne.

'For', wrote Brantôme, 'he who held her prisoner in a very short time became her prisoner, although he was very brave and valiant. Poor man, what did he think he could do? Hold as his prisoner, subject, and captive one whose eyes and loveliness could enchain and bind to her all the rest of mankind like convicts?'

To have received Canillac into her royal bed would not have seemed to the Queen too high a price to pay for her freedom. But, with her usual practical sense Marguerite, if she did allow him this favour, did not leave matters there:

'We, Marguerite, by the grace of God Queen of Navarre, only sister of the King, Duchess of Valois and Etampes, Countess of Agenois, Rouergues, Senlis and Marle, Lady of La Fère and the lands of Rieux, Rivière, Verdun and Albigeois, etc., in consideration of the very exceptional and agreeable services we have received and hope to receive from Jean de Beaufort, Marquess of Canillac, which we will never be able sufficiently to reward . . . in witness of the constant remembrance of his good offices . . . have given to him, give, and make over to him and his heirs all our rights over the county of Auvergne and other lands of the said Auvergne belonging to the Queen, our very honoured lady and mother, which should and must in due course belong to us, as much owing to the portion and legitimate inheritance due to us as for the 200,000 francs that our said lady and mother bestowed on us in our marriage contract, but which she has never since paid,'—a nice and typical touch.

In promising Canillac such generous rewards, Marguerite at the time possessed nothing but her justifiable though doubtful expectations on Catherine's death. However, this did not prevent her from assuring him of further sums, 'payable as soon as it becomes possible to us', and this curious document ended: 'As for certain good reasons we did not wish to have this matter handled by notaries, we wrote and signed it by our own hand. Given at Usson in the year 1588, on 8 September.'

Apparently only Marguerite's signature was in her own hand, and for this reason some later historians regarded it as a forgery, but since it was never implemented this is slightly irrelevant. It has a ring of truth about it as showing the enormous price, which, if need be, Marguerite was prepared to pay for Usson and her freedom.

The greatest service rendered her by Canillac, however, was his defection from Henri III and adherence to Guise and the League. This was Marguerite's real triumph. By the beginning of 1587 she was no longer a prisoner, and in any case she had no immediate intention of leaving Usson. At the end of January Canillac went to Lyons, and there he wrote to Guise, offering him his services, which were gladly accepted.

In spite of Usson's grim reputation and situation, very soon after her arrival there and her seduction of Canillac Marguerite found this eyrie the perfect refuge both from the King her brother and the King her husband that she had so long been seeking. Having so brilliantly won over Canillac by her charms and wiles, at last she was in full command of her situation. On 14 February the Duke of Guise wrote a letter to the Spanish Ambassador, Mendoza:

'I do not wish to fail to inform you that the negotiations I began with the Marquess of Canillac have been entirely successful, and that for this reason the Queen of Navarre is now living in all security. I am delighted by this good news, not only for her sake, but also for the acquisition this gives us of a great number of places and castles which assure us of the whole of Auvergne, and also because it puts an end to the tragic plots that were being made, involving her death, which, when you are informed of them

in detail, will make your hair stand on end. You will then understand what effect this event has had on the King of France, seeing that the Marquess has discharged the garrison that His
Majesty had installed there, which was the first evidence of his
loyalty that I demanded from him.'

Canillac went even further, for, having handed over Usson to
Marguerite, he joined the forces of the League under the command of the Duke of Mayenne, Guise's younger brother. Marguerite was freed from her obligations towards him on 28 April
1589, when he was killed during the Siege of Saint-Ouen. His
widow did not become a great Court lady, but instead settled
down quite happily at Usson as Marguerite's chief lady-in-waiting.

Impregnable as her fortress, with its twenty watch-towers,
appeared to be, Marguerite did not overlook the possibility that
the King might attempt to attack it. She replaced the Swiss Guard
and the remainder of his garrison by troops with whom Guise
supplied her. She was in constant communication with Randan, the Governor of Auvergne, and other Leaguers fighting
against the Huguenots and the King's men. She even laid in
sufficient provisions to last out for two years in the event of Usson
being besieged.

But Henri III, although still only in his thirties, was becoming
increasingly maniacal—in some respects almost senile—and had
lost his hold over the French people, who hated and despised him,
his bed-*mignons* and, alternating with his debaucheries, his
masochistic religious practices, flagellations and the rest. Everywhere, and in Paris especially, his abdication was being publicly
demanded. Joyeuse was killed in the Battle of Coutras in 1587;
Epernon, increasingly insolent, even to the extent of incurring
the Queen Mother's hatred, was acting as if he were Viceroy, in
command of the Crown's attenuated forces. Henri III had neither
enough money nor troops to match those of his opponents. Guise
and the League had nearly the whole of Catholic France behind
them; Navarre and the Protestant faction were still in active combat. Both sides were dependent on foreign aid: Guise on Spanish

gold and men, Navarre on German mercenaries paid for him by Elizabeth I of England.

Two major events involving these two Powers had considerable bearing on French affairs.

The first of these was the beheading of Mary Queen of Scots at Fotheringay on 18 February 1587. She had been Marguerite's sister-in-law, the widow of King François II, her beauty and charm one of the outstanding adornments of the brilliant Valois Court when Margot was still a little girl. Mary was a Lorraine, and her relatives made strenuous but futile attempts to rescue her. Her tragic fate was a warning to Marguerite never to relax her own vigilance. Knowing her danger when first she arrived at Usson and fearing that the method used to eliminate her would be poisoning, she ordered that all food served to her was first to be tasted by one of her women. Fortunately for them both, no such 'accident' occurred.

The second event that changed European history at that time occurred in July 1588, when the Great Armada, fitted out by Philip II of Spain for the invasion of England, was wrecked in a terrific storm off the Irish coast. Spain never recovered from this blow and with it the decline of Philip's career as the invincible Catholic King began to set in.

Henri III occasionally had certain flashes of perspicacity. Debauched and degenerate as he undoubtedly was, like all the Valois he was not a fool. One of his correct opinions was his conviction that the English would defeat the Armada, in which case the Guises, who depended almost entirely on Philip of Spain for arms and funds, would be irretrievably weakened in their campaigns. The King would then be able to deal with those traitors without fearing the revenge of their Spanish backers and an invasion of France.

Before the Armada set sail, however, Henri III's position was becoming more and more precarious. During the years 1587 and 1588 the Queen Mother, by then nearing seventy, old and ailing, was still travelling from one end of the realm to the other, from south to north, alternately bargaining, haggling, and signing away more lands and strongholds to Navarre or Guise, hoping against hope that one side would join her to defeat the other, but to no purpose. Navarre would not yet renounce his Protestantism; Guise was planning to place on the throne, which Henri III would be forced to abdicate, the old Cardinal of Bourbon, so that it would not be occupied against the will of the French people by that heretical Bourbon, Henry of Navarre.

His victory at Coutras was followed by those of the Leaguers at Vimory in October and Aumeau in November. Both sides were exultant; the only losers in these battles that were tearing France to pieces were the King and the French people.

Nevertheless, Henri, having lost faith in his old mother's capacity to settle matters by negotiation, took a strong line with the Duke of Guise, forbidding him to enter the capital, where he was so tremendously popular that he was called the King of Paris. Guise defied his monarch and arrived there at the beginning of May. Henri retreated to the Louvre; once again the Queen Mother tried to make peace between her son and Scarface, whom, after all, she had known since he was a child and who always behaved towards her with courtesy bordering on affection. But in vain. The King refused to receive him and on 12 May, fearing that the people of Paris were about to rise against him, Henri decided to leave for Chartres under the protection of his Swiss Guards. Only Guise's intervention prevented their massacre by the mob. Friday, the 13th, was the Day of the Barricades, when the Parisians erected them in order to prevent the King's men from passing through the streets. The old Queen fearlessly did so, traipsing back and forth from the Louvre to the Marais, visiting Guise and holding him in conversation whilst her precious son escaped. The Duke's words to her when news of this was brought to him in her presence, were prophetic: 'Madam, now I am dead! Whilst Your Majesty keeps me occupied here the King leaves, to my perdition!'

Guise could at that moment, and in his own interests should, have made himself master of Paris, but he preferred to await the outcome of the Armada's attack—which he naturally expected to succeed—before overthrowing the King by force and placing the Cardinal of Bourbon on the throne.

After the destruction of the Armada, Henri III ran true to the Valois tradition. He had insufficient troops, but he did have a body of assassins known as the Forty-five. It was freely rumoured in Paris that the Duke of Guise was to be murdered at the King's orders, but when he was warned to be on his guard, Scarface, the hero of so many battles, replied contemptuously: 'I am not afraid of that one. I know him well and he is too much of a coward.'

He forgot the murder of his own father, the first Duke of Guise and greatest Scarface, by Poltrot de Méré; he forgot the assassination, ordered by Catherine and Henri, of the Huguenot leader, Admiral de Coligny, that led to the Massacre of St Bartholomew.

In his own opinion and according to his family tradition, Henri was completely justified in despatching this enemy and traitor by the same method, since no other was available. Catherine was at Blois, in bed with a serious chill. Her son showed little gratitude for her years of utter devotion to him, nor for her political slavery and consent to that former crime, which forever stained her historical image.

On 23 December 1588 the Florentine envoy, Cavriana, was visiting Catherine when Henri III came to see the sick Queen Mother. He asked the Ambassador how she was feeling.

'I answered him that she was well and that she had only taken some slight medicine. Going towards her then, with the most confident mien and the calmest manner in the world, he said to her, "Good morning, Madam. I beg you to forgive me. Monsieur de Guise is dead and will be spoken of no more. I had him killed in order to forestall the same plan he had formed towards myself. I could no longer tolerate his insolence," and he continued, "I now intend to be king and no longer a captive and a slave, as I have been from May 13th until this hour,"' and, added Cavriana, 'I left full of thought, reflecting on how sweet must be revenge, in order thus to revivify a mind and light up a face.'

Next day Catherine, still in bed at Blois, learned of the murder of Guise's brother, the Cardinal of Lorraine, and the imprisonment of the Bourbon Cardinal. Henri III had forgotten St Bartholomew. His mother had not. Filled with anxiety, the old Queen rose from her sick-bed in order to visit the Bourbon Cardinal and to promise him a safe conduct. She received little thanks from him for this well-meant gesture. After the two old people had wept a little together for their unfortunate country, 'the Cardinal reproached the Queen', wrote Héritier, 'for her deceits, her fine words, her illusory guarantees, her thousand false promises'—a not altogether unfair summing-up of her activities over the past thirty years—'without which the Lorraine brothers would not have been killed, nor he himself have been a prisoner'.

'The defeat of this final hope'—of coming to some arrangement with the Cardinal to save the King from the consequences of these murders—'was the end of Madam Catherine.'

The Queen Mother died of pneumonia at Blois shortly afterwards, on 5 January 1589, aged seventy.

L'Estoile supplied a picturesque epitaph to her end:

'She died . . . on the eve of the Feast of Kings [Twelfth Night], a date fatal to those of her House, for Alessandro de Medici was killed on that day, as well as Lorenzo de Medici and others. . . . As for Blois, where she had been adored and venerated as the Juno of the Court, no sooner had she drawn her last breath than nowhere did they pay any more notice to her than to a dead goat:

> Elle enfanta trois rois et guerres civiles,
> Fit bâtir des châteaux et ruiner des villes.

Historians will never agree about Catherine de Medici. Her admirers, of whom Héritier is the most erudite and convincing, claimed that she spent her whole life in the struggle to unite France in peace and strength, that her first thoughts were always for the good of the realm, which she administered as Governess for so long. Her adversaries took the opposite view with equal conviction. They claimed that Catherine's whole policy was Machiavellian, based on the principle, 'Divide and rule'. By fostering the mutual hatred of Catholics and Huguenots, she fought to keep power in her own hands and her three sons—all physically and mentally degenerate—on the throne of the Valois, to the appalling suffering of the French people, Catholics and Protestants alike, throughout the Wars of Religion that marred their reigns.

No doubt the truth lies between these two extremes. Catherine was a woman of outstanding physical and moral courage, of infinite patience and industry, intelligent and erudite, yet wildly extravagant and calculatingly cynical. She used the debauchery of the Court and of her sons as an instrument of policy, her 'Flying Squadron' as sordidly as a brothel-keeper. Although she gave birth to ten children, after the death of her husband, Henri II, she had no personal sex-life; all her urges, with one exception, were sublimated into her lust for power.

The exception was her morbid passion for Henri III. She also had some affection for her two elder daughters, although she married them off, as she did Marguerite, for reasons of policy. But since that was the common custom of Royal Houses at the time, this was not held against her, except by her youngest daughter. In her old age Catherine appears to have had considerable affection for her granddaughter, Christine, the daughter of the Princess Claude, Duchess of Lorraine. It was to this granddaughter that in her testament the Queen Mother left all her personal property that did not go to Henri III. Marguerite was not even mentioned in her mother's will. By her own conduct in recent years, she had cut herself out of it.

When the news of the Queen Mother's death reached Marguerite at Usson, happy and safe by then in her fastness, she did not grieve too much for her. Throughout her life, ever since her brother Henri had repudiated her girlish affection owing to the influence of de Guast, and especially during the past two years, Marguerite had suffered too many unkindnesses from her, culminating in her betrayal at Ibois, to feel her death as a personal loss. In her Memoirs she made her resentment quite clear, and in her later letters to the Queen Mother even more so. One of the last of these, written in November or December 1586, was an indignant repudiation of the libel—believed at the time by everyone at Court—that at Carlat she had given birth to an illegitimate son, a deaf-and-dumb child, fathered by Aubiac:

'MADAM,

'Since my misfortunes have driven me into such misery that I no longer desire to live, may I at least hope that you will take steps to preserve my honour, which is so clearly linked with your own and that of all those to whom I have the honour to be related . . .' and she begged the Queen Mother to provide her with 'a lady of quality and worthy of belief, who may testify to my condition and who, after my death, will be present at my autopsy, in order that she may then testify to the state I was in . . .'

—to the fact that she was not, nor ever had been, pregnant.

At that time Marguerite's thoughts were often morbid, quite naturally in her dangerous circumstances. After the death of Aubiac, whom she had loved and depended on as her last protector, she might well have considered suicide a greater relief to her than murder by poisoning. But her physical and mental vitality—inherited from her mother—were still far too great in her early thirties for her to give way for long to such melancholy intentions. And after she had gathered her wits together and so brilliantly turned the tables on Canillac, there was nothing very serious for her to fear.

Marguerite's last source of anxiety was suddenly and shockingly removed when on 1 August 1589 King Henri III of France met the fate he had only so short a while previously dealt out to Guise. He was mortally wounded at Saint-Cloud by the dagger of a fanatical Dominican monk, Jacques Clément, and died of this attack.

When Canillac took Marguerite to Usson as his prisoner, she was thirty-three, still young, beautiful, and desirable. She was to spend nearly twenty years there, gradually and inevitably becoming an obese, middle-aged woman. Her increasing obesity does not, however, seem to have been due to self-indulgence. Although from a modern point of view the enormous banquets that were customary, especially in Court circles, well into the nineteenth century appear to confirm the unbridled gluttony of all those who partook of them—and Catherine de Medici was notoriously a prodigious eater—on the evidence of her later portraits Marguerite's stoutness was more likely due to some glandular or hormone deficiency, possibly hyperthyroidism. Such a deficiency might also have been the reason for her sterility. Scaliger showed considerable acumen when he wrote, centuries before the discovery of the endocrine glands and sex hormones, that 'the Queen is too fat [*grasse*] and never had a child'.

Her girlish beauty, which had been so great an ornament of the Valois Court, faded year by year like that of any less exalted female. The days of the great lovers—La Molle, Bussy, Chanvallon—were long past. Aubiac was already in a much lower social and seductive category. Yet Marguerite was still and remained almost to the end of her life in love with love, seeking emotional and erotic satisfaction. Although her enemies cruelly libelled her in many instances, the nymphomania she showed in her later years did give them some basis for their scandal-stories.

As she aged Marguerite developed certain curious resemblances, both in her sexual life and in her ever-increasing religious piety, to her brother, Henri III. The great lovers were succeeded by a series of bedmates of markedly humbler origins, recalling the *mignons* who had so ruthlessly exploited that King's proclivities. At Usson the Queen of Navarre chose her favourites for their youth, looks, and virility, showering gifts on them, minor titles, settlements, and presents, and marrying them off, as the Kings whose daughter, sister, and wife she was, married off their mistresses.

One of the first of these Usson favourites was Claude François, the son of a local coppersmith, whose sister was not even a lady-in-waiting, but one on the Queen's women-of-the-bedchamber. Marguerite, who always loved music, according to Brantôme, played the lute and also had, when young, a pretty singing voice. At Usson she took a great interest in her chapel choir. Perhaps young François also had a good voice and showed the necessary talent, or perhaps this was merely a pretext for taking him into her service, and appointing him her choirmaster. Very soon he became her secretary as well as her admitted lover, was ennobled under the title Lord of Pominy, and took full charge of her household. This affair appears to have lasted for six or seven years.

Marguerite married off Pominy for form's sake to one of her maids-of-honour, Michelette de Faugières. Allegedly he fell from the Queen's favour for being too devoted a husband!

His successor, Date, was of even lower birth, the son of a carpenter of Arles, a strikingly handsome Provençal boy who had entered the Queen's service as a page. The fact that he was young enough to have been her son did not restrain the passion Marguerite felt for him. He too was ennobled and given the title of Saint-Julien, and Marguerite made a rather surprising match for him. The bride she chose was a woman of thirty-four, one of her ladies-in-waiting, the daughter of that Marzé, the brother of Lignerac, whom Henri III had appointed Governor of Carlat during Marguerite's enforced residence there after her flight from Agen. The fact that Marzé's daughter was in Marguerite's service seems to prove conclusively how unjust as well as cruel Aubiac's execution for allegedly poisoning her father had been. When the Queen arranged the match between Jeanne de Lignerac and her favourite she endowed the bride with a substantial dowry in reward for 'her good and agreeable services' to her, both at Carlat and Usson. No doubt it was made clear, this time, that such services need not include the consummation of her marriage to the royal bedmate.

In spite of her turbulent past, her tarnished reputation, and the break-up of her marriage, Marguerite remained on excellent terms with her sister-in-law, Elisabeth of Austria, the widow of Charles IX, who was very wealthy. Whether or not Elisabeth secretly envied Marguerite, she did not resent her conduct as the Queen Mother and the King had done. For some years she provided her with an income to relieve her more pressing needs, though not nearly sufficient to cover the upkeep of Usson, the wages of the soldiery, the salaries of the members of the household, and Marguerite's innumerable charities and endowments of nunneries and monasteries. There was a regular procession of beggars to Usson from all over Auvergne, for the Queen of Navarre's generosity was famous throughout the region, and no one was ever turned away from her gates empty-handed.

Very soon more agreeable visitors found their way there, including many of the most eminent intellectuals of the day—poets, philologists, and philosophers like Scaliger. They were regally entertained, and at the banquets Marguerite gave for them, hours were spent in learned discussions of Plato, the Fathers, or lighter subjects, such as the poetry and plays or romances of the day. Marguerite's library contained more than 300 volumes, including translations from the Greek as well as Latin, Spanish, and Italian works, which she read as easily as French. According to Brantôme, if a book interested her she would not put it down until she had finished it, often reading far into the night. Her librarian was a woman, Montaigne's niece.

Owing to a riding accident which had lamed him some years previously, Brantôme had been obliged to retire from Court to his country seat, where he spent his time very contentedly writing his reminiscences—many of them amusingly bawdy—in semi-anecdotal, semi-historical form, partly recollections of incidents he had himself witnessed or portraits of individuals such as Bussy d'Amboise, whom he had greatly admired. Of all the glamorous ladies and princesses he had known at Court his greatest and most abiding devotion was given to Marguerite of Valois, with whom he was clearly more than half in love, although as a well-trained courtier he was far too well aware of the gap between their stations to have expressed his feelings in any but the most generalized terms:

'In her adversity she did me the honour of writing to me fairly frequently, I having had the presumption to send for news of her —but after all, she was the Daughter and Sister of my Kings. When I inquired after her health, which I was glad and happy to know was good, in her first letter she wrote to me as follows:

'"Thanks to your inquiries of me (which were less surprising than agreeable to me), I realize that you have kept the affection for our House that you always showed us. The little that is left of a miserable shipwreck will always be at your service, and I am very happy that Fortune has not effaced me from the memory of my oldest friends, one of whom you are.

'"I knew that like myself you had chosen a quiet life, and I regard as fortunate those who are able to lead it, as by the grace of God I have been able to do for the past five years, He having provided me with an ark of refuge in which the storms of these troubled times, thanks be to God, cannot harm me, and where, if some means remains to me to be of service to my friends, and in particular to yourself, you will find me entirely at your disposal. M.'"

This letter quoted by Brantôme was written some time in 1589 or 1590. Four or five years later Brantôme sent Marguerite his *Eloge de Marguerite de Valois, Reine de France et de Navarre, Fille unique maintenant restée de la noble Maison de France.* This was partly an anecdotal biography of the Queen as he had known her for most of her life, and partly a song of praise of her beauty, intelligence, courage, and unlimited generosity. He also deeply admired her exquisite taste and recorded for posterity the splendid dresses and jewels she had worn on certain great occasions in the past. His enthusiasm went so far that he even dared to challenge and deplore the Salic Law, which barred Marguerite from succeeding to the throne of France owing to her sex. No doubt she herself was deeply grateful to him for expressing her own feelings in the situation to which she had long ago had to resign herself.

But when Brantôme sent Marguerite this literary tribute he could not have known that he was enabling her to win a form of immortality of an entirely different kind. For it sparked off her decision to tell her own story, in the form of her Memoirs. In the covering letter she sent him with the first instalment of these, she said that she thought he would be pleased to receive them from the person who knew the facts best; she was also induced to write them because of 'five or six mistakes you made ... when you speak of Pau and my journey to France, the late Marshal de Biron ... Agen, and also the departure from here of the Marquess of Canillac.'

'I shall write my Memoirs', she continued, 'to which I shall not give a grander name, although they might deserve that of history, for the naked truth they will contain, without any ornamentation, for I do not consider myself able to provide that, nor have

I at present the necessary time to do so. This work of an afternoon's leisure will therefore come to you like a little bear, a heavy
and unsightly mass, for you to lick into shape. It is a chaos into
which you have already managed to bring some light. There
will be another five or six days' work to be done on it. It is a story
that is indeed worthy of being edited by an honourable gentleman, a real Frenchman, of illustrious descent, attached to the
Kings my father and brothers, related to and intimate friend of
the most distinguished and excellent women of our time, to whose
company I also have the honour to belong.'

It would have been fascinating to have had Marguerite's own
account of the events at Agen—for which Brantôme put all the
blame on Mme de Duras—Carlat, and Usson, when she freed
herself from Canillac and took over the fortress from him. It has
been suggested that she did in fact write these later instalments,
but that they were lost. Most authorities, however, take the view
that she deliberately abandoned the whole plan, breaking off her
story at the time of her separation from Henry of Navarre in
1582, when she left Nérac for Paris at the command of Henri
III. It would have been too embarrassing for her to have continued it, to have had to admit her adherence to the League which
put up such a stubborn resistance to Navarre, at a time when they
were negotiating their divorce and the terms on which she would
grant him his freedom.

Nor, in spite of her claim, can the Memoirs be regarded as
history, a literary form that is and should be detached, objective,
and impersonal. Marguerite was in every way utterly unqualified
for it. She was incapable of any but the most subjective,
emotional, and intensely personal reactions. Whenever the facts
did not suit her she did not hesitate to arrange their presentation
in her own favour. Yet there was undoubtedly a great deal of
truth on her side when she described herself as the victim of
Fortune and circumstances beyond her control, dating all her
subsequent misfortunes from the time when her brother Henri,
on his return from Poland, and under the influence of de Guast,
repudiated her girlish affection.

No, Marguerite's literary talent was not that of an historian, but of a born diarist, one of the greatest by any standard. Her memory of certain events was almost photographic, her observation extraordinarily acute, her sense of drama and humour unerring. The horrors of St Bartholomew's Night were crystallized for her in the events passing in her own bedroom; her description of them brings the terrifying scene to life with more vividness than any objective account of the general massacre could possibly do. And this was her most brilliant gift—her capacity to paint a picture in such rich and glowing colours that it would remain a shared experience between herself and her reader.

The Académie Française was founded by Richelieu only twenty years after her death, and it was these matchless qualities that it paid tribute to when it pronounced the Memoirs of Marguerite de Valois to be one of the masterpieces of French literature.

18 *The Happy Divorce*

Henri III was wounded by Jacques Clément on 1 August, but did not die immediately. His life could hardly be described as edifying. According to the chroniclers, his deathbed was in the best tradition.

He sent for his brother-in-law, heir and successor, Henry of Bourbon, King of Navarre.

'"My brother," he said to him, "you see what your and my enemies have done to me. Take care that they do not do the same to you"—a prophetic warning, since in due course Henry met a similar end.

' "But as it pleases God to call me," the King continued, "I am happy to die with you beside me. This is the will of God, who has cared for this realm, which I am leaving to you in a very troubled state. When God's will has been done, the crown will be yours. I have ordered all my officers to recognize you as my successor." The King of Navarre was on his knees and weeping. Having embraced him, Henri III gave him his blessing.' He then bade all his gentlemen draw near and made them swear loyalty and obedience to their new ruler. He was still in full consciousness, for he even warned Navarre that he would have a great deal of trouble if he did not change his religion, adding: '"I pray you to do so, as much for the good of your soul as for the welfare I wish you."'

Henri III died at 2 a.m. on 2 August 1589, aged thirty-eight.

Henry IV, as Navarre then became, was left, not with a kingdom, but with a kingdom to reconquer. Although the Guises were dead, the League was still very much alive. In the previous year they had proclaimed the old Cardinal of Bourbon King Charles X. Owing to Henry's continuing apostasy, the Pope favoured this ecclesiastical pretender. In spite of the destruction of the Armada, the Spaniards were not yet prepared to withdraw from France, into which they had poured so much gold. Henry still had his Huguenots, of course, and was also joined by some of the less fanatical Catholics of the Political Party. Many members of the aristocracy, following tradition, were also pledged to the legitimate successor and monarch. Nevertheless, in a series of battles that continued to ravage France, Henry only succeeded in recapturing his kingdom by tearing it piecemeal from his enemies.

At Usson Marguerite heard of his victory over the Duke of Mayenne at Ivry on 14 March 1590. The defeat and death of her protector and ally, the Count of Randan, Governor of Auvergne, and one of the principal Leaguers, occurred next day at Issoire, quite close to her fortress. Time and again the battles in the south came near enough to Usson to cause her to tremble. 'The Queen', wrote Father Hilarion de Coste, 'was hoping for little and fearing everything, for all around her were flames and uproar.' And besides, she was having troubles enough of her own.

At the beginning of January 1591 there was a short but sharp revolt among the troops of Marguerite's garrison, apparently led by the Captain of the Guard. A bullet was fired at her, which was mercifully stopped or deflected by her voluminous skirts and many petticoats. There appears to be no detailed account of this incident. Marguerite's only reference to it was much later, when in 1609 she requested Pope Paul V to grant her permission 'to build an altar of gratitude, as Jacob did ... for my miraculous deliverance from a very great danger when I was at Usson, at the time of the greatest troubles in this realm, when my castle having been attacked by revolting troops, and only the summit of the keep still remained to me, that night in His great mercy He gave me victory over my enemies, saving my life and fortress.'

Perhaps the troops had gone on strike because their wages were overdue. For Marguerite was so short of funds that she was obliged to melt down her gold and silver, sell more of her jewels at a great loss in Italy, and borrow where and when she could at usurious rates. Her financial difficulties were not only due to her extravagance. Henry was not paying the Queen's allowance, and when Catherine had cut her daughter out of her will, she was deprived of the income from the landed estates in her maternal line to which she had an hereditary right.

Catherine left these—the comtés of Clermont and Auvergne, the baronies of La Tour and La Chaise and the comté of Laura-guais, to Charles of Valois, her illegitimate grandson, of whom in her old age she had become very fond.

This boy was the bastard of Charles IX and his lovely Hugue-not mistress, Marie Touchet, who, had he been legitimate, would have succeeded his uncle, Henri III. He was handsome and brave, and in 1590 King Henry IV, who admired young men as dashing and courageous as himself, appointed him Governor of Auvergne in succession to Randan. Marguerite had been fond of Charles when he was a child at Court, but not unnaturally bitterly re-sented him having supplanted her and, as she saw it, usurped her rights in her mother's will. Charles was then still only eighteen, spoilt and ambitious, and married to the daughter of the Gov-ernor of Languedoc. Marguerite, fearing that he might attempt some move against Usson, was anxious to have a contact in his household through whom she might learn of his plans. As it happened, several of her late brother François' former secretaries had taken service with him, including a crafty and intriguing character called La Fin la Nocle, whom she assured of her affec-tion for her nephew, possibly in the hope that Charles would re-store to her a part, at least, of her inheritance. But her hope of this was not fulfilled.

When Henry of Navarre succeeded Henri III he was thirty-six, in the height of his vigorous manhood. After the reigns of the three degenerate Valois brothers, this strong, brave, intelligent, witty and magnetic Bourbon swept on to the throne of France like a breath of fresh air. But although with the passing of his homosexual predecessor the *mignons* were out, on the new King's accession the mistresses were in. Very soon the male harem at Court was succeeded by a female one.

Henry's sexual activities, his uncontrolled lechery, had caused Marguerite a great deal of unhappiness throughout their life together. From Charlotte de Sauves and poor Fosseuse to the arrogant Corisande, his intriguing mistresses had made her existence a misery.

For ten years Corisande dominated this lusty royal lover, although, in spite of his protestations of undying devotion, neither he nor she expected him to remain physically faithful to her. By the end of that remarkably long period, however, the King had tired of her and had no intention of making her his consort. And when an opportunity occurred to break with her, Henry accepted it with alacrity. He was very fond of his sister Catherine, who had lived under his protection all her life, and in her early thirties was still unmarried. Corisande was scheming to make a match between her and the Count of Soissons, and this intrigue of hers, to unite his Protestant sister to a Catholic nobleman, was Henry's feeble pretext for finally dismissing her in March 1592, with the curt declaration that he would never tolerate anyone who tried to separate his sister from him.

By then Henry had at least one other mistress, but his subsequent affairs were transient until he met the beautiful Gabrielle d'Estrées, twenty years younger than himself and one of the loveliest girls of her time. Henry lost his heart and head over Gabrielle as he had never done until then. Although one or two of her predecessors had borne him illegitimate daughters, he still had no son: a son was his most passionate desire. Gabrielle gave him two boys; the eldest they grandiloquently called Caesar, the second Alexander. Henry was determined to marry Gabrielle and to legitimize Ceasar, so that he might one day succeed him.

The royal mistress was installed in the state becoming a queen; Caesar was, although unofficially, regarded as the future Dauphin, and Alexander was in fact given the appellation 'Monsieur', usually bestowed on the King of France's second legitimate son. Unfortunately for Henry's intention to share his throne with this adored family, there still remained his wife, the Queen of Navarre, to be reckoned with.

On 26 July 1593 the King of France at last took the decisive step that Catherine and Henri III had in vain for so many years urged on him. His struggles to reconquer France had finally convinced him that the French people, and especially the influential Parliament and citizens of Paris, would never accept a Protestant monarch, and that peace would not be restored until he bowed to their wishes. In consequence, Henry IV returned to the Catholic faith at St Denis, and in February 1594 he was annointed and crowned in Chartres Cathedral.

Henry was fortunate in having exceptionally able and trustworthy ministers, notably Duplessis-Mornay and Sully, who became famous for his reorganization and reconstruction of France. Whilst the King was fighting his way into power and by his conversion winning over the people, these Protestant statesmen were planning for the future security of the Bourbon dynasty. In order to ensure this, it was necessary, as they saw it, for the King to produce a legitimate heir.

Duplessis was an elder statesman, who had known and served Henry long enough to be able to speak to him frankly. According to his Memoirs, one day he pointed out to his monarch 'all the risks he was running by having so many frivolous affairs, in which he was endangering his body, soul, and reputation'. Henry replied in his usual joking manner:

'Well then, why doesn't somebody think of getting me married off?'

'By all means, Sire,' Duplessis answered, 'but do not think it strange if we have apparently not thought of it, for first we will have to get you unmarried.' And he added: 'As you recognize the need to strengthen your State by doing so, with your permission I will deal with the matter.'

The problem was not, however, a simple one. Wishing to avoid a scandal, the King and his advisers rejected the plan of attempting to divorce the Queen of Navarre for adultery. And, strangely enough, the argument for the annulment of the marriage they decided to put forward might have been suggested by Marguerite herself. According to canon law, if one of the parties to a marriage was coerced into it against his or her will, then it was not a true marriage made in Heaven, and might be dissolved. Nothing was more certain than the fact that this law applied to the marraige made by Catherine and Charles IX between Marguerite of Valois and Henry of Navarre, entirely against the reluctant bride's inclinations. It was therefore decided to send Erard, the official in charge of the Queen's business, to interview her at Usson on her husband's behalf and to persuade her to take the necessary steps for her divorce.

Marguerite had no desire to resume marital relations with Henry; in any case, it was most unlikely that, had she done so after her late thirties, she would have produced an heir to the throne. There was therefore no reason why she should not grant the King the dissolution of their marriage which several years previously had so completely broken down in fact, if not yet in law. There was every reason from her point of view, however, why she should avail herself of this God-sent opportunity to secure her own financial future. So, with no hard feelings but with feminine common sense, she set herself to deal with this business in a business-like manner.

The two main demands Marguerite was making in exchange for her petition for the annulment were that the annual allowance of 50,000 francs she received as a Daughter of France during her Royal brothers' lifetimes should be continued, and that Henry should also agree to pay her debts, which by then had amounted to the huge sum of 250,000 *écus*. Henry was only too willing in theory to comply with these conditions, but the King of France was still almost as short of funds as he had been as King of Navarre.

Marguerite wrote Henry three letters—the first on 10 November 1593, the second in July 1594, and the third in the following

November again, pointing out to him more in sorrow than in anger that none of the financial arrangements he had agreed to make for her had been implemented, and, more and more pressed for money as she was, begging him to expedite the matter. He had also offered her a safe residence, but with regard to this proposal, Marguerite made it clear that she intended to remain at Usson. In order allegedly to reassure him, but at the same time to make it clear how hard it would be to force her out of her refuge, she gave him a detailed description of it. Had he seen how she protected herself?

'I am sure that although you might laugh at the timidity natural to my sex, you would agree that God alone could remove me from it, and that I have good reason for considering this hermitage to have been miraculously provided as an ark of refuge for me. . . .'

Now that Marguerite and Henry were in complete agreement in wishing to have their marriage annulled, they were again on the best of terms, as they had been during their perilous years together in the Louvre. Neither of them, of course, was disinterested. The King again called her 'my dear' [m'amie], whilst Marguerite knew all about his liaison with Gabrielle, congratulated him on the birth of his children, and even offered to make them her heirs.

Henry had made Gabrielle Marchioness of Monceaux, and later Duchess of Beaufort. Referring to her by her first title in a letter to him of 24 January 1595, Marguerite wrote how pleased she would be 'to show this honest woman that I will always be glad to be of service to her, and throughout my life to love and honour those whom you love . . .'.

Two years later, on 24 February 1597, she wrote a very long letter to Gabrielle herself, explaining that whatever her enemies might have reported to the Marchioness and the King, she was only anxious to be of service to both of them. The real purpose of this letter, however, in which she would speak as frankly to her as if she were her sister, was to enlist Gabrielle's influence in persuading Henry to make some immediate provision for her, since she had not received any income or revenues for the past year, and her creditors were incessantly tormenting her. Moreover— and this was the crux of the letter—Marguerite wished to leave Usson, which she could not do without His Majesty's consent:

'For now all my affairs so urgently need my personal attention, and my necessity is so pressing, that it is no longer possible for me to remain here, where I am so far away from all my resources.' She suggested that at the King's pleasure she would travel 'to one of my residences in France, as far as maybe from the Court, in order that I may there attend to my affairs. I will be greatly obliged', Marguerite concluded, 'if you will inform me of his will, which for me will be permanently binding, as permanent as my very grateful affection for your own merits', and she signed herself 'your very affectionate and most faithful friend, Marguerite'.

But it did not suit the King that the Queen of Navarre should leave Usson, where she was living in almost forgotten privacy, to reappear in public before their divorce had gone through. Even when he had regained his freedom, his marriage to his mistress and her elevation to the throne at his side would be a delicate enough matter.

Neither did it suit Marguerite to proceed with her petition until she had obtained from Henry the necessary financial guarantees on which her whole future security depended. If the Pope granted her the annulment before she received any settlements from her husband, there was no certainty that the King would afterwards keep his generous promises to her. She therefore played hot and cold, assuring him in her letters that she was more than willing to fulfil his wishes, but alternately signing and then cancelling two or three such petitions.

The Pope, Clement VIII, was in no hurry either to grant his freedom to that notorious heretic, Henry of Bourbon, who had so recently returned to Mother Church solely and cynically for political reasons, and who only sought to have his matrimonial bond dissolved in order to make his mistress queen of France and their bastard son heir to the throne.

Nor were Henry's own statesmen in favour of this prospect. In their view, it was necessary to the stability of the monarchy that

when the King did re-marry he should do so according to traditional royal convention, wedding a Catholic lady of impeccable
virginity who by descent and connections would be a suitable successor to Marguerite of Valois.

But as Mariéjol aptly wrote, 'Henry IV was a lucky man'.

Marguerite had written to him on 9 April 1599, refuting her
enemies' charges that she was deliberately holding up the proceedings. On that very day their dilemma was dramatically ended
by the sudden death of Gabrielle d'Estrées—so fortunate in the
circumstances that it was assumed by many that she must have
been poisoned. The royal mistress, who was again pregnant, was
spending Easter in Paris, where she was staying in the house of
Sebastian Zamet, an Italian banker. The French were in any
case convinced that all Italians were poisoners, but Gabrielle died
of a stroke, possibly an embolism, after giving birth to a still-born
child.

Henry's ministers immediately informed Marguerite of this sad
event, begging and urging her to proceed with her petition. In
reply, she wrote a very frank letter to Sully, saying that she was
now hoping the matter to be settled, since it would be so 'for the
satisfaction of the King and all those good Frenchmen who, you
tell me, so ardently wish him to have legitimate children who can
succeed without opposition to the Crown he has saved from ruin'.
And then at last she put all her cards on the table, continuing: 'If
hitherto I raised doubts and difficulties, you know better than
anyone else the reason for it, since I did not wish to see in my
place such a common baggage, unworthy of possessing it. But
now that, thanks to Heaven, matters have changed (and I have no
doubt of the King's discretion, nor of the wise counsel of his good
servants in making a suitable choice), when he will have given me
the necessary security regarding my rights and titles, my station
and way of life (for I wish to spend the rest of my days in bodily
and mental comfort and tranquillity, as you and the King can en-
able me to do), and I will do everything you may advise me to that
end.'

Marguerite's contemptuous description in this letter of the
King's late mistress as a 'common baggage', after writing to her

as affectionately as if she were her sister, is one of those rare instances when one catches a glimpse of her true feelings, until then concealed by the flattering turns of phrase she was obliged to use, even to the King's mistress, in order to gain the security she so desperately needed. Her reference to her station and her way of life was meant to remind the King, through his Ministers, of her intention to go on living in the regal manner to which she had always been accustomed. It was natural enough that, when she was about formally to renounce any claim to be accepted as Queen of France, she should be poignantly and regretfully conscious of the fact that she was the daughter, sister and wife of kings.

Marguerite signed her final petition on 24 April, and in the following July the French Ambassador to the Holy See presented it. The Pope then instructed his legates in France to hear the evidence of the parties. Henry appeared before them, but in a touching letter to Duplessis Marguerite begged that she might be excused from doing so, and be allowed to give her evidence in private, which she would do 'quite voluntarily and with no regrets', but such a public ordeal would be so upsetting that she knew she could not endure it, 'and my tears might induce those Cardinals to assume that I was under some duress or constraint which might harm the result the King desires.'

This request was granted, and Marguerite's evidence was taken at Usson. On 11 November her grateful ex-husband wrote to her that 'I shall have more care for you than ever, and will prove to you on all occasions that I am not only your brother in name, but also in fact . . . being very satisfied by the ingenuity and candour of your behaviour and hoping that God will bless our remaining days by our fraternal friendship and the general happiness of the people. . . .'

He meant it, and kept his word. On the following 29 December by letters-patent the King confirmed that his ex-wife should continue to bear her title of Queen of Navarre and Duchess of Valois, enjoy the revenues due to her from the estates that formed part of her marriage settlements, and agreed to pay her debts.

From that time until his death, Marguerite's and Henry's

relationship could not have been a more pleasant one. Her Memoirs make it quite clear that although they were physically so incompatible that they loathed one another they otherwise appreciated each other's unusual qualities. Henry genuinely admired Marguerite's intelligence, and during Charles IX's and Henri III's reigns constantly made use of it in his own interests. Marguerite admired his dash and courage. During her first stay at Nérac, their Court had been one of the most brilliant in Europe. When his mistresses did not poison his mind against her, Henry was as fond of Marguerite as if she were indeed his sister. Although it was six years before she finally proceeded with her petition, when once Henry granted her the security for which she had had to fight so hard she was happy and willing to serve him.

The final dissolution of his marriage having been promulgated on 17 December 1599, the King's Ministers began eagerly to seek him a suitable second wife. Meanwhile, however, Henry had not been leading a life of celibacy. Only six weeks after the death of Gabrielle d'Estrées he again fell violently in love. The girl was twenty—Henriette d'Entragues. She was the stepsister of that ambitious young Charles of Auvergne, whose mother, Marie Touchet, after Charles IX's death, had married Balzac d'Entragues.

Charles and Entragues saw in this latest infatuation of the King's a splendid opportunity. When he first met Henriette, Henry's divorce from Marguerite had not yet taken place. Knowing that when he was in love the King would concede anything to satisfy his lust, Henriette's stepbrother and father prompted her to insist on the highest price before she lost her virginity to him.

Henry did not hesitate. He presented Henriette with 100,000 écus, made her Marchioness of Verneuil, and even gave her a written promise of marriage on condition that she produced a male heir. Sully, to whom this foolishly compromising document was passed, tore it up. Henry then wrote it out again. If it was implemented, Henriette might aspire to become queen. Meanwhile, she was installed in the Queen's apartments at Fontainebleau.

At last the appropriate bride for the King of France was found.

She was Marie de Medici, a distant cousin of Marguerite's on her mother's side, and a niece of the Pope. The customary haggle took place regarding her dowry. Henry, still impoverished by years of civil war, demanded one million *écus*; the sum finally agreed upon was 600,000.

The King's second wedding took place by proxy. On 16 October 1600 the Master of the Horse, Roger de Bellegarde, was sent to Florence—Henry remaining with Henriette at Fontainebleau —to marry Marie de Medici on his behalf. With a sigh of relief, Sully was able to say to his impetuous master: 'Sire, we have married you off at last!'

And indeed they had. The new Queen of France arrived at Lyons on 2 December; her husband the King joined here there on the 9th. Henry made no bones about waiting for the nuptial blessing on his marriage, but leapt into his bride's bed on the very night of his arrival. Within nine months and a couple of weeks, on 27 September 1601, Marie produced the longed-for heir, the Dauphin who was to become King Louis XIII.

A new era, the seventeenth century, was setting in. Henry had overcome the League and the Spaniards. By the Edict of Nantes in 1598, he had re-established full liberty of conscience for his former co-religionists, the Huguenots. After all those fifty years of dreadful civil wars during the Valois reigns, under the new Bourbon dynasty France was at last facing peace and prosperity.

Nor was there any longer any insincerity in the mutually affectionate letters that passed between the Court and Usson. Marguerite had cordially welcomed the new Queen Consort to France, and on the birth of the Dauphin she wrote to Henry:

'MONSEIGNEUR,
'Like the most grateful of all those in the humble service of Your Majesty, you will allow me, after having with all my heart thanked God, to rejoice with you that by His grace He has given you a son. Every good Frenchman will rejoice with you; but the happiness I know this will give Your Majesty, to which I join all my vows and wishes, gives me particular pleasure, since I imagine that no one, excepting those to whom it matters most, can share it as completely

as myself, who, thanking God a thousand and a thousand times over, requests and begs Your Majesty to keep in your good graces also. Your very humble and very obedient servant, sister and subject,

'MARGUERITE.'

Reading between the lines of this letter, one senses the inevitable regret Marguerite was feeling when she wrote it. She herself had been unable to give Henry and France an heir. But in due course she was to love and be loved by the little Dauphin as dearly as a second mother.

Early in 1600 Henry had written to tell her that Marie was pregnant. The King also warned Marguerite through one of his local adherents that Charles of Auvergne might be preparing to attack Usson.

On 17 March Marguerite wrote to thank him:

'As for my wicked nephew, that ill-advised youth has several strongholds hereabouts, which belonged to my late mother, and which he usurped from me' and which, in the King's interests 'would be better pulled down than left standing'. She was determined that by God's grace Charles would never set foot in Usson, 'and I no longer recognize him as my nephew so long as he remains Your Majesty's enemy'. Moreover, she was asking the King's permission to apply to the parliaments to have the late Queen Mother's will rescinded, and her rights in her estates restored to her.

When Henry married Marie de Medici, Charles's stepsister, Henriette d'Entragues, the Royal mistress, had been frustrated in her ambition to become Queen Consort. But her father, Balzac d'Entragues, still held that compromising promise of marriage the King had so foolishly given her. And Charles joined in the conspiracy against the new Bourbon monarchy of which the leader was Marshal de Biron, son of the old Marshal whom Marguerite had known at Nérac.

Biron was arrested at Fontainebleau on 14 July 1602 and executed in Paris a fortnight later. But this did not end the conspiracy, of which the new leader was the Duke of Bouillon, the former Viscount Turenne. For his part in it, Charles of Auvergne had been sent to the Bastille for a few months; on his release he returned to Auvergne, where he immediately joined Bouillon.

These events prompted Marguerite to write to the King:

'At this time, when God has granted you children and one sees —what one would never have dreamed of—such monstrous characters that they can conceive of patricidal designs against a prince such as Your Majesty, . . . I would humbly beg you to allow me to renounce the title of Queen in order that such pernicious creatures cannot in future use it as an excuse in any sense to disturb the security of your children, and to agree that I should call myself after my duchy of Valois, which is also the name of my House. . . .'

But whilst touched and grateful for this gesture, the King saw no need to deprive his former wife of her rightful title.

In the autumn of 1602 Marguerite was also engaged in a very different kind of correspondence, a legal action she was bringing against her former secretary, Choisnin, who had insulted her at Carlat and betrayed her to Henri III. She was suing him for the moneys he had filched from her at the time of her flight from Agen. In a very long letter of 5 November she formulated her whole case against 'this wicked man' who had stolen between 15,000 and 16,000 *écus* from her at that time. Marguerite had a remarkable ability to state a case clearly, as she had shown so many years ago in the Louvre, when she drew up Henry's defence for him.

In all her correspondence with the King until then Marguerite had over and over again expressed her passionate devotion, gratitude, and loyalty, so that the letter she wrote him on 19 November 1603 is almost breathtaking in its outraged pride and justified indignation.

Henry had inadvertently committed a blunder which provoked it. Charles of Lorraine, Duke of Mayenne and younger brother of the late Guise, had succeeded Scarface as head of the League. After Henry finally defeated Mayenne at Ivry in 1595, he surrendered body and soul to the Bourbon King. Henry, whose fame rested in no small degree on his generosity to such beaten enemies, rewarded Mayenne by conferring on him the 'baronies of Aiguillon, Montpezat, Sainte-Livrade, and d'Olmerac', which were in fact part of Marguerite's appanage as Countess of Agenois.

'To the King my Lord and brother—
'My Lord,
'To you alone, as to my superior to whom I owe everything, I have surrendered everything; to my inferiors, to whom I owe nothing, I will surrender nothing.'

And, continuing in the same proud strain at great length, the Queen of Navarre reminded her former husband that she had renounced the prospect of becoming Queen of France, 'not for lack of courage and understanding, but for the very great affection I have for Your Majesty and the good of your State', but that the Duke of Mayenne would never with her consent obtain possession of those lands and the rights that went with them and that were part of her dowry, to which she had an inalienable right, which the King himself had recognized in the deed drawn up in 1599 to replace her marriage contract.

Marguerite also wrote to M. de Lomenie, the King's secretary, protesting even more strongly, declaring that 'M. de Mayenne must stop wanting the impossible and coveting other people's possessions, and request from the King what one may expect from a King and not from a tyrant'. And she concluded with no false rhetoric:

'Good God! must one endure so much trouble to hold on to one's own? This persecution has lasted long enough; I became ill with displeasure at the King's last two replies, which were so far from justice and the support His Majesty had promised me in retaining all my possessions', ending by begging him, if the King did not read her letter, to draw his attention to it.

As the result of these vigorous protests, Henry gave way; the Duke's heirs were allowed to keep the title of Aiguillon, but Marguerite retained all her previous feudal rights and authority over these domains.

It was not until June 1604 that Henry was able to obtain the evidence inculpating his mistress, Henriette, her father, d'Entragues, and her stepbrother, Charles of Auvergne, in the Bouillon plot. Charles was re-arrested in Auvergne. The liaison man between the conspirators and the Spaniards who were financing this latest attempt to overthrow the French dynasty was an Englishman, Thomas Morgan, who was also arrested. The charges against them were that Bouillon was to provoke risings in Auvergne, the Limousin, and Quercy and, in exchange for Spanish gold, Toulon and Marseilles would be handed over to Spain. The infant son of Henriette and the King, the Marquess of Verneuil, whom Henry had legitimized, was to replace Queen Marie de Medici's son as Dauphin and successor to the Crown.

Entragues naturally enough based this claim to place his grandson on the Throne on the promise of marriage Henry had so foolishly given his daughter. He was now obliged to divulge its hiding-place—'in a little glass bottle enclosed in a larger one, carefully sealed and wrapped in cotton, then firmly inserted into the thickness of a wall' in Entragues' residence.

On 1 February 1605 the Count of Auvergne, Entragues, and Henriette were put on trial, together with Thomas Morgan. The men were all sentenced to beheading; the King's mistress was to be permanently confined in the convent of Beaumont-les-Tours. Henry, however, either because he still loved Henriette, or was guiltily aware that he had never intended to keep his promise to marry her, which was now safely in his keeping again, to be destroyed, revoked her sentence and spared her father's life. The Count of Auvergne had proved himself too dangerous a troublemaker to set free and, although he was not executed, he was sent to the Bastille for eleven years.

The downfall of Auvergne was a godsend to Marguerite. Henry authorized her to proceed against him, and her case for the revocation of Catherine's Will was then before the Paris Parliament. She therefore explained to the King that she needed to return to the capital to follow it through. Henry was by then doubly grateful to her. She had given him his freedom, and, far from showing any bitterness towards his new wife and family, had written most affectionately to Marie and promised to make the Dauphin her heir, a promise she scrupulously fulfilled. And through her spies she had kept the King well informed of the activities of Biron and his fellow-conspirators in the southern provinces. So he told her that she had his permission to leave Usson and would be welcome in Paris.

Marguerite had been quite sincere in describing Usson as an ark of refuge during the first years she spent there. Civil war was then raging all around her. But after Henry had recaptured his country and prosperity began slowly to return to France, the attractions of her lonely retreat inevitably palled on her.

From her letters to the King, it is clear how eagerly Marguerite leapt at the chance he graciously gave her of returning to the great world, which fundamentally was her natural setting, but which by then had almost completely forgotten her. Henry was still perhaps a little nervous of the reactions that the reappearance of the last of the Valois might provoke, and was anxious to know where she intended to make her new home.

On 30 January 1605 Marguerite wrote to him, first reminding him again of her intention to leave all her property to the Dauphin, 'hoping soon to be at Villers-Cotteret, where God granting I shall go as soon as I am a little recovered from the serious and violent illnesses that I suffered from all last year,' without, however, mentioning what these were. But by the beginning of May she had changed her mind, asking that her residence at Boulogne-sur-Seine be returned to her: 'the air there being healthier for me than that of Villers-Cotteret, which, my lord, like everything else of mine is Your Majesty's, and will be more convenient as a hunting-lodge. If you will therefore return it to me [the house at Boulogne] I will have it furnished and decorated and, God willing, will go there before the end of September. . . .'

This residence of Marguerite's, known as the Castle of Madrid, was in the Bois de Boulogne. For several years previously it had been used as a centre for the royal silk-weaving industry, but was then again vacant.

Fearing that at the last moment the King might change his mind regarding her departure, Marguerite decided to leave early in July. When she set out, accompanied by her lover, young Saint-Julien, and her retinue, she was escorted to the borders of Auvergne by the entire local nobility.

So, after spending nineteen years in that remote eyrie, Marguerite at last came out of Usson. With her innate sense of drama, she appreciated the contrast between her arrival there as a helpless prisoner and her departure, with all her rights and magnificence restored to her, and a fitting reception awaiting her along the way to her new residence at Boulogne.

Nor did she neglect to thank God for her new lease of life.

Before leaving Usson she arranged that her local charities there should be continued in perpetuity.

19 La Reine Margot

From D'Artenay, on her way to Paris, Marguerite wrote to Henry:

'I have left your castle of Usson safely in the hands of an old and trusted gentleman, the master of my household, guarded by my Swiss and the soldiers who served me during the time it pleased God for me to dwell there. I also left Mme de Vermont there, to keep them all in mind of their duties.'

This woman, whom she had previously sent to Paris on special missions during the divorce proceedings, had become a kind of confidential secretary to Marguerite at Usson, where she lived with her husband and sons, exercising a great deal of power over the establishment.

'It is', Marguerite continued, 'an important stronghold, and I have ordered them to allow no one to enter it unless sent by Your Majesty, with letters bearing your personal seal ... it is a stronghold that could ruin the whole country if it fell into bad hands.'

Henry agreed with Marguerite that Usson was potentially a menace. He intended to blow it up, but this was not done until 1636, during the reign of Louis XIII.

Throughout her trip Marguerite wrote to the King day by day. He had sent Sully to meet her at Cercottes, and from Etampes she wrote on 18 July that she would travel as fast as she could on her next stage—'in order to give less trouble to M. de Vendôme, whom Your Majesty is sending to meet me.'

For, having accepted the inevitable return to Paris of his former wife, Henry spared nothing to make her welcome there with all the honours due to her. The first of these was to send the Duke of Vendôme to receive her on arrival at the Castle of Madrid. This Duke was a child of eleven, the boy Caesar whom Gabrielle d'Estrées had borne, and whom Henry would dearly have loved to succeed him had it been possible. Marguerite, writing to thank him for this flattering gesture, expressed her admiration for the little Duke—'whose physical beauty [was] as perfect as his intelligence [was] beyond his years . . .'.

But a discordant note was added to the account of Marguerite's resplendent reception at Boulogne. This was provided much later by Scipion Dupleix, a former secretary of Marguerite's who, after her death, became one of her most notorious and scurrilous libellers, described by a contemporary as an 'infamous viper' for posthumously besmirching the reputation of 'this great Queen'. According to Dupleix, the gentleman-in-waiting who opened the door of Marguerite's coach and helped her to alight from it was, of all people, Chanvallon, 'whom she had formerly loved more than she should have done, so that this reception was an insult to so great a princess'.

Chanvallon had been a Leaguer, and, like so many others, had become a loyal supporter of Henry IV and been favoured by him. Yet one cannot imagine Henry's sense of humour—coarse as it frequently was—leading him to play such a malicious trick on Marguerite after otherwise honouring her so highly. And there is no other evidence to support Dupleix's statement, which, like many of his assertions regarding his former employer, was so obviously inspired by spite and malice.

In fact, the King himself called on his ex-wife on 26 July, when they spent three hours together. This was their first meeting since Marguerite had left Nérac twenty years previously. They were both now middle-aged—Marguerite certainly sadder, and Henry in many respects mellower and wiser. Without any difficulty, they immediately re-established their former friendly brother-and-sister relationship.

Marguerite was longing to meet the little Dauphin, her heir, and Henry sent him to visit her on 6 August. He was almost a baby, still only five, and when his governess brought him to her, to her huge delight he called her *'Maman-fille'* ['Mummy-girl']. Next day Marguerite joined his father at Saint-Germain, where they heard Mass together; she brought the Dauphin a little Cupid with diamond eyes, seated on a dolphin. Until the end of her life she loved him as if he had been her own son.

Although she had repeatedly assured the King in her letters from Usson that all she wanted was to settle down quietly at Boulogne, having arrived so near to Paris Marguerite, of course, found it quite impossible to stay away from the capital. Her first formal call on Their Majesties took place on 28 August. The King came halfway across the great court of the Louvre to receive her, and later, apparently, scolded Queen Marie, who had not thought it necessary to advance beyond the great staircase to greet her royal sister. Nevertheless, the two wives of Henry IV were soon on the most affectionate terms. Marguerite was invited to Saint-Germain, where on one occasion, the Queen being in bed, the King sat at the foot of her bed, cuddling the Dauphin, whilst Queen Marguerite sat on the floor beside it—a truly touching domestic scene.

L'Estoile was a less defamatory gossip than Dupleix:

'The arrival of Queen Marguerite in Paris, where she had not been seen for twenty-four or twenty-five years, and her appearance at Court, so suddenly and hurriedly that it seemed she could not get there fast enough . . . caused a great deal of talk. It was said that on her arrival the King asked two things of her: firstly, that for the sake of her health she should no longer turn day into night and night into day; secondly, that she should restrain her generosity and practise a little more economy.

'She replied to him that in the former case she would do her best to please His Majesty, although owing to her lifelong habits she would find it very difficult; but regarding the latter, that would be quite impossible, as she could never live otherwise, having acquired the habit from her mother, all the Medici having been noted for their wild extravagance . . .'.

Soon Marguerite bought a residence in Paris, the Hôtel de Sens, a splendid Renaissance building, where once again she kept open house for all the most brilliant intellectuals of the day, and also received a deputation from the Parisian citizenry, who came to welcome back and pay homage to the last of the Valois.

But even there and in middle age melodrama pursued Marguerite.

On 5 April 1606 she was returning in her coach from hearing early Mass, accompanied as usual by Saint-Julien, her lover. As she was about to get out he was shot dead at her feet, at point-blank range. Marguerite nearly went out of her mind with shock and rage at this senseless murder of her *mignon*.

'From Paris, 5 April 1806'.
'To the King my Lord and brother—
'MY LORD,

'An assassination has been committed at the door of my house, in my own sight, quite close to my coach, by a son of Vermont, who drew a pistol on one of my gentlemen called Saint-Julien. I humbly beg Your Majesty to have justice of him and to show him no mercy. If such wickedness is not punished no one will be able to live in security. . . .'

This letter, which she wrote almost immediately after the murder, she sent to the King by her personal messenger, M. de Fourquevaut.

The murderer, who escaped on horseback, but was soon captured, was a lad of eighteen, the son of that Mme de Vermont whom Marguerite had left in charge of her household at Usson. His motive was not sexual jealousy, and there was no suggestion that the boy was in love with the fat, rouged, middle-aged Queen in her little blonde wig. His hatred for Saint-Julien was apparently due to the belief that the favourite was trying to oust his mother from her appointment. When shown his victim's body, young

Vermont was defiantly unrepentant, demanding that it should be turned over so that he might make certain that Saint-Julien was dead; otherwise, he said, 'he would have finished him off'. Seeing that this was unnecessary, he was apparently perfectly happy to die in his turn, which he did the next day, on the very same spot, outside the Hôtel de Sens, by order of the King.

Marguerite personally witnessed his execution from a window. She then pursued his mother, whom she had so long trusted, with the utmost vindictiveness. Some years previously she had made over the Convent of Rouergues, in an isolated district, as a gift to her. She now petitioned the King to have Mme de Vermont permanently banished there, accusing her of witchcraft and of having been in league secretly with the Count of Auvergne and Spain. Henry granted Marguerite's request, but, according to L'Estoile, in his usual cynical fashion begged her not to grieve so insensately for her lost favourite, since, he told her, there were plenty of gallants at his Court as handsome as Saint-Julien, and he would be pleased to provide her with more than a dozen whenever she liked.

Following the King's jest, the Parisian lampoonists also made hay with the incident; several satirically coarse verses were circulated about it, some of which were pasted on the walls of the Hôtel de Sens. Marguerite, like Catherine de Medici, seldom took offence at such populist attacks, and even occasionally found them amusing. This time, however, the shock and grief at her loss were too much for her; she left the Hôtel de Sens the night after Vermont's execution and never returned there.

Nor did she remain much longer at the Castle of Madrid, which she gave back to the King when she bought herself a new country house at Issy. This she was able to do because at long last, on 30 May 1606, the Parliament of Paris restored to her all her rights that her mother had willed away. This good news was brought to her whilst she was hearing Mass at Saint-Séverin, and she was so delighted by it that she left in the middle of the service to have a *Te Deum* of thanks sung at the Cordeliers.

And Marguerite also immediately carried out her promise to make the Dauphin her heir. Whilst retaining the income from her estates during her lifetime, she settled on the future king the counties of Auvergne, Clermont, and the rest of the lands returned to her, with the express stipulation that they should remain Crown properties, so that they might never again be willed away from the monarchy.

With her debts temporarily paid and her revenue restored to her, Marguerite embellished Issy at huge expense in Renaissance style, modelling the gardens on those of Fontainebleau, which she loved. Her own residence was nicknamed the 'Olympus' and quite close was a smaller one, the 'little Olympus' which in a short time housed the latest favourite, a handsome young Gascon called Bajaumont. Marguerite made fun of him and herself, declaring that he was one of the stupidest young men on earth, but nevertheless found it impossible to live without a lover in attendance.

Marguerite was allegedly the author of a trivial dramatized dialogue entitled *La Ruelle mal assortie*, between a lady called Uranie and her cavalier, who was quite unusually stupid, as well as unusually handsome. This was first published in 1644. Some authorities consider that she whiled away a boring afternoon at Usson by writing it. The stupid, handsome lover, however, bears such an obvious likeness to Bajaumont that it more likely dates—if she wrote it at all—from her country pastimes at Issy.

Issy was a country retreat, but all the more since her long banishment from the capital Marguerite was the most Parisian of *parisiennes*. She therefore built herself a truly regal residence on the left bank of the Seine, immediately opposite the Louvre. The site she acquired for this purpose was a very large one, consisting of two islets as they then were between the rue de Seine and the rue des Saint-Pères, the rue Visconti and the quai Malaquais, and part of the former Pré-aux-Clercs, which was converted into an elaborate park. (The rue des Saint-Pères was named after the convent of Augustinians that Marguerite established there.) The palace faced the quai Malaquais, with its main entrance in the rue de Seine; there were three buildings with slate roofs, the chief of which was surmounted by a dome and a lantern. There was an impressive courtyard, with a double staircase leading up from it. Marguerite took up her residence there in 1608.

None of her former habits changed, although everything was done on a more magnificent scale. At her nightly banquets she continued to entertain the leading intellectuals and the conversation was of a high standard. Marguerite liked to choose or suggest some lofty subject for discussion during the meal, and to listen to these learned debates whilst she was waited upon by her gentlemen-in-attendance. After dinner there would be a concert, when songs set to verses composed by the Queen might be performed.

The palace on the left bank was linked to the Louvre by the new bridge, the Pont Neuf, completed in 1606. Marguerite's most famous entertainment was given in honour of the King and Queen and, according to L'Estoile, cost 4,000 *écus*. And when Their Majesties themselves entertained on a grand scale, it was Queen Marguerite whom they consulted and who revived for them the glories of her mother's Court. Marie de Medici was not conversant with the great French tradition of such entertainments; the King remained at heart a roughneck and a soldier, still despised by many members of the older aristocracy as a provincial upstart. He and his courtiers were all born, as one contemporary put it, 'in a century of iron'—the period of almost incessant religious warfare when for days and weeks on end they lived in uniform. Henry never became more addicted to culture and the arts than when he first married Marguerite of Valois. He was also naturally, like all the Béarnais, a saver rather than a spender. But, being King of France, it was necessary that from time to time he should display the requisite magnificence, and in this connection he again found his former wife as useful as in the old days. And nothing pleased Marguerite more than to revive some of the former great spectacles, ballets, and masques on such occasions.

But at this closing period Marguerite again showed her resemblance to her late brother, Henri III, in dividing her interests with equal prodigality between the profane and the sacred. It was then that she remembered her vow during that night of peril at

Usson to build an altar of thanksgiving, like Jacob's, if she survived it. And although the monastery she founded around it no longer exists, it is still commemorated in the name of the present rue Jacob. Her charities became legendary; she visited hospitals and the poor, and endowed several girls without means with dowries. She took under her protection the Irish refugees in Paris, and on one occasion, when she was visiting the church of the Jacobins, found on the doorstep an unfortunate young Irish woman, who had just given birth to a baby boy. 'She wished', wrote L'Estoile, 'to hold the infant in her arms, and, hearing that M. de Montpensier was present, she asked him to be the child's godfather, and gave it the name of Henri.'

Had the last years of Queen Marguerite's life consisted only of such edifying secular and religious activities as enjoyment of philosophy and literature, the giving of sumptuous entertainments for the Royal Family, and the pouring out of charity, she would not have gone down to history as 'La Reine Margot', besmirched by malicious gossip. But she refused to be her age, and still dressed as if she had kept her beauty and her figure, becoming a positively huge caricature of her former loveliness. Her grief at the death of Saint-Julien had aroused more mockery than sympathy; and this mockery was even sharper when her later favourite, Bajaumont, fell ill. Henry, who had visited Marguerite, apparently to express his sympathy in her anxiety, jokingly remarked to the maids-of-honour in her ante-room: 'Pray for Bajaumont's recovery, for if he were to die, *ventre-saint-gris!*, the Queen would take a dislike to this house, too, and I would have to buy her another!'

Bajaumont was tuberculous, and his doctors warned the Queen that he should be spared excessive physical fatigue. When he died young, like millions of consumptives before a cure was found for tuberculosis, Marguerite's libellers attributed his death to the Queen's nymphomania. She was certainly excessively jealous of him, forbade him the least dalliance and dismissed from her service the daughter of the Count of Choisi, by whom he appeared to be attracted. The ostensible reason given by Marguerite to her father was that his daughter's behaviour had been unseemly, to which the Count retorted that 'Had you, Madam, behaved as well as she has, you would still possess the Crown that you lost.' And on 10 May 1608 Henry wrote to Marie that 'I have no news except that yesterday Queen Marguerite beat Bajaumont, and that he wants to leave.'

There is no evidence that Marguerite made any physical demands at all on her last favourite, whose name was Villars, whom she chose to succeed Bajaumont because he had an exceptionally lovely singing voice. On one occasion she took him across the river to the Tuileries gardens, so that Queen Marie might listen to him. And Villars certainly did not resent Marguerite's interest in him. For when she fell seriously ill he vowed that if she recovered he would make a pilgrimage on foot from Paris to Our Lady of Victories at Senlis. Marguerite did recover, and Villars duly set out to fulfil his vow, followed by the Queen in her coach. As she grew older, Marguerite tended to become eccentric, like all the Valois. She, who in her youth had been the queen of fashion, in defiance of the new mode still clung to the styles of her own most glamorous period, and insisted on dressing up poor Villars like a gallant of the Valois Court, a La Molle or Bussy, so that he became the butt of mockers, who referred to him coarsely as 'le roi Margot'.

The Court on the left bank of the Seine had little better reputation than Marguerite's former residence presided over by Mme de Duras, whose alleged immoralities had led to the Queen of Navarre's banishment from Paris by Henri III. Henry IV was more broadminded than his predecessor, and merely referred to it jokingly as a brothel.

The King himself, however, continued to maintain what was virtually a harem in the Louvre, his legitimate and illegitimate children all living and playing and quarrelling together on the same landing. The constant succession of his mistresses and bastards was inevitably a source of anxiety to the Queen. On several past occasions when he was in love, Henry had wanted to legitimize one or the other of his mistresses—Fosseuse, Gabrielle d'Estrées, Henriette d'Entrangues—and Marie felt no certainty that he might not wish to do so again. She decided that her own protection against any such impetuously foolish plan of his lay in her coronation and consecration as Queen of France.

Henry was then planning a new war against Austria and Spain and was intending himself to lead an expedition into Belguim, ostensibly to support his allies, the German Protestant princes. But in fact his motive was a twofold one, for he was then madly in love again, at the age of fifty-six—this time with Charlotte of Montmorency, the wife of the Prince of Condé, who had taken her to Brussels, out of the King's lascivious reach. Henry appointed Queen Marie as Regent during his proposed absence from the kingdom, but she, well aware of his secondary motive for it and determined that there would be no second divorce in the Bourbon family, insisted on her coronation before his departure.

Quite naturally, Marguerite, who if their lives had turned out differently would then have been Queen of France at Henry's side, found it distasteful, to say the least, to be present at the coronation of her successor. But the King found her presence indispensable in order finally and publicly to establish the Bourbon dynasty as successor to the Valois in the eyes of the nation, and his word was her law. So Marguerite could only insist on the fullest recognition of her royal prerogatives on this occasion: she would wear a queen's crown and a cloak entirely embroidered in gold fleurs-de-lis, the Lilies of France. The King agreed that she might wear the crown, since he had confirmed her title as Queen; but as regarded her robes, she was to wear a dress of silver brocade, edged with only two rows of gold fleurs-de-lis, with an ermine stole encrusted with jewels. This was exactly the same costume as had been assigned to the elder daughter of the King and Queen Marie, the little nine-year-old Princess Elisabeth. And when the procession was formed it must have been an odd if still magnificent sight to see the little Princess in front of the stout old Queen of Navarre, both of them wearing exactly the same dresses, although Marguerite also had a train of purple velvet carried by two young Counts, which she afterwards bestowed on the Church of Saint-Sulpice as an altar-cloth.

After Marguerite had been ceremonially greeted by the King and taken her place, he remarked with his usual irony that he was sorry she had had to get up so early, and looking round at the dazzlingly dressed company that filled every corner of the Cathedral of Saint-Denis on this solemn occasion, Henry—who could never be entirely solemn—remarked that it made him think of the Day of Judgment, and what a shock they would all get if the Judge did appear!

He himself was nearer to it than he then realized.

For the Queen's Coronation took place on 13 May. Marguerite left on that same evening for her country seat, Issy, where she was planning to spend her fifty-seventh birthday with the usual festivities on such occasions. Dupleix, who was with her there, with a courtier's desire to say something pleasing, drew her attention to the fact that 14 May was a lucky date, and quoted some military victories and other instances to prove it. No sooner had he done so than the news was brought to Marguerite of the murder of Henry IV by Ravaillac, a frustrated religious fanatic, tragically fulfilling the forewarning Henri III had on his death-bed given his successor.

The nation was stricken with fury, horror, and sorrow by this tragedy. And in spite of later studies of Henry's personality and reign, throwing into relief his faults and defects as much as his gifts, he has remained and will always remain Henry the Great, a symbolic national idol to the French. Certainly, with his virtues and vices, he was wholly a man. The most remarkable among the former was his outstanding courage; and if his exceptional sexual appetite seemed exceptionable to some of his compatriots, the majority admired and probably envied him for his freedom to exercise it. Henry, who in early childhood had led the life almost of a peasant, was a forerunner in his day for realizing that peasants, common soldiers and other humble folk, so generally ignored and despised by their superiors, were human beings like himself, and intending that they should have a fowl in their pot every Sunday. Basically he was a countryman and a soldier, far happier in camp than at Court, and always resisting female domin-ation, even when he was in love. He was astute to the verge of cunning, and handled Catherine de Medici and Henri III with remarkable cleverness, evading every net they spread for him after his escape from the Louvre. He realized very soon that Marguerite, with her unusual intelligence, could be very useful to him, and until she left him never ceased to exploit her. He treated her abominably during the Fosseuse episode and whilst he was under Corisande's spell. But as soon as they were divorced and during the whole of their later years they were the best of friends. Henry winced at Marguerite's uncontrollable extravagance, but he was sincerely grateful to her for her generous acceptance of Queen Marie and her utter devotion to the Dauphin, and showed his gratitude by giving her all the financial and social security for which she craved.

After the King's tragic death the friendship between his two widows, his ex-Queen and the Queen-Regent, became closer than ever. Whenever Marguerite appeared at Court she was received there with the fullest honours, and as soon as Marie emerged from deepest mourning she visited Marguerite at Issy, on 8 July, when, wrote L'Estoile, 'she was offered a magnificent and sumptuous collation'.

The new little King, Louis XIII, still only a child of ten, was Queen Marguerite's heir and the apple of her eye. To her infinite pride and delight, when he was crowned in Rheims Cathedral, Marie invited Marguerite to act as one of his sponsors, and she was also godmother to his younger brother, Gaston, Duke of Orleans.

Very soon after Marie became Queen Regent, France's foreign policy underwent a radical change. After all the embittered struggles against Spain under the Valois dynasty a reconciliation took place between the two Powers. As usual, this was cemented by arranging marriages between the royal children of both Houses. Louis XIII married the Spanish Infanta, Anne of Austria. A year later, in 1612, the Duke of Pastraña, who was the son of that legendary beauty, the Princess of Eboli, came to ask the hand of the little Princess Elisabeth for the future Philip IV of Spain. (Her younger sister, Henrietta Maria, later married Charles I of England.)

The great reception, banquet and ballet for this Spanish grandee did not take place in the Louvre, but in Marguerite's palace across the Pont Neuf. It was the last and most magnificent of all her grand entertainments there. Rows of seats in the shape of an amphitheatre were erected all around the great hall, and there the Queen of France, the Royal Family, the Ambassador, and all the Court and guests took their seats to watch and enjoy the dancing and singing. Marguerite made a glittering appearance in a gown of silver brocade with long split sleeves, covered in rose diamonds, with ropes of pearls and diamonds in her wig and a superlative diamond necklace over her large bosom.

Marie de Medici was, however, a bad Regent, ill-advised by Concini, a rascally Italian favourite whom she foolishly trusted and promoted. The aristocracy, the clergy, and the Third Estate, representing the citizenry, were soon in revolt against the corrupt and tyrannical government, and affairs of State were not stabilized until in due course the great Cardinal Richelieu became the grey eminence behind the throne and the unchallenged governor of France.

During those uneasy earlier years of Louis XIII's reign Marguerite did all in her power to support the monarchy, endeavouring with some success to persuade the aristocratic rebels to return to the Bourbon Court. One of her last letters to this end was written by her to the Duke of Nevers, on the basis of 'the close friendship' she had formed with his mother, 'as everyone knows'. This lady was the pretty and naughty young Duchess of Nevers who had been in love with that fantastic cavalier, Coconat, when Marguerite had been in love with La Molle, and with whom she had fetched away their heads after their execution all those long years ago. Her appeal to her friend's son was successful in bringing him back to Court.

Her next political activity at this closing period of her public life was to attend the last session of the States-General in the autumn of 1614. On 17 November she wrote a long and one of her most persuasive letters to Cardinal de Sourdis, President of the clerical party in the States-General, pointing out to him the danger of provoking the Third Estate, to the detriment of the good of the realm.

At this assembly, however, Marguerite, then aged sixty-one, caught a chill from which she did not recover. Towards the end of March in the following spring it was clear that she would not live much longer. Rather sadly and typically, her final official transaction was to sell some of her non-entailed estates for 32,000 *livres*, for she was as deeply in debt as ever.

On 26 March her Grand Almoner, the Bishop of Grasse, warned her that her end was approaching; with another typical gesture, the Queen expressed her gratitude to him by making him a present of her silver plate. She received the sacraments the next day and died at eleven o'clock that night, 27 March 1615.

The poet Malherbe wrote a mean little note about her lying-in-state:

'M. de Valves went to see her. As for me, I will take it for granted, for there's as big a crowd as at a ballet and it is not so pleasurable. The Queen said that she intended to pay her lawful debts, for if she did not do so she feared that she would come and haunt her at night. She thought that her debts would only amount to 400,000 *livres*; but it is said that she owed more than 200,000 *écus*. This morning the Queen's chamber was so full of creditors that one was unable to move.'

Marguerite dictated her last testament on 25 March, confirming the bequest to the King and the Queen Mother of all her possessions; she enjoined on them to pay her debts and the pensions of her gentlemen- and ladies-in-waiting and various other officials, as well as the six months' wages and salaries that were due to them.

Yet there was one secret which was not divulged in Marguerite's Will. She ordered her heirs to carry out certain wishes and instructions she had confidentially given to two of her most trusted officers, Maître Bonaventure Quentin, Master of her Household, and Maître Jean Boissieux, her private secretary, which she had not cared to disclose to the lawyers drawing up the official document. These two servants observed their Queen's last instructions with such scrupulous loyalty that it was never known what these orders were. Possibly they related to bequests to persons of low degree, such as her last favourite, Villars, whom the Queen would have thought it unbecoming for a Daughter of France to name in her will.

Marguerite's coffin was placed in the chapel of her residence, since the Augustinians' church containing the Jacob's altar was not yet finished. Although the Court went into full mourning for her, Louis XIII and Marie de Medici were too preoccupied by current affairs, and possibly too ungrateful for her loyalty and generosity, to arrange for her final disposal for more than a whole year. Then the coffin was taken to Saint-Denis at dead of night, without any ceremony or even escort beyond a couple of the King's archers, so that on arrival there the monks at first refused to accept it, not believing that a Daughter of France could be brought to her last resting-place in so miserable a manner. The Valois Chapel in which it was placed was pulled down in 1719, when the tombs of Marguerite's parents, Henri II and Catherine de Medici, were transferred to the Abbey church. Marguerite's remains mysteriously disappeared and have never to this day been recovered.

But Marguerite de Valois needed no physical resurrection. Even in her lifetime her legend had begun, and throughout the centuries it has never ceased to fascinate her countrymen. Her libellers and calumniators fastened on it with the tentacles of an octopus. According to Aubigné, she was the reincarnation of the Scarlet Woman, the Whore of Babylon. According to Dupleix, the number of her known lovers was twenty-two and included her three brothers, Charles IX, Henri III, and François of Alençon, with all of whom she was alleged to have committed incest whilst still in her teens. She was also alleged by him and those prepared to believe him to have had two illegitimate sons, one by Chanvallon, 'Father Angel', and the other a deaf-and-dumb child by Aubiac at Carlat.

These poisonous libels and calumnies are no longer accepted by reputable French historians. And Marguerite's noblest epitaph was the tribute paid to her by Cardinal Richelieu in his Memoirs:

'She was the greatest princess of her time, daughter, sister, and wife of great kings, yet despite these advantages she became the plaything of Fate, was despised by those who should have been her subjects, and saw another in the place she herself should have filled. Her wedding, which should have been an occasion of public rejoicing, and bring about the reunion of the two parties which were dividing the kingdom, was on the contrary an occasion of general mourning and the renewal of crueller warfare than previously; its celebration was St Bartholomew's Night, the screams and agony of which resounded throughout Europe; the blood of the massacred was the wine of rejoicing; the banquet, the flesh of the innocent intermingled pell-mell with that of the guilty. She saw her husband in danger of his life; they were discussing whether or not to kill him, but she saved him. . . .

'This war ended, but from time to time broke out with renewed violence, like a fever which recedes and then returns again. In such a situation they were inevitably from time to time on bad terms; suspicion based on false rumours such as are very common at Court . . . separated their hearts, as the necessities of the times kept them physically apart.

'Her three brothers died one after the other during those miserable wars; her husband succeeded to the Crown, but since she had no part of his affection he gave her none in his good fortune. For reasons of State he took a second wife to give him the children she could not bear him. But whereas lesser women burn with envy and hatred against those rivals who occupy the place to which they claim a right, so that they cannot bear to meet them, and still less the children with which God blessed their marriages, she, on the contrary, gave all her possessions to the Dauphin and made him her heir as if he were indeed her own son; came to Court, lived opposite the Louvre, and not only visited the Queen, but until the end of her days paid her all the honours and duties of friendship that she might have expected from the least of princesses.

'Her lowly station was so highly raised by her goodness and royal virtues that she was never despised for it. True heiress of the House of Valois, she never gave anything away without apologizing for giving so little, and the present was never so large that she did not wish she could have given more ... and she would rather give to an unworthy recipient than fail to help one who deserved it.

'She was the patroness of men of letters and enjoyed listening to them; they were always at her table, and she learned so much from them that she spoke better than any woman of her time and wrote more elegantly than her sex warranted. And as charity is the queen of the virtues, so this great Queen crowned hers by the giving of alms with such generosity that there was not a religious house in the whole of Paris, nor the poorest of the poor, who applied to her in vain.'

Marguerite of France was above all *une grande amoureuse*—a great lover. She understood as few other women, and certainly no other queens have done, the Platonic ideals of the Good, the Beautiful, and the True. She took her love of beauty—physical beauty—too literally, but paid dearly for her excesses in the suffering they brought her. Her life at times had the rich Rabelaisian flavour, the Gallic humour, of sixteenth-century France. Her brother, Charles IX, had once contemptuously nicknamed her 'La Reine Margot', but in the course of time this nickname became one of tolerant affection by the French people, and intrinsic to her legend.

In her courage, pride, and stubborn endurance she was a Daughter of the Medici, the Valois, and of France. But in her feminism, honesty, lack of inhibitions and repressions, she was 400 years ahead of her time—a woman of the future, a woman of all time.

Sources and Acknowledgements

'A man will turn over half a library to make one book.' *Dr Johnson*.

My sources are given below. First and foremost are and must be Marguerite's own Memoirs. But as she arranged her reminiscences to suit her own views and her status as a Daughter of France they cannot be regarded as wholly definitive. Nor are they complete.

The Memoirs are, however, largely complemented by Marguerite's considerable correspondence, especially her letters to Chanvallon, those written during the years she spent at Usson, during the negotiations for her divorce, and her later years in Paris. With regard to the love-letters, most of her French biographers consider these as partly spurious, i.e. re-written and embellished by their writer at a much later date. I feel, however, that they do on the whole accurately express the passion she had for Chanvallon, even if she did furbish them up subsequently from the copies she had preserved.

It would have been impossible for me to have written this book had it not been for the intensive and detailed studies and research by Marguerite's two most distinguished French biographers, Merki and Mariéjol, as well as the excellent notes and commentaries in his edition of the Memoirs by Caboche. I have quoted none of these eminent French scholars directly, but I have frequently quoted from their works excerpts from earlier commentators, such as L'Estoile, Aubigné, Dupleix, etc., whether favourable or unfavourable. Any historian interested in the minutiae I have omitted (when they did not seem to me sufficiently significant to be included) is referred to those authorities.

This account does not claim to be a history of the Wars of Religion, nor of the Valois dynasty, nor of the reign of Henry IV. These have only been dealt with from Marguerite's own points of view or in so far as they affected her life and emotions.

Marguerite de Valois, *Mémoires*, published in the following editions: Jean François Broncart, Liège, 1713; M. F. Guessard, Paris, 1842; Charles Caboche (Charpentier) Paris, 1860, and *Correspondence*, M. F. Guessard (as above) and many sources quoted by subsequent French authors.

Brantôme, *Mémoires et Eloge de la Reine Marguerite*, Jean François Broncart (as above).

Charles Merki, *La Reine Margot et la Fin des Valois* (Librairie Plon) Paris, 1905.

Jean-H. Mariéjol, *La Vie de Marguerite de Valois* (Librairie Hatchette) Paris, 1928.

Paul Rival, *La Folle Vie de la Reine Margot* (Firmin-Didot et Cie) Paris, 1929.

Jean Héritier, *Catherine de Médicis* (Fayard) Paris, 1959; English translation by Charlotte Haldane (Allen & Unwin Ltd) London, 1963.

I am greatly indebted to the copyright owners and publishers of the above works for permission to translate and quote certain passages from them.

I am, as ever, most deeply indebted to the Librarian and staff of the London Library for invaluable assistance in research and the loan of books.

Notes on translation

Marguerite's Memoirs are written in varying styles, at times more or less formally, at others quite informally, according to whether she felt she was writing 'history' or a personal and intimate account to her friend Brantôme. In translating my quotations and extracts from them and also from her correspondence, I have tried to keep as closely as possible to her very personal style. It is interesting to note how many colloquialisms have survived both in French and English from much earlier periods and I have retained those used by Marguerite. Another example is the Duke of Guise's letter to Mendoza, in which he wrote that the plots being concocted against the Queen of Navarre, 'when you hear of them will make your hair stand on end'. Marguerite often repeated herself, sometimes at length, and where it seemed indicated I have eliminated such repetitions. She also wrote, as did Catherine de Medici, without much concern for punctuation; I have therefore occasionally shortened her longer sentences and paragraphs in order to simplify them for the reader. I have followed the same principle when quoting Brantôme and other of her contemporaries.

The spelling of proper names has varied from century to century with other modifications in French spelling. The outstanding example in this case is that of Harlay de Chanvallon (as Marguerite spelled it in Guessard's edition of her letters) later becoming Chamvallon and finally Champvallon. I decided to retain Marguerite's own spelling in this case. Other proper names are as given in Larousse.

I thought it more convenient for the reader to give the English equivalents of the French titles whenever possible, and I have done this. The outstanding exception, however, is Catherine de Medici, as it appeared positively affected to describe her as Catherine of Medici. The French spell Medici with a terminal 's'; the pedantically correct English would be de' Medici, but the apostrophe seemed to me superfluous and merely tiresome to the eye.

There is absolutely no pleasant English equivalent for the French *Noce vermeil*; preferring accuracy in this instance to aesthetics I have therefore translated it literally as the 'Bloodstained Wedding'.

As Henry of Navarre spelt his own name with a 'y' as in English, I have also done so, especially since it helps to differentiate between him and the other two Henris—Henri III and Henri, Duke of Guise. On his accession Henry of Navarre became Henri IV of France.

A map of late 16th century France showing places mentioned in the text

MARGUERITE'S FAMILY TREE

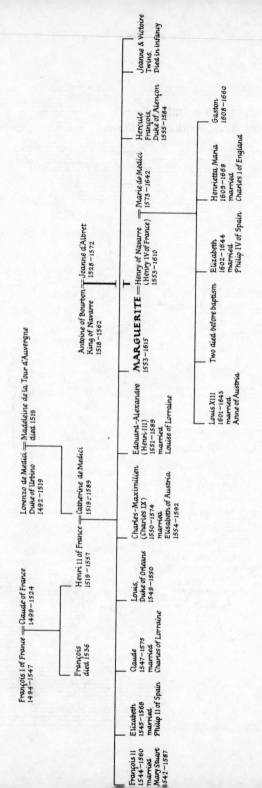

Index